RY

D0388896

SEASONS OF THE SPIRIT

THE ARCHBISHOP OF CANTERBURY AT HOME AND ABROAD

ROBERT A. K. RUNCIE

excerpted by
JAMES B. SIMPSON

WILLIAM B. EERDMANS PUBLISHING COMPANY
GRAND RAPIDS, MICHIGAN

For
The Most Reverend Timothy Olufosoye,
I Archbishop of Nigeria,
a gracious host
in a beautiful land

Copyright © 1983 by William B. Eerdmans Publishing Company
255 Jefferson Ave. SE, Grand Rapids, Mich. 49503

Library of Congress Cataloging in Publication Data

Runcie, Robert A. K. (Robert Alexander Kennedy),
1921-
Seasons of the spirit.

Includes index.
1. Anglican Communion —Addresses, essays, lectures.
I. Church of England. Province of Canterbury. Arch-
bishop (1980-   :Runcie) II. Simpson, James Beasley.
III. Title.
BX5006.R8625   1983   252'.03   83-1734
ISBN 0-8028-3589-9

Other books and compilations by James B. Simpson
Best Quotes, 1954
The Hundredth Archbishop, 1962
Contemporary Quotations, 1964

With Edward M. Story
The Long Shadows of Lambeth X, 1969
Stars In His Crown, 1974
Discerning God's Will, 1979

CONTENTS

Ecumenical guests at Archbishop Runcie's enthronement included England's Cardinal Archbishop, Orthodox and Free Church dignitaries, and the Reverend Billy Graham at right.   RNS

PREFACE

I commend this book as an exegesis of the faith of Jesus Christ as interpreted by my friend, Robert Runcie, Archbishop of Canterbury. Its publication marks the first time that his sermons, addresses, and personal observations have been assembled in a single volume.

You will find some interesting references to Anglican tradition as well as the very human touch that Dr. Runcie imparts in all that he says or writes. I suggest you read straight through — the book offers a comprehensive picture of the life of a modern Archbishop. Afterwards you will find it of value to go back to various portions to meditate on pertinent issues that he raises. He and I come from very different traditions, and we hold different views on some things (for example, the Eucharist), but we both love the same Christ.

I was privileged to attend the Archbishop's formal enthronement in Canterbury Cathedral nearly four years ago. Since that time, our paths have frequently crisscrossed as he carries out his work as spiritual head of the Anglican Communion — that widespread congregation of twenty-seven church bodies that one writer has called "an ecclesiastical clone of the United Nations." In that role it is clear that he gives himself completely to the present moment, wherever he may be. The record of these widespread involvements constitutes a knowledgeable introduction to a world leader whose picture we often see in the press and whose statements we often read. Relaxed but tenacious, Robert Runcie speaks with wit and deep insight into the ambivalences or contradictions of our lives.

Minneapolis, Minnesota
30 August 1983

BILLY GRAHAM

ix

INTRODUCTION

IN 1958, when I was still a leisured layman, I completed a European trip by stopping in London. The reason, I suppose, was partly to extend my vacation and also to renew associations from the time when I had been a graduate student living abroad.

There was more at stake than a holiday and sentiment — for, as I was to learn repeatedly in the ensuing years, we have no awareness of fate leading us into fresh interests and deeper involvements in life.

What was to be a consuming adventure began when, by chance, I encountered an American friend employed by the Episcopal Church Foundation in New York. He remarked that the Lambeth Conference of bishops from throughout the Anglican Communion had just been concluded. Since I was still a layman, with no thought of entering a seminary, he went on to explain that the bishops had been convening every ten years or so, since 1867, at Lambeth Palace where the Archbishops of Canterbury had resided since about 1200. He told me so much that he eventually said he would like me to see Lambeth.

So it was, a few days later, that I strode into the spacious courtyard and toured the library. Then I went off for a weekend at St. Margaret's Bay in Kent.

"Have you visited Canterbury?" asked my host.

"No," I answered, "besides, the Archbishop lives in London."

"Well, he lives in Canterbury, too, hard by his Cathedral," he replied. "You certainly shall not miss *that!*"

True to his promise, he called me early the next morning and we set out with his chauffeur, Shrimpton, at the wheel. I savored the narrow country lanes and then, suddenly, the majestic gray facade of the Cathedral.

Since that long-ago August morning I have been deeply interested in everything about Canterbury, especially those chosen few who bear the ancient title, Archbishop of Canterbury.

The following week, back in London, I came across a book entitled *The Archbishop Speaks*. It was "the selected addresses and speeches" of Geoffrey Fisher, then in the 13th year of his 17-year primacy. The volume is before me now, still a part of my library after various moves over a period of two decades.

In time I became a "Fisher fan," always puzzled at how a man could be regarded as vastly interesting and amusing when abroad but as a harsh schoolmaster by his own clergy. "He changes the moment his plane touches down in England," said one of them. My interest easily carried over to Dr. Fisher's successor, Michael Ramsey, and I bent willingly to the task of writing the first biography ever done on a living Archbishop of Canterbury (*The Hundredth Archbishop of Canterbury*; Harper & Row, 1962). It was a memorable winter in which I met Fisher and Ramsey as well as Donald Coggan, then Archbishop of York, and Robert Runcie, who was principal of Cuddesdon Theological College in Oxfordshire—all names now solidly linked with Canterbury.

The true measure of a man may well be in how he meets a stranger—especially one, such as myself, who turns up from overseas seeking confidences and facts. That moment of judgment came for Robert Runcie and me early in 1962. He was caught up in his job as "Princeps" at Cuddesdon (now called Ripon College, Cuddesdon) and vicar of the village church. If anything, I was an intruder, a voice on the telephone. I asked tentatively if I might come to Cuddesdon, then went off on further investigations into Ramsey's years in Lincoln, Durham, and York. Winding up in Oxford (Ramsey's younger sister lived there), I again telephoned Professor Runcie.

"Oh, yes, I remember you," he said—and that instant, cordial response became the keynote of our whole relationship.

In other quarters I was regarded with suspicion and silence, but Professor Runcie was open and helpful. A visit was arranged, and I took a bus from Oxford. The college was a clump of venerable stone buildings alongside a road winding through flat countryside. I stayed two days, not long enough for what turned out to be a charming place. We spoke at once of how little it seemed to have changed since Ramsey's days as an ordinand.

"There goes my old gardener in his gaiters," Runcie remarked.

Neither of us imagined that, in another decade, such gardeners would have passed from the scene and Runcie himself would be in gaiters — episcopal gaiters as Bishop of St. Albans (1970-80).

I remember spending the night — a cold, dark, windy night — in a second-floor bedroom of the Runcies' house that looked across a lawn to the college. Mrs. Runcie was also welcoming, the pretty mother of a year-old son. (He was recently graduated from Cambridge and his sister, Rebecca, was in her second year at Durham.) It was the couple's first home outside Cambridge where he was Dean of Trinity Hall and married to a don's daughter. Indeed, Professor Runcie had come a long way from Liverpool where he was born 2 October 1920, the youngest child (second son) of an electrical engineer, a Presbyterian, and an Anglican mother who had been a hairdresser on Cunard liners.

My stay at Cuddesdon was highlighted by exceptionally responsive and helpful students (they located the Cuddesdon *Pie* of 1927-28 and Ramsey's minutes as secretary). The services in the chapel and village church were unusually reverent. I even found time to walk along a lane, a few wan stars relieving inky blackness, to watch a dart game in the local pub. A day later, in Oxford, the late Austin Farrer, Warden of Keble College, brought my book into focus: Ramsey's whole life fell into place with sense and shape and soul.

Nearly 20 years later, almost to the day, I again met Robert Runcie. He had become Archbishop and was making his first tour of America. I had become a priest-journalist and had contrived to cover his transcontinental trip. As we flew westward over the vast plains, bound for San Francisco, I mentioned my stay at Cuddesdon.

"Oh yes, I remember you," he said — and we resumed the same easy gamut of talk we'd known in 1962.

It was my privilege to be with the Archbishop throughout his time in the United States. I was with him again, later in 1981, when the Anglican Consultative Council met in Newcastle and I called on him at Lambeth. In the spring I accompanied him for two weeks in Nigeria, which has the largest Anglican body outside England.

During a subsequent stay at Lambeth I began to compile these addresses at a desk in the spacious conference room. ("Thou hast set my feet in a large room," said the Psalmist.) The great portraits of former Archbishops were stored there while the central corridor was being painted. They provided extraordinary company and inspiration. The large, framed likenesses of Ramsey and Coggan leaned against my worktable. The other Primates of this century — Davidson, William Temple, Lang, and Fisher — eyed me from across the room. Behind me and along the front of the room were the 19th-century worthies — Sumner, Longley, Tait, Benson. Meanwhile, across the Thames, Big Ben struck the hours as people came and went at Lambeth during the Falkland Islands crisis and uneasy preparation for the historic visit of Pope John Paul II.

Admiring the ornate frames and solemn countenances, including a sketch just started of Dr. Runcie, I realized anew that English monarchs, defenders of the faith, have been fortunate in appointing to Canterbury the finest of the clergy. Whether skilled as theologians or administrators, they are excellent preachers and even better after-dinner speakers. They have been equally at home in the pulpit and at the banquet table, endlessly perfecting what is a recognized art in *Anglia hilariset antiqua*. Moreover, their texts *read* well. But the really striking thing was the variety of podiums awaiting an Archbishop — stately cathedrals, legislative chambers, hotel dining rooms, embassies, schools. Indeed, the panorama of pulpits and places in which a Primate speaks is only surpassed by the variety of topics discussed. Their ability is astonishing in its sweep — solemnly pronouncing, preaching, teaching, and pleading, or jocularly laughing. All of it is done — one or two or three occasions a day — interspersed with meetings and appointments.

Each Archbishop has, of course, his own personal style. The present incumbent has a simplicity of speech enhanced by warmth and eloquence of delivery. The way he structures what he says, leaning heavily on outlining a subject and presenting it point by point, reflects his professorial past. At the same time, Dr. Runcie takes pains to set his remarks in the context of the past. He uses his research material well, telling with relish some obscure tale about the very organization to which he is speaking or relating with wit an amusing story about a predecessor. It is a careful approach that gives his remarks a sense of perspective and a built-in attitude that no one, even an Archbishop, should take himself too seriously.

The Runcie primacy is well into its fourth year, bringing with it more and more invitations that the Archbishop wants to accept even as he fills the engagements that are expected of the occupant of the office. Rising to the occasion, Dr. Runcie sustains a tradition; with scholarship, lightheartedness, and deep sincerity he builds endless goodwill all over the world. The ransom for his widespread mission is probing, periodic analyses (usually anonymous) by the religious and secular press. Except for the post-war Falklands address — when he spoke of compassion more than victory — he is, as they say in the trade, "getting good notices," as several of the assessments herewith excerpted will bear out. In both speech and appearance, he lends himself well to succinct description such as the *New Yorker's* recent observation of him as "a tall, cheerful-looking man with puffs of gray hair fanning out at his cheekbones."

I acknowledge with gratitude the cooperation of the Archbishop and his associates, most especially his chaplain, The Reverend Richard Chartres, and the Adviser on Anglican Communion Affairs, Terry Waite, MBE. The virtues of patience and perseverance I attribute to Deaconess Inez Luckraft, the Archbishop's secretary, and her fellow workers — Caroline McLintock, Rosemary White, Hazel Christmas, and Celia Hore. There are days when they deftly move and rearrange paragraphs or even whole blocks of materials — "cannibalizing," they call it. They are faithful keepers of the huge accordion-pleated file marked "Public Utterances" from which we have drawn most of this book. It is a realistic reflection of our times and a foretaste of what people in widely scattered parts of the world may expect to hear from an interesting, articulate Archbishop.

JAMES B. SIMPSON

St. Michael's Church, New York City
Holy Cross Day, 1983

SEASONS OF THE SPIRIT

OBERT RUNCIE'S THOUGHTS ABOUT HIS NEW JOB:* The Archbishop of Canterbury is primarily in the business of truth, morale, trust, compassion, and integrity. But one of my chief fears is of being a platitude machine.

If there is a word to describe my feelings it is "trepidation."

I am fortunate to be succeeding Donald Coggan. He has helped to change the atmosphere in which the Church confronts its problems and opportunities. His emphatic and unruffled way of speaking, his evident and unshakable faith, has helped the Church of England to recover its nerve. There can be no debate about the debt the Church owes to its 101st Archbishop and his wife also.

By coincidence I shall be in Canterbury next week. I shall look forward to seeing places I knew when I was stationed at nearby Eastwell Park during the hot summer of 1944, preparing among the orchards and under the doodlebugs to go across to Normandy.

Every Archbishop must scrutinize his use of time. If he gets caught up in too many committees and good causes, his involvement degenerates into a mere formality. If minutes and memos form too large a part of his daily diet, he will lose the capacity to speak anything but platitudes about the world outside the Church ghetto.

*Statement issued by the Church Information Office, 7 September 1979, shortly after Dr. Runcie had learned of his appointment but more than six months before his enthronement.

← *Anglicans the world over were introduced to their new Archbishop through a family photograph made on the morning of his enthronement. Standing in front of their weekend residence, the Old Palace, with Canterbury Cathedral in the background, the group includes, left to right, Rebecca Runcie, a student at Durham University; the Archbishop; Rosalind Runcie, called "Lindy," a Cambridge don's daughter who married the Archbishop in 1957; and James Runcie, a 1981 Cambridge graduate who has been working as a director in repertoire theater.*

Robert J. Anderson

3

I shall be particularly on the alert to prevent this happening, conscious that this is the sort of thing you say before you take up a post and then find out how strong the pressures are. But at this stage I am determined not to succumb to them. I will give this area of my new responsibility close scrutiny to see what can be shared and what can be dropped.

It is clear that the Archbishop can no longer assume that he will be heard and heeded as of right on the great issues of national life. But he must comment, and, if he is to be speaking effectively, he must make sure he sees a wide cross section of people both from outside and inside the Christian Church.

He must have a team that has a varied experience of contemporary English life. It is only in this way that he will be able to give an informed and searching commentary on events and controversies.

Above all, in a complex world he must not be too quick to speak. The hollowness of ringing declarations and general moralizing divorced from a direct experience of the doubts and difficulties of ordinary people is only too evident.

Our Anglican Communion has set its face against a Papal style of leadership, and I know the importance of developing the closest consultation between leaders of the Anglican Churches.

As Chairman of the Anglican/Orthodox Discussions, I have been very concerned with ecumenical relations.

7 September 1979

Anglican Communion

SALVE

THE news that Robert Runcie, Bishop of St. Albans since 1970, is to be the next Archbishop of Canterbury has been greeted with universal acclaim, though it took *The Church of England Newspaper* an issue or two to decide whether it fully shared in the general euphoria. The Archbishop-designate, his wife, and his children took their sudden overexposure to the media with remarkable grace and unfailing good humor. Then, and since, there has been an air of expectancy, as though Kennedy was preparing to succeed Eisenhower. It is the kind of expectancy which is aroused when one generation succeeds another: Archbishop Coggan was already in holy orders, and holding a senior teaching post in the Church when war broke out in 1939, and was taking up the Principalship of a theological college as the war ended. Bishop Runcie came to ordination after the war, with his character and personality necessarily shaped by experience of involvement in front line warfare. It is no disrespect to his predecessor to say that the new Archbishop is unmistakably a man of the post-war world and of the post-war Church. He stands in the ecclesiastical and intellectual tradition of Charles Gore and Michael Ramsey though he wears the traditional Anglo-Catholic colors with a late twentieth-century difference. He manages to walk, with remarkable nonchalance, the tightrope between tradition and openness to new ideas — as is shown by his skill in retaining the profound confidence and goodwill of Orthodox church leaders in a period when their confidence in the Anglican Communion has been shaken and, equally, by his encouragement in his own diocese and elsewhere of an attitude to ministry which transcends the traditional categories, and points the way to a wider sharing of responsibility for ministry within the people of God. If it sometimes appears that his radicalism is of the cultivated rather than the natural variety — time and Canterbury will tell. The fact that he has, in recent years, been so much absorbed by his commitment to the Orthodox and his chairmanship of the Central Religious Advisory Council of the BBC and IBA has limited him to comparatively rare appearances on the synodical stage and not much has been seen of him in the Church Commissioners' corridors. But he has done enough in the Synod — a battle in his early days as a Bishop over the future of the theological colleges; a most skillful retreat, having marched the Synod to the top of the hill [over disputes] about South India, to old, carefully prepared positions; and forays and skirmishes on a variety of subjects from divorce to world development — to demonstrate that he is at ease there. He is a bonny fighter and witty. . . . Meanwhile, he has the prayerful support of the whole Church as he prepares to take up his new office.

T CANTERBURY FOR ENTHRONEMENT AS 102ND ARCHBISHOP AND PRIMATE OF ALL ENGLAND: Sermon text: St. Luke, Chapter 1, Verse 32: "And the angel said to Mary, 'Jesus shall be great and shall be called the Son of the Highest, and the Lord God shall give Him the throne of His father David.'"

Jesus was given a throne. That means He was given authority, but authority of what kind, and how did He come by it? On the day of his own enthronement, an Archbishop does well to ponder such matters, which touch not only him but the whole Christian community. The Church exists as an embodiment of Jesus Christ. It exists to express God's love for men and to draw men to an ever deeper love of God.

We are doing this work as we become more like Jesus Christ. Our proper authority comes by being like Him and our way to a throne must be like His way.

Of course the Church has often tried to take short cuts to authority, enforcing respect and obedience by wordly means and so obscuring the face of God. I have inherited a substantial supply of weapons which once equipped the Archbishop's private army. Men of power sat in the Chair of St. Augustine and their pikes now decorate the walls of Lambeth Place; they have become museum pieces.

But the temptation to gain the Church's end by using the world's means is still with us. We are tempted to organize ourselves like any other party or pressure group, to establish sharper dividing lines between those who are members and those who are not, to compete more aggressively for attention from the public, to recruit new members with a strident self-confidence which suggests that we have nothing to learn, to persuade with a loud voice rather than with the quiet reasons of the heart.

Salesmanship may seem a sensible strategy for securing the Church's prosperity and survival as an institution. I do not wish to be misunderstood. Any Church which does not make demands on those who call themselves Christian, and which does not desire to draw others into the company of those who know God and love Him, is deaf to the resounding commission of the Lord which has just been read.

We have spiritual treasure in the words of life; but it matters desperately how our treasure is shared, how those ends are pursued and how the Church seeks to exercise authority. Aggression and compulsion was not the way of Jesus Christ, the homeless wanderer, the Son of God who came among us in the form of a servant and shared our suffering.

When you are a friend to everyone, whether they belong to your group or not, when you have felt suffering, poverty and sickness, not necessarily in your own person but by being a friend to those who suffer, then you are led into a depth of love which the hard-boiled never glimpse or attain. This deep unsentimental love — part toughness, part sensitivity — has in itself an authority which makes people question and change the way in which they are living. You can see it in the life of our contemporary, Mother Teresa of Calcutta. She is almost powerless, but she speaks and acts with Christ's own authority. She is hugely influential in a world distracted and confused by the strident clamor of pressure groups and rival theories.

If the Church acts as if it possessed its answers to life's problems tied up in neat packages, it may be heard for a time. It may rally some waverers; but its influence will not last. It will confirm others in their suspicion and hostility. To them it will mean that the Church, like every other human institution, is making a bid for power. Even when we speak, as we must, the life-giving truths in the precious words of scripture handed down to us, those words can lack authority because what we are will deny what we say — and we will not be able to understand deeply ourselves what we are saying.

For the Church to have the authority of Jesus Christ, it must not merely repeat the definitions of belief distilled by our fore-runners — vitally important though this is. The Church must live now as Jesus Christ would live now.

Like Isaiah of old, we must begin by admitting that we have fallen short of the vision which is given to us; but his response was "Woe is me for I am a man of unclean lips and I dwell in the midst of a people of unclean lips." This penitence should be a constant note of our life in the Church. Today [the Feast of the Annunciation] we celebrate the response to God's call made by a young woman of no great family or education. She was able to hear God speaking in a way which was, and is, not possible for the worldly-wise with the crust of success which cakes the eyes and covers the ears. "How shall these things be?" Wonder, longing, obedience are the mixture in Mary, the first to respond to the call of God in Christ.

So the strange authority of Christ's Church begins not in the assumption that we possess all the answers but in our recognition of our poverty of spirit. From that can come a real longing to hear God speak. One of the major themes of the New Testament is that a sense of possession gets in the way of spiritual growth. Our lives must be full of longing as we struggle to become more Christlike.

One task which is going to occupy much of my time is gaining some knowledge of the worldwide Anglican Communion. There are nearly 70,000,000 Anglicans spread in every continent with a great variety of styles of life. I am soon to attend an enthronement in Central Africa of an Archbishop for a new French-speaking Province of the Anglican Communion. Archbishop Bezaleri will be enthroned in very different circumstances. No cathedral, let alone trumpets there.

This service in Canterbury, so carefully prepared, so magnificently beautiful, speaks eloquently of the glory of God and the dignity which God gives to men by loving them. Its pageantry speaks, too, of English tradition of which we are rightly proud — countries, like individuals, only thrive if they are loved, and I am proud of a religious tradition which, in attempting to blend freedom and religious conviction, has colored a nation's life and sometimes been paid for in blood.

But it may be that the simple service to which I shall go in Africa will prove more eloquent about the uncluttered way in which the Church should live now, about the unpretentious character of real Christian authority.

There is no place in our understanding of authority for the Archbishop of Canterbury to visit Africa like some reigning monarch descending on a viceroy. I will be there to share what we have in England with our brothers and sisters, and to learn what they have to teach us about personal discipline and sacrifice, and about the fresh joy of being a new follower of Christ.

The same approach will be vital in relationship with other Christian churches. It fills my heart with great hope to see so many Christian leaders assembled here, from every part of the globe.

And it would be insensitive if I did not share the shock at today's news of the murder of Archbishop Romero [in El Salvador], a sober reminder that life and death for the Gospel are still the way Christians are called to change the world.

The vitality and spiritual energy represented here could be a great force for world peace and social justice. Much is being done already, but we are hampered by our divisions, and the worldwide Christian Church will not be able to speak with the authority of Christ until it speaks with one voice. Few would dissent from that, but how is it to be achieved?

I believe that negotiations aimed at merging institutions have only a limited usefulness without the sort of work in which I have had a tiny share in recent years as across ancient theological misunderstandings and sharp political frontiers we have tried to discern the mind of Christ. Brotherhood grows not only by two people obsessively discussing each other's personality but by two people looking in the same direction, working together and experiencing new things together.

A humble willingness to work in this way and to accept disappointment when progress seems slow has been a mark of the ministry of both my predecessors, Archbishop Ramsey and Archbishop Coggan. They both saw that true Christian Unity came from the sheep rallying to the call of the Master and not from the sheep deciding to huddle together against the storm.

Christ does not only draw us closer to our fellow Christians. If we are to be followers of Him, we will be led into friendship with the host of thoughtful and honest men and women outside the Church who are aware that the world is out of joint, perilously close to famine and war, that the streets are more and more dangerous for the weak, that families are breaking up, perhaps their own lives are in a mess. Christ draws us close to many people who seek God and who may be doing His will more effectively than those who can say to Christ, "Lord, Lord."

You know how sometimes in an English garden you find a maze. The trouble is to get to the center of those hedges. It is easy to get lost. I had a dream of a maze. There were some people very close to the center, only a single hedge separated them from the very heart of the maze but they could not find a way though. They had taken a wrong turn right at the very beginning and would have to return to the gate if they were to make any further progress. But just outside the gate others were standing. They were further away from the heart of the maze, but they would be there sooner than the party that fretted and fumed inside.

I long to be able to speak while Archbishop with men and women who stand outside the Christian Church. I would say to them, "You can teach us so much if together we could look for the secret of the mazelike muddle in which the world finds itself." I ask for your prayers that I may be given the grace to speak like that and listen.

But I must stand also not at the edge but at the very center of the Christian company as supporter and encourager — and my particular heroes among those who speak for Christ and follow His way are found in places where priest and people, men and women, of different ages, change the atmosphere of their local community, drawing people to Christ by the authority that their honesty and love and service win for them.

This way of living and sharing, admitting our own failings and our longings, is not what people expect from those who sit on thrones. "Speak out, condemn, denounce" is what is expected. But the throne of Jesus is a mercy-seat. It stands firm against all the vileness of the world but it stands also for compassion. The way of Jesus means reverencing people whether they belong to our party or not. The strategy of Jesus means changing lives with love.

This is a hard way and people tend to want it only in theory. The cry is "the Church must give a firm lead." Yes, it must — a firm lead against rigid thinking, a judging temper of mind, the disposition to oversimplify the difficult and complex problems. If the Church gives Jesus Christ's sort of lead it will not be popular. It may even be despised for failing to grasp the power which is offered to it in the confusions and fears of our contemporaries.

But it will be a Church not only close to the mind of Jesus, it will find itself constantly pushing back the frontiers of the possible.

"For with God nothing is impossible." And it will be a Church confident with the promise of Jesus: "Lo I am with you always, even to the end of the ages." That is why this is a service of glorious celebration.

But the personal dedication around which it revolves is a dedication to the way of Jesus Christ, and the support of all who share with me in this day will find no better expression than in the personal dedication of all who can follow with me in that way.

It is not just the Pontifex — that rather grand title which simply means "bridge builder." We are all to be the bridge builders in the world — the bridge between God and man, found for us in the face of Jesus Christ — the bridge between the Jesus of history and the living Christ of our experience — the bridge between Christian and Christian — the bridge between Christians and a world where our allies will be the God-seekers, the peacemakers, and friends of the poor.

But if you would seek to put the world to rights, do you begin with some other person or with yourself? It is a day to remember that the confrontation of God with man calls out not the interest of the spectator but the fresh and renewed response of the seeker. "Here am I, send me. I am the Lord's servant. As you have spoken, so be it."

25 March 1980

Chair of St. Augustine, Canterbury Cathedral

T CANTERBURY ON THE FIRST EASTER AS ARCHBISHOP: Any religious building is a remembering sort of place. Into it we bring memorable human things: birth, marriage, death, our flickering communion with God, and our fragile relationships with each other, so that they may be deepened and directed. How strongly true that is of such a place as Canterbury Cathedral.

But what we remember is *always* the touchstone of our character. The musician remembers melodies, the artist pictures, the financier figures, the loyal family man birthdays, anniversaries, and get-well cards. If you don't remember, it shows you don't really care. The first followers of Jesus Christ were called Christians because they remembered Jesus Christ. They remembered him deeply, easily, tenaciously. It made them the people they were.

But what did they remember? That He welcomed and accepted people, that He forgave and broke through conventions as to who was good and praiseworthy or who was bad and blamable. He didn't speak of the masses but of "a certain man" or "a certain woman." They remembered that He loved not in a sentimental way but in a way that was stronger than the destructive forces of life — violence, bigotry, sickness, even death — so that He was able to absorb them and turn them to increase the total output of goodness in His world. Circumstances never mastered Him. He mastered circumstances. They remembered that He pointed beyond Himself to His Father's world — and He made words like Heaven or the Kingdom of God no longer seem hollow.

As they remembered Jesus Christ, they found that new life sprung up within them so that they, too, were given the power to be forgiving and caring, to engage and transform the forces of evil, to fight for the New Jerusalem — and so, in spite of terrible failures and treachery, it has continued through history. Today in San Salvador — its very name means "The Saviour" — in the conflicts of Ireland, or in personal and domestic crises, there are those who care

13

and redeem and fight for a vision because they remember Jesus Christ.

Now this is astonishing — that someone who lived over 2,000 years ago should be so remembered that it makes such a difference. And the secret? The New Testament never simply says "remember Jesus Christ." That is a half-finished sentence. It says "remember Jesus Christ is risen from the dead."

6 April 1980

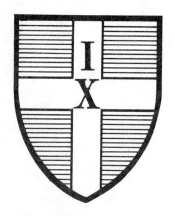

← *White and gold enthronement cape was made by a versatile woman from St. Albans, Jenny Boyd-Carpenter, who also tends Runcie's prize pigs.* Church Information Office, London

OD AND THE IRON HORSE," A SERMON AT CANTERBURY CATHEDRAL MARKING THE 150TH ANNIVERSARY OF THE CANTERBURY-WHITSTABLE RAILWAY: On May 3, 1830, at 11:25, the bells of this Cathedral rang out, guns were fired, and almost the whole population cheered, waving banners proclaiming "Prosperity to our City." With the Mayor and Corporation bravely in the front coaches, what can claim to be the first passenger railway journey started out from Canterbury. In 41½ minutes, pulled by *Invicta*, the train glided into Whitstable Station. On return to Canterbury, a large dinner party concluded with the singing of *Non Nobis Domine* — "Not unto us, O Lord, but unto Thy Name we give the praise." It was not perhaps a very ecclesiastical occasion, but I believe it had some fundamental religious ingredients to it. So I welcome you to this Cathedral, built by pioneers of faith for pilgrims and citizens — the right place to commemorate a remarkable moment in our history. . . .

In one sense it all seems to belong to another world, and the whole story of steam and the railways exercises in the present day the fascination of romantic nostalgia. . . .

But we should not be ashamed of encouraging a sense of history and romance — that unfailing cordial for drooping spirits. It can put new heart into us. There is more to be said about the railway story than seeing it as a slice of antiquarian interest. There are strands in it which speak very much to our condition today. The men who fathered the railways of Britain and, therefore, the whole world, were pioneers — using materials they knew little about, operating in a medium entirely new — and they were creating out of the unknown a new dimension of civilization, the social effects of which were not possible to guess. They characterized those who have fearlessly brought

"God and the Iron Horse" was reprinted as a booklet by the Association of Railway Preservation Societies, The Station, Sheringham, Norfolk NR26 8RA.

new truth and life to the human enterprise, a thread running strongly through our Bible: Abraham journeying with the Children of Israel, the Wise Men planning their journey not only by the star but by political events, and the strategy of St. Paul who established his centers for the Christian mission at the crossroads of trade and saw the seminal significance of cities and their relationship to the surrounding countryside. . . .

Through it all we see that faith is not believing lists of things or hoping the worst won't happen. Nor is it mere human dreaming. It is staking your all for what you believe, trusting beyond human expectations, and converting dreams into change. . . .

Travel as a consumer industry has been a mark of civilization. A world at peace is likely to be a world that travels. . . .

Travel is an expression of the human spirit, a precious freedom. Perhaps we should remember among the secular saints Thomas Cook and his ilk who took travel from the privileged and gave it to the people. From travel, whether within or between nations, there can grow the exchange of ideas and understanding and tolerance on which alone can be built the peace and understanding for which we all yearn. . . .

Boasting of the achievements of our people, which is a natural thing to do, can easily glide into arrogance — that way lies the trouble. Hence we begin as they did 150 years ago in a spirit of *Non Nobis Domine* — "Not unto us, O Lord, but unto Thy Name we give the praise." And we start our celebrations in a setting where we are constantly reminded, "Everyone to whom much has been given, of him shall much be required." What is required of us?

Faith to do battle with a sort of cynical fatalism which afflicts us.

Partnership of a wider and deeper sense than ever before.

Peace and proper use of the discoveries and talents of the human race.

It is for these gifts that we pray, and also that our affectionate memories may be converted into a momentum which characterized those early pioneers and without which in our own day we should not be worthy to be their successors.

3 May 1980

T BUKAVU, ZAIRE, FOR THE ESTABLISH-
MENT OF THE CHURCH OF THE PROV-
INCE OF BURUNDI, RWANDA, AND
ZAIRE: Today, when a new province of the Anglican
Communion is being created and a new Archbishop enthroned, we
first of all look to Jesus who ascended into heaven, having won the
battle against sin and evil. Like good farmers, as many of you are,
we prepare to turn our hands to work and to the preparation of the
ground so that the Holy Spirit of God may continue to work in all
fullness.

How can we prepare and continue to plant? Many years ago, a
young Jewish man scratched a message on the wall of a ghetto: "I
believe in the sun, even if it does not shine; I believe in love, even
if I do not feel it; I believe in God, even if I do not see Him."
Today, when we are all together from so many different places, it
is not too difficult to have faith and to feel the nearness of God.
Soon, this day of rejoicing will pass and to each of us will come the
day and time of testing, the day when we cannot see the sun, when
the rains do not fall, when we feel and experience hate, and when
God seems far away. It is during such days that faith takes on a new
meaning; it is during such days that we really need the fellowship
of the Church, both within and beyond these borders. . . .

When a new province is made, we are not creating a separate
lake or pool. A pool, when the waters are still, will soon turn dark
and stagnant. When a new province is made, in one sense the Christians of that province join a river. They put themselves alongside
Christians throughout the world, and together they move forward
towards the Kingdom of God. At quiet points along the river there

---

← *Pope John Paul II makes a point in conversation with the Archbishop
on their first meeting when their paths crossed in Ghana in the spring of
1980. They met again two years later when the Pontiff visited Canterbury
Cathedral.* Press Association Ltd.

are pools which are still and deep, but they are constantly refreshed by new waters. At other points the river surges along with tremendous energy and life. The different moods and expressions are all part of the new river, the one Church throughout the world. . . .

In love, we welcome this new province to the Anglican Communion. We ask you to accept us as we are. Together, let us look to heaven where Christ reigns on high; together, let us tend the earth, that we may work for the kingdom of justice, truth, and peace. Together, let us link our hands around the world. . . .

April 1980

N ARCHBISHOP LUWUM OF UGANDA: When Archbishop Luwum died, a missionary had a dream. He was standing in Africa. In the distance he saw a fire. As he approached, he saw that in the midst of the fire was an African, but he was not being burned, and he heard a voice which asked him to place his own hand in the fire. Not all Christians are called to be martyred for the sake of their faith, but all are called to touch the living fire of the Holy Spirit, and to be touched by that fire.

May 1980

Church of Uganda

T WORCESTER FOR THE 13TH CENTE-
NARY OF THE DIOCESE: In this Diocese of
Worcester we can celebrate and give thanks for the
promise of Jesus of power from on high by pointing to
the remarkable achievements and personalities of the last 1,300 years:
Bosal, the first Bishop, a simple monk called to great responsibilities;
Dunstan, the scholar and reformer of monastic life; Oswald, builder
of the first Cathedral; Wulstan, suppressor of the slave trade; and in
more recent times we remember Henry Pepys who brought his
evangelical seriousness to bear on early 19th-century rural lethargy,
and Henry Philpot, who directed the Church's attention to the needs
of the new industrial areas and encouraged restoration of Holy Communion as the heart of the Church's life. Jesus' promise of power
from on high has flowered in buildings of great beauty, notably the
Cathedral itself. The Spirit has also flowed into a concern for the
spiritual beauty of individual lives, and a zeal for education. . . .

I believe that little of lasting value can be achieved without faith
and the Spirit, but I am aware that the common opinion is very
different. For so many, the Christian faith is seen as at best an
amenity or an agreeable hobby, or at worst a tedious irrelevance.
This dismissive view of Christianity is portrayed at present at many
bus stops where you see an advertisement for a certain fizzy drink
which pictures a clergyman — dare I say, obviously C of E? — with
a plate of sandwiches perched insecurely on his knees and a scared-
rabbit grin on his face as he is handed a cup of fizz with the inquiry,
"one lump or two?" It is a harmless and ineffective characterization
illustrating the image which many good-hearted and quite well-
disposed people have of the Church. You would never have described
energetic builders and reformers like Wulstan in these terms.

Last Sunday I shared the Eucharist in Africa on a football ground
with Bishops from Uganda and Zaire gathered around the altar with
their people. There was plenty of fizz in their worship I can tell you,
and you would never dismiss them as being of no consequence in a

21

crisis. Their faith is the ingredient of hope and confidence in a society falling apart.

Indeed, real faith is emphatically not a luxury item or a minor asset. It is an essential spring of solid achievement. Such a fact is not easy for modern men to grasp. We have grown used to discussing all our problems without reference to the dimension of faith and the Spirit. Too often the problems of our national life are analyzed in narrowly economic or political terms, but there is no mere financial or political formula that can overcome the fear and selfishness that distort all human life and society. Man is not meant to live locked up in himself. He can only give the best of himself when he is turned to a center beyond himself, and when he is attached to God. . . .

The faith of Jesus Christ releases a Spirit into the world which creates and builds and overcomes ingrained fears and the cynicism that nothing else can combat. It is just as much true now as it always has been. . . .

Fear not, neither be afraid: the promises of Jesus have not failed over 1,300 years in this place, and they will not fail in the centuries to come.

18 May 1980

← *The Cathedral Church of Christ and the Blessed Virgin Mary, Worcester, Province of York, is the seat of a diocese dating from the year 680.* British Tourist Authority

T A LUNCHEON GIVEN BY THE ASSOCI-
ATION OF AMERICAN CORRESPON-
DENTS IN LONDON: I've been genuinely surprised
by the extent of interest taken in my appointment by the
media. I don't think the Archbishop of Canterbury is by definition
a popular figure; as part of the Establishment and very much one of
the hierarchical ingredients of the Establishment he is inclined to be
a judgmental figure. He lives in a palace — well, actually he has two
palaces — and one that is peculiarly shut up, I always feel.

Somebody told me that in passing Lambeth Bridge one day he
asked what that was and pointed to Lambeth Palace with its twin
towers. The taxi driver answered, "I think it's one of the prisons,
I think it's one of the female ones." Well, I hope, during my time
at Lambeth, to make it one of the open places that people will be
able to visit, because there are treasures there. But it stands, it almost
seems visibly, for privilege as the office seems to stand for judgment.

I think an Archbishop has very much to make his way, and
therefore I don't think the coverage of my appointment is just cu-
riosity about a new Archbishop or even a spin-off from a very different character, the charismatic Pope John Paul whom I met in
Accra. I believe it is part of a renewed interest in religion and in the
Christian faith. . . .

Why? Well, I think that there are opportunities in three areas
for the Church to try to capture the general interest which I sense.
It's been said again and again that there is a disenchantment with our
capacity to solve our problems by technology alone, politics alone,
economics alone. And there is a search for meaning in the face of
contemporary lostness.

Now, whether the Church, in a day of disenchantment with
institutions, can pick up some of that search and meet it is the first
question which occupies my mind. I believe at the moment the Anglican Church has something specific within this area because it's

never entirely lost touch with the mainstream of educational, intellectual, and cultural life of the country. . . .

Throughout history it has also been cautious about defining faith too precisely. . . .

And then I think it's tradition, the Anglican tradition, which believes itself called to handle new knowledge because God speaks not only through the Church but through the world and through the enlargement of ethical horizons. . . .

Secondly, the Anglican Church has always attempted to hold together different strands in religion — the tradition, the experimental, the prophetic. The danger is, of course, that we should be either counterfeit Catholics or counterfeit Protestants. But I want a church which doesn't see Christian unity as an end in itself but as an agent in the service of the unity of mankind. . . .

And the third opportunity I list is opportunities in compassion. . . .

I believe that kindling awareness and trying to reduce to personal and immediate terms some of the really long-range and intractable ethical issues are of far more importance than some of the issues of private ethics which are so much more easily bandied around. . . .

That's my vision of the Church. I don't believe the Church of England or the Anglican Communion is *the* Church. It is *part* of the one Holy Catholic and Apostolic Church throughout the world, and, if it's going to find its soul, it may have to do quite a lot of dying here and there to do so.

29 May 1980

RESIDENTIAL ADDRESS TO THE GEN-
ERAL SYNOD OF THE CHURCH OF ENG-
LAND: A new Archbishop of Canterbury is quickly
aware that he has assumed the mantle of great men. But
a newcomer is soon cheered and encouraged by a growing sense of
the inner unity and spiritual resources of the Church. He comes to
realize the riches he has in people — gifted bishops, priests, and laity — as well as a readiness to serve. And he is also aware of the
yearning of those who speak for Christ to speak together.

At the last Synod, a kindly question was posed about steps to
relieve the load of the Archbishop's work, and one or two recent
press announcements about appointments I've made have appeared
under the heading of "easing the Primate's burdens." While I recognize the goodwill, it is not quite how I see the matter. They give
the impression of someone who will just about struggle on if a few
burdens are lifted. My view is that the Archbishop of Canterbury
has some special opportunities to serve the Church, both in this
country and overseas, and so I have enlarged my staff to enable me
to respond more creatively to these opportunities. . . . People do not
want directives from Lambeth but personal contact and an informed
interest in the life of the other churches of the Anglican Communion.
Hardly a day passes without visitors and messages from Iran, South
Africa, Uganda, Singapore, and other areas. They are expressions
of an Anglican tradition that combine a lively sense of interdependence and a unity in the essentials of faith. It is a tradition that
transcends political frontiers.

If the Archbishop is to have a role in that worldwide community
he must be well informed and able to maintain personal relationships
with individual Anglicans spread over the globe. These are the reasons why I have appointed an Assistant for Anglican Communion
Affairs [Terry Waite, MBE].

At the same time it is easy to become intoxicated by interconti-
nental vistas and to lose touch with local congregations and parishes.

Chesterton's observation, "Nothing is real unless it is local," has been for some years one of my cherished shibboleths. I believe it, and therefore I have particularly relished my work in the Diocese of Canterbury and I look forward to becoming a familiar figure in Stodmarsh, Wickambreux, Wormshill, and other parishes of the Diocese. I am determined to follow my predecessors in a regular round of Confirmations, Institutions, and other parochial celebrations. Where I shall be delegating more is in the area of diocesan policymaking and appointments.

The Archbishop, then, is fortunate enough to have experiences both of small country parishes and exuberant gatherings in African football stadiums. He is a personal bridge between parish and province; also at the local level he is a link between the various elements which make up the rich diversity of the life of the Church of England. Moreover, he has the privilege of being heard through the media by the great number of sympathetic but unattached well-wishers in the country as a whole. Bishops, the central agencies, theologians, clergy, and laity have sometimes been in conflict, and it is an important part of the Archbishop's responsibility to help with weaving together their varied insights into a presentation of Christ's Gospel that can draw out the altruism and spiritual energies of the uncommitted. The Archbishop can't have a Colossos but he can have a Chief of Staff who moves easily between Church Commissioners and Synodsmen, who understands something of Bishops as well as minority groups. That's why I have risked the wrath of the Diocese of Bradford by the appointment of Bishop Hook to be one of my associates.

With these sessions we come to the end of a General Synod and to the completion of a decade of synodical government. It is a time for reflection. When Archbishop Temple and the Dean of Canterbury, Dick Sheppard, founded the Life and Liberty movement neither had much patience with legal structures, ecclesiastical bureaucracy, or parliamentary-style assemblies. Sheppard remained amazed that he, of all people, should have wanted an Act of Parliament and a church legislative body. He wanted them only as a way to set God's people free from the complexity of the past so that they might know a Christian liberty and the release of new spiritual energy. William Temple had a vision of a Church where there would be a sharing of

material resources, freedom to develop new ways of worship, a new search for Christian unity, and a renewed mission to the nation.

. . . Looking back on our work together, I do not regret *all* of the recent public reaction to liturgical reform. It is a reminder that the worship of God not only expresses the life of the Church but can nourish the soul of a people. The power of sacred association penetrates into deep affections of the heart and stirrings of the conscience, and those who cling to what they know do so from no unworthy motives. Nor can someone who has travelled, as I have, in countries hostile to Christianity, be unaware of the power of an ancient liturgy to carry faith from age to age. We must not fail to recognize the new life that has come to so many of our congregations through a greater understanding of liturgy and of being given a share in its action.

I hope over the coming decade that it will be possible for the different rites, both old and new, to be compared with each other. I hope it will be easier once again to have a Prayer Book in the home and to bring it to Church. I hope that a varied and balanced teaching ministry may be built upon our Prayer Books, all of which reflect a worldwide Anglican face. Above all, I hope there will be a readiness of people and priest so to think and plan together about the ordering of worship that it can lead, in many other areas besides liturgy, to freshness of the Christian life.

8 July 1980

← *(Top) At Eucharist marking the start of General Synod, left to right: Edward Carpenter, Dean of Westminster; Archbishop Runcie; Queen Elizabeth; and Archbishop of York, Stuart Blanch, who retired from office in August 1983.* Times of London

(Bottom) Greeting the Queen Mother on her 80th birthday celebration at St. Paul's. RNS

T ST. PAUL'S, LONDON, FOR CELEBRA-
TION OF THE QUEEN MOTHER'S 80TH
BIRTHDAY: As life goes on, we play a larger and
larger part in making our own faces . . . which reflect
our attitude to life. The Queen Mother's is a face with its share of
the dignity that comes from suffering, but is also full of life, affection, and a zest for new things or people . . . a face of deep but
unparaded faith, of one equally able to worship in a splendid cathedral or in a simple Presbyterian church over the border. The Queen
Mother has continued to speak and stand for abiding virtues and to
express her confidence in things that are pure, lovely, and of good
report. . . . She reminds us of a deep religious truth: if you want
to know the inmost nature of God, you must look not so much to
rules, commandments, and principles, important as they are, but at
the faces of those who love God and whose lives have been nourished
by Him. Faith, hope, and love that are deep and nourishing are
God-given. They come in full measure to those who are turned in
the direction of God, *and it shows.*

15 July 1980

T THE LONDON DINNER OF THE FREE
CHURCH FEDERAL COUNCIL: I understand
that the tradition of these dinners started in the 1930s,
and that they have been held to welcome each new Archbishop of Canterbury and to say farewell at the end of his time.
Therefore I hope for your sakes that Archbishops do not change too
frequently! . . .

Among the encouraging messages and letters which I have received on taking up my office, I treasure above all perhaps a poem
which was composed by a Methodist and sent to me. It was entitled
An Archbishop at His Enthronement (with apologies to T. S. Eliot):

> This is not all what I had in mind at all
> When I was seized by the ear, as you might say,
> And hauled out of my safety into a life
> Which I imagined would be somewhat different.
> I thought of some sort of martyrdom perhaps,
> Ecstasy possibly, the Poor my blood brothers —
> And total self-abnegation; now here I am
> Coped, mitred, and croziered, like a totem.
> On a throne; inter pares, yes, but certainly Primus.
> Multitudinous activities, all through official channels,
> Multifarious meetings with representatives,
> And heartfelt spontaneity seized by the Media,
> Examined, interpreted, twisted, falsified.
> One could be tempted to self pity.
> That would be betrayal — tribes need a scapegoat.
> Miter, Cope, Palace, Chauffeur, and all.
> Is it possible that this is the martyrdom you had in mind?

Well, the understanding spirit of one Christian talking to another
undergirds that poem, and it is a fine expression of Free Church
friendship. Much publicity has been given to my close links with
the Orthodox — I reckon that I have embraced more beards than
most in this country — and my frequent trips to Eastern Europe have
given me much opportunity to admire the courageous witness of

particularly the Baptists and the need for that sort of witness alongside the more reticent and traditional witness of the Orthodox. . . .

But tonight I would like to assure you that the formation of my own faith owes more to the influence of the Reformed tradition. . . .

I can still remember three sayings which I have often quoted to illustrate the reception of fundamental doctrine by the growing child. They all came from my Presbyterian grandfather. Whenever he saw travesties of the Christian faith — either Orange Day riots in Liverpool or unctuous Archbishops — he would ask, "What has that to do with Jesus of Nazareth?" There's the appeal to true authority for you. Nor do I forget the care with which he prepared for his quarterly Communion, with spats and flower-in-buttonhole, and called it "The Occasion."

. . . Later, though now an Anglican, I spent four years in a Scottish regiment with a Presbyterian padre, and will never forget his preaching of the Word.

You see that my debt to the Free Church tradition is considerable, and if I had to put into a sentence what distinguishes the Christian from the non-Christian, I would give an answer that I received once from the Salvation Army, "A Christian always carries about with him a sense of indebtedness — any goodness he may achieve or any virtue he may possess is all a response to what God has done for us in Jesus Christ." . . . However, loyalty to truth and the call to Christian unity do not always go hand in hand. Be as ecumenical and as warmhearted as you like, I can never be united with you if the condition is that I believe what I disbelieve. . . .

Differences of belief now run through, and not simply between, denominations. That is a contemporary fact. . . .

The choice for the future is not between a loyalty to truth and indifferent amiability. It is a question of discovering a common loyalty to the Gospel and the unity which God longs to give us on that basis. . . .

The future really depends on getting the best things caught, for it is an old adage that religion is caught not taught. And it simply means that if love, not power, is to rule the world, Christians must be an infectious people.

10 September 1980

T BIGGIN HILL ON THE 40TH ANNIVER-
SARY OF THE BATTLE OF BRITAIN: Now-
adays, people are inclined to be cynical about heroism
or embarrassed by it. . . .

One of the most dangerous fashions of our time is the tendency
to belittle human beings, to reduce them to the lowest common
denominator of greed and self-interest, and to deny the element of
altruism and even heroism in the human character. It's dangerous
because, if you can sneer at heroes, you can convince yourself that
everyone is nearly always out for himself. I give thanks for the
heroism displayed in 1940 as an antidote to that kind of denigration.
I also give thanks unashamedly for the victory. . . .

Yet wars do not in themselves solve the deepest problems of
human life: at best, they give us a breathing space in which we can
build and work for a world in which war will seem an obscene
irrelevance. . . .

Unless we use the time our force has bought us to turn our love
into aid and development programs for the poor and hungry, then
our children may have to face conflict on a scale and of a ferocity
that could not be imagined in 1940.

Love your country. Love God. Love mankind. Each one of
these commands by itself contains great dangers. Love of country
without love of God or mankind can turn us into rabble-rousing
chauvinists. The love of God which does not overflow into love of
our neighbor is arid and sterile. The love of mankind without the
hope born of faith in God can bring us close to despair as we reflect
on the stormy history of this century and what people have inflicted
on each other. Taken together, love of country, God, and mankind
compose a vision worthy of work and struggle.

12 September 1980

T THE CANTERBURY DIOCESAN SYNOD, THE PRESIDENTIAL ADDRESS: The problem of many who speak on faith is not so much how to communicate but a clearer idea of what they have to communicate. So often, what is paraded seems to be either too simple to be true or too complicated to be communicated. . . .

I believe we have reached a stage when faithful Church people are not sufficiently steeped in Gospel perspectives and the Christian tradition to make the critical and qualifying emphasis the priority. . . .

Too often we have been immobilized by a sense of the complexity of things and a cloud of conflicting witnesses has concealed things which have never been more obvious to eyes which have been given sight by Christ. . . .

We have a particular opportunity now, at a time of liturgical consolidation, marked at the last Synod by the presentation to the Queen of the completed *Alternative Service Book*. The experimentation that backs up the book, which I believe to have been essential, has only been achieved at some cost. Perhaps part of the reason why the present generation is less alert to the Gospel resonances than any previous one is because of the plethora of liturgies and translations of the Bible. Now is the time once again to concentrate on steeping the Church in the Gospel perspective and restoring phrases to people's minds which will illuminate their everyday experiences. We shall indeed be impoverished if we have moved away from the old Bible and Prayer Book phrases and have nothing which can take their place. So we need first to work away at clarity in belief. But along with it goes the call for genuineness, the call for the life of a Church or individual to be aligned to the faith that is declared.

22 November 1980

34

T KENT UNIVERSITY, AN OPEN LEC-
TURE: Caution advises that, as a response to the title
suggested for this lecture, "Church and Society," I should
present a quasi-academic meditation on the various models
offered by history of how Church and Society have coexisted and
interacted. It would be disingenuous to pretend, however, that the
Archbishop of Canterbury has very much leisure for such speculations. He is a participant in the contemporary drama of relations
between Church and Society in this country. . . .

[In that role] yet some elements of the vision remain. The Crown,
which makes an incalculable contribution to the unity of the country,
is even more visible by television and is wedded to the Church of
England in birth, marriage, coronations, and deaths. Bishops are
still appointed by the Crown and still sit in Parliament, each of whose
sessions opens with prayer; and, under the provisions of the 1944
Education Act, Christian worship is still obligatory in state schools.
It is notorious, of course, that the provision is widely ignored, but
it is still on the Statute Book. . . .

The responsibility for religious education is not invariably given
to believers, and so-called value-free education often amounts to the
propagation of a corrosive scepticism, a reduction of religious faith
to the phenomenology of different cults. We have not made up our
minds, however, whether to dissolve the Church/State partnership
entirely and to admit that England has ceased to have a fundamentally
Christian, homogeneous culture or purpose and has become a geographical expression. I would not wish to hurry people into a
decision. . . .

Since we are poised between the world of the Christian incubator
and that of the neutral State, it would help to be clearer about the
issues involved. Some Anglicans, particularly clergy, manifest a sense
of guilt at having a privileged place in society, in government, and
education. They believe Christianity is incompatible with intimacy
with the rich and the powerful. They earnestly desire disestablish-

ment. I have much sympathy with their views, but those who hold them must be prepared to see the State becoming more rigorously neutral in its attitude to competing world views while holding that the Christian witness of a Church, untrammelled but also unsupported by the plausibility lent by a State connection, will be more effective in society as a whole.

An example of where we are on the line is the law relating to suicide. Its status as a criminal offence was abolished, but it is still illegal to assist or encourage people to take their own lives. In the Christian tradition, it is absolutely impermissible for the believer to commit suicide; he is usurping the prerogative of God Himself. For those, however, who do not believe in God as the author of life and for whom life has become a burden to themselves and others, why should they not have the right to decide to end it and why should they not be assisted to do that in as painless a manner as possible? Clearly the State would have a right to legislate on moral matters if the order of society was involved. . . .

But do we really want to surrender all ideas that the State should help build a social context for citizens which would be positively conducive to virtue and even to the vision of God? . . .

We ought to know what we are saying when we disclaim any wish to share further in the partnership which has profoundly marked English society for more than a thousand years. I suspect the divorce will be carried through, but I do not say that with any self-destructive, pseudo-apocalyptic excitement, but with a determination to make the best of present opportunities without lamenting the past or despairing for the future. . . .

As for the statistics of declining allegiance to the Church of England, they are well known but difficult to interpret. The core of regular worshippers is about one twentieth of the population. Those who attend about once a month are about a tenth, but nearly six out of ten people still have a C of E identity disc hung 'round their necks. As Archbishop I do not find the situation satisfactory, but I believe that it is following the way of Jesus Christ not to proceed by condemnation and to see the Spirit sometimes more clearly at work in those who would rarely feel at home in a church than in some of those whose religious practice is more assiduous. . . .

How precisely does the national Church serve its wider constituency, and how real is the sense of attachment still admitted to by such a large proportion of the population? It seems to me the Church still provides evocative symbols, perhaps especially in its buildings. Their reproduction on a myriad of postcards and calendars, set in glades and gentle vales, still points to their power to focus a sense of Englishness which has retained its potency when the uniforms of imperial glory are tattered and even ludicrous. If you have ever tried to close a church you have discovered how deep the foundations lie in popular affection and how many people who have never darkened the door feel themselves involved. Large numbers of people continue to make use of the Church's ceremonies as well. The rites which mark the turning points in life — birth, marriage, and death — where the Church still offers venerable and resonant words, help to give dignity and significance to our existence. . . .

[Whatever the case] the distinctiveness of Christ's way of looking and living needs to be reasserted in a distinctive community life and language.

December 1980

Kent University

T CANTERBURY CATHEDRAL ON HIS FIRST CHRISTMAS AS ARCHBISHOP: For the last few weeks, as I have crossed Lambeth Bridge, I have been able to see the bare concrete bones of a swiftly rising new building. A workman has put a Christmas tree on one of the corners. It appears to spring right from the concrete and has set me thinking about Christmas and its meaning.

For most people in the West today, the natural habitat is not grass or trees but concrete. It is the favorite material for the social engineers who have achieved so much in the last century. Certainly the housing and living standards for the majority of the population have improved greatly, but there are obvious dangers in the process whereby the planners take more and more detailed powers to manage the life of the individual and determine his environment.

The most obvious concrete symbol of that is the high-rise block itself. It seemed to satisfy certain planning requirements — economical in cost and space but intensifying loneliness and broken-down old communities. Floor upon floor they rise, like cell-layers in a great coral reef of humanity, mutely communicating the message that the individual human unit is insignificant. What has happened was not the objective of the planners. They were responding to increased population pressure and shortage of space. One of the most terrifying things, however, about the apparatus of the modern state is that it seems to have a life of its own. All of us, planners and planned for, seem to be victims, immobilized by the complexity of things. Concrete stands for the monolithic and oppressive aspect of all states in all times.

In His day, Christ was no stranger to it — ". . . A decree went out from Caesar Augustus that all the world should be taxed." In telling of the birth of Jesus, the Gospel writers surround the manger, not only with shepherds and wise men, but also with menace and darkness.

Concrete, the symbol of a hard and inhuman outside world, is also reflected in the personal lives of individuals. Herod will seek the young child to destroy Him. The New Testament actually refers to hearts of stone and to men's hardness of heart and shows Our Lord grieving over it. Look around, but even more, look inside, and you will see that the heart of concrete is not merely a New Testament figure of speech. . . .

You might be thinking this is not a very Christmassy sermon, but Christ was born into this world, into a setting which was in many ways far worse than our own. Concrete within and without. . . .

Yet, for all that, it is God's world (and) there are always forces at work in the world, hardly perceived, but breaking up the inhuman concrete and letting in more light and life. I remember, at the end of World War II, seeing Hitler's proud achievement, the concrete Autobahn, cracked and with grass growing through it. Again in Germany, outside the city of Berlin, there is a great mound, made of the rubble of the devastated capital. It is called the Kreuzberg; its ugliness has been transformed by a carpet of grass and now it is used by contemporary Berliners as a ski slope. Water and grass seem very puny, but they stand for the forces in the world constantly at work breaking up the concrete. . . .

God speaks to us in the Christ-child, and there is nothing like babies for melting the hardhearted. The Light of the world looked so frail, but He was shining in darkness and it did not overcome Him. . . .

Whoever set up that Christmas tree near Lambeth so that it seems to sprout from the concrete pillar has provided a startling image of the deepest meaning of Christmas. Hope of this sort means that Christians are free to act to change the world, where others are immobilized by the sense of how complicated everything is and how strong are the moulds and patterns which dominate our lives. Christianity does not give us detailed answers to our many problems, but it does give confidence in the power for good in the world, and it saves us from becoming people whose attitudes are set like concrete. . . .

That's what God intended, that's what He revealed in His Son. That's what we celebrate at Christmas.

25 December 1980

PONTIFEX OR GRASPER OF NETTLES?

LAST year's preface exulted at the prospect of Robert Runcie as Archbishop of Canterbury — witty, it called him, "a bonny fighter," and "skilled in walking tightropes." Now, a year later, we have seen all these things, and so much more. . . . He has established himself as a public figure, nationally and internationally. There is a dignity about him, a quiet sense of humor, a freedom from pomposity. He can command attention on a great occasion in a cathedral and hold it — and yet minutes later he can appear at ease sitting outside on the grass talking to children. He has a remarkable sense of occasion and of what is fitting. At his Enthronement amid the glitter, the gold, and the trappings of state, there was in his sermon a pondering, a meditation almost, upon the strange authority of Christ's Church, beginning "not in the assumption that we possess all the answers but in our recognition of our poverty of spirit. From that can come a real longing to hear God speak. . . ." When he appeared before the General Assembly of the Church of Scotland, there was appreciativeness of his Scottish forbears, and of Scottish spirituality, but also a clear and uncompromising affirmation of that Anglican spiritual tradition in which he is rooted, and of which the Archbishop of Canterbury is the chief bishop and guardian. Before Queen Elizabeth the Queen Mother, celebrating her eightieth birthday, he spoke with feeling and for the whole community, making a sermon from her face and quoting Dame Julian of Norwich, "All shall be well, all manner of things shall be well." He has spoken, too, upon great public issues and about the problems of the Church and the Churches. Before his own Diocesan Synod, he has affirmed his belief that the time has come for the Church to "firm up its faith" — to decide what the real issues are and where it stands on them. Nettles, he has said, have now to be grasped.

Nettles there are in plenty, both in Church and State. He must do his share of the grasping and the uprooting. His form in his first year as Archbishop encourages us in the belief that he can and he will. Meanwhile, he has been equipping himself with the human aides he needs for his multifarious tasks. His chaplain and his secretary came with him from St. Albans. He has inherited his predecessor's lay assistant, his press officer, and his foreign relations experts. Two fresh appointments make up the team; one is an adviser on international Anglican affairs who, incredibly, is a former member both of the Church Army (of the Church of England) and of the Vatican Secretariat. Finally, there is the presence — considerable in more ways than one — of the new Lambeth chief of staff, Bishop Ross Hook, who has given up the bishopric of Bradford to put the wisdom of forty years of ministry in different parts of England at the service of the new Archbishop. It is indeed a strong team.

T THE HOUSE OF LORDS ON THE IN-
TERNATIONAL YEAR OF DISABLED PEO-
PLE: The disabled are a special care of the churches
because Christians cannot regard them as on the edge of
society or objects of pity but as those who are at the center of the
discovery of depth in trust, love, and sharing.

I know a block of rather soulless flats in which lives a crippled
man who cannot move from his room. The door is always open: it
is with the so-called handicapped person that the desperate and lonely
housewives or the unloved children can find attention and unselfish
interest. The care of the handicapped always draws out unsuspected
qualities from those engaged in it, and when you minister to others
they minister to you. . . .

My Lords, I believe that the International Year of Disabled
People offers an opportunity for us to display two examples of growth
in partnership within our society: first, a partnership between the
professional services and the strength and vigor of voluntary action;
and, secondly, a partnership between disabled people and the rest of
us which recognizes how much we have to receive from them. In
days when confrontation, polarization, and protest increase, I suggest
that such robust partnerships may remind those at the center of
government that while they struggle to solve our economic problems,
there is also a moral imperative without which we shall never achieve
the recreation of a real community life for our people.

14 January 1981

T GLOUCESTER ABBEY'S 1,300th ANNI-VERSARY: Your Bishop lured me here with the sug-gestion that I would be the first Archbishop of Canterbury to return here since St. Theodore, the seventh occupant of my office, helped to consecrate the Abbey Church in the year 681. I did not, however, need much persuading to come to this beautiful part of England, to experience the warmth of your welcome, and to join you in your thanksgiving for thirteen centuries of Christian life.

In Gloucestershire you have a rich tradition to celebrate. The spirit of Christ has flowed into fine buildings, dignified worship, and men and women of vision and energy such as Osric, the founder of the abbey; Cyneburgh, the first Abbess; Serlo, the Norman rejuve-nator; and my unfortunate predecessor, Dean Laud. There is so much to give thanks for that it could become overwhelming. The profusion of forms taken by the Spirit of God makes it desirable for us to go back to the simple beginning, to make sure that we get our bearings straight.

In surveying the vast achievements of the Church here — in art, in education, in care for the poor and needy — I was struck by the extreme position represented by one of your Bishops. It is a choice piece of 18th-century invective. I speak of Bishop Warburton who grudgingly admitted that "the Church, like the ark of Noah, is worth saving, not so much for the unclean beasts and vermin that almost filled it and doubtless made the most noise and clamor in it, but for the little corner of rationality that was as much distressed by the stink within as by the tempest without." I would lay claim to a rather better opinion of my fellow passengers than he expressed!

Behind all the weight of centuries, however, it is salutary to look at the simple strategy pursued by Osric and his collaborators at the beginning of the story of the Church in Gloucester. It was to produce such a flowering of Christian life that the saying "as sure as God's in Gloucestershire" became a proverb.

Osric was a practical man of affairs, an underking, administering the province of Mercia which then, in 681, had within living memory been a pagan kingdom torn by conflict with other English states. Osric's response to troubled and insecure times was to found a community dedicated to prayer and the building up of a fellowship in the Gospel.

What about prayer? The Church is frenetically planning, surveying, drafting, reporting, and consulting. Much of the effort is worthwhile, but I see more and more clearly that, if we rely simply on the worldly or common sense that has brought us to this point, we have no superior wisdom to offer a world already choked with information to the point of indigestion. Prayer is our door into God's way of seeing the world; it gives us hope and the freedom from fear that leads to unselfish action when instead we might be tempted to spend our energies clinging onto our possessions and achievements in a disintegrating world. Prayer is the most practical activity in a world like ours.

But this kind of praying must be grounded in the fellowship first given us in the picture of the band of apostles in the Gospels — the fellowship that enables its members to taste and see the Gospel in action. Some modern spiritual talk seems to be commending an isolated course of spiritual self-improvement, just like an adolescent building up his biceps in private. Christian prayer roots us in the life of the Father who goes out to embrace a needy and distracted world in the arms of His Son. In turn His Son brings back to the Father the outcasts he has befriended. Our prayer, if it is to be in the Christian spirit, must share in that dynamic quality.

We are all involved in this work in a fellowship in the Gospel that does not identify, say, the clergy as those religious professionals to whom alone the principal task of the Church is delegated of being with God for the sake of others and with other people for the sake of God. Osric was a lay ruler; his religious community was headed by an abbess, and his heirs and beneficiaries were bishops. We shall not be true to our calling if we do not see the Church's task of being Christ's body, His eyes and hands in the world, as a task we all share.

The beginnings, then, were prayer and a fellowship in the Gospel. I believe little of lasting value can be achieved without them, but I am aware that common opinion is very different. For so many, Christianity, prayer, and the community of faith is seen as, at best, an amenity or an agreeable hobby, or at worst a tedious irrelevance. Even though this Cathedral Church is packed with people, it would be idle to deny that the influence of the Church in our society has declined in recent years. But perhaps it is not fanciful to see the decline as a necessary stripping to basics — the vision that Osric knew. It is essential if the Church is to be worthy to present Christ to the next generation. Just as prayer and the community of faith were the bases for growth and solid achievement in the troubled and semi-barbarous England of the seventh century, I believe that they are springs of hope for the future.

The situation is not an easy one for modern Christians to grasp. We have grown used to discussing all our problems without reference to the dimension of prayer and the Spirit. Too often, the problems of our international life are analyzed in narrowly economic or political terms. Yet there is not a mere financial or political formula that can overcome the fear and selfishness that distort all human life and society. Humankind is not intended to live locked up in itself. It can only give the best of itself when it is turned to a center beyond itself and when it is attached to God.

Those inherent attributes, fear and selfishness, are partners. You don't have to be a gloomy moralizer to see them very active in our own day. If you live locked up in yourself and in your possessions — or dwell on the interests and concerns of your family or group — you embrace a way of life that breeds fear. Indeed, there is much fear abroad in the land. I hear people express fears of loss of position and privilege, fears of other people, races, and groups. If you make your own individual happiness and prosperity the center of your life, then you are bound to create hostility in the world as you look out at other people in a competitive or envious light. Also, if you invest everything you have in your own limited life and in your own material prosperity, then you are committing yourself to something that must end in death.

God's children were meant to love and to give themselves to God. They were intended to love their neighbors as fellow creatures of God. If we really are centered on God because the Spirit is active within us, if we are really praying, then there will be no room for the fear that comes when the defense of our own castle walls is our own priority. If we are in love with God, then there is no room for a selfish attitude to God's other children.

Take Gloucestershire, for instance, which in the seventh century was on the edge of the civilized world. It was in "the country of the white savages," as we were called by the inhabitants of Southern Spain. These many years later we still see that our Christian love and service must carry us into a way of looking and living that sees brothers and sisters in Christ in every part of the world.

Sharing in the prayer of Jesus Christ releases a spirit into the world which creates and builds and overcomes ingrown fears and the cynicism which nothing else can combat. We are surrounded today, both in the stones of this ancient Cathedral and in the lives of all the believers who have gathered here, by evidence in plenty of the power and vigor of the prayers and the Spirit which have reshaped the world. Through us, through our prayer and fellowship in the Gospel, the spirit of Jesus Christ desires to express Himself more and more fully for our own age, to reshape it anew. To be faithful followers and witnesses of Jesus, we must place Him at the center of our love and our hope and our strength.

11 February 1981

← *Gloucester Cathedral*   British Tourist Authority.

T THE GENERAL SYNOD'S DEBATE
ON COVENANTING WITH OTHER
CHURCHES: . . . I am eager to see wounds in English Christianity healed, [and] I owe much of my up-
bringing and education to Free Church influences. . . .

So I inevitably feel a kinship with the Free Churches, who have
responded to the call issued from Lambeth earlier this century that
they might be one with us in an episcopally ordered Church. But
what sort of bishops would we have — clusters and committees of
them, undermining the very notion with which I have been reared
that episcopacy means finding at the center of our operations not a
committee, but a person, ever reminding the Church of its center
on a person? What sort of energy-consuming bureaucratic quagmire
lies in store behind the easy phrase "common decision-making?" . . .

It must be remembered that the Roman and Orthodox traditions
are just as advanced with some Protestant conversations, especially
on the Continent. A unity ticket issued from Canterbury must be
routed via Geneva as well as Constantinople and Rome. And then,
next, do the proposals safeguard the catholic episcopal order, being
in communion with the bishop? It is a *sine qua non* of Anglican
involvement in unity discussions with nonepiscopal bodies that the
historic episcopate is nonnegotiable. Yet does that commit Anglicans
to the narrow tractarian pipeline theory of the transmission of
orders? . . .

In this as in other areas it is clear that the rights of conscience
of bishops, clergy, and people must be safeguarded. So I believe I
can commend the proposals and vote for them, and welcome the
substantial move which the Free Churches have made to meet us.
But frankly, there will need to be some changes in us as a Church
and in how we regard these proposals if they are ever to inspire us
rather than make us feel, as it has been expressed so often in recent
weeks, what a bore we have got to go into all this business of cov-

enanting. We must stop thinking of one last heave to achieve an ecclesiastical semimerger. . . .

I look for a comprehensive spirit in any Church which goes into covenant. But it will require from us a much deeper faith than we yet have in the Divine Grace which, as the old Byzantine liturgy has it, always heals what is wounded and makes up what is lacking.

25 February 1981

TATEMENT AT THE GENERAL SYNOD'S DEBATE ON HOMOSEXUAL RELATION-SHIPS: The Gloucester Report has not received a very warm welcome from those who would like the Church to sound a clear blast on the trumpet on either side of the argument. But at the very least I believe that the authors of the report deserve congratulations for the way in which they have skillfully marshalled medical and social data to explode prejudices still commonly maintained. I hope the report will be used to promote the kind of informed discussion that will combat the silly insinuations and innuendos, the casual contempt and unthinking mockery of homosexuality that so often pass for discussion of the subject even, alas, in Church circles.

Often in the field of race relations, for example, or care of the handicapped, we are able to point to an evolution in public attitudes and understanding. I am not certain that such is the case in public discussion of homosexuality. I believe the situation may even have deteriorated since the last century.

It was about 1897 when the word homosexual was first used as a noun by the psychiatrist Havelock Ellis, and he apologized for such bad usage. Until then people spoke of homosexual acts and not homosexual persons, and that was one of the reasons why students and others in the 19th century could write letters to one another with expressions of affection few would dare to use today.

Once we were encouraged by Freud to define people in terms of their sexual feelings the danger was there of tyrannically imposing the categories *heterosexual*, *homosexual* on a range of relationships and feelings that cannot be categorized in such a banal and crude way.

One of the results has been the eclipse of friendship as a profound spiritual relationship which inspired some of the greatest art and writing in the ancient world. I detect much ungenerous suspicion surrounding friendship in our own day, and I am reminded of that passage in C. S. Lewis in which he pleads with us not to judge close relations between persons of the same sex by any crude *a priori* theory.

Kisses, tears, and embraces are not in themselves evidence of homosexuality. Hrothgar embracing Beowulf, Johnson embracing Boswell, a pretty flagrantly heterosexual couple. And all those hairy old toughs of centurians in Tacitus, clinging to one another and begging for last kisses when the Legion was breaking up. All pansies? If you can believe that, you can believe anything.

It is not, of course, the demonstrative gestures of friendship among our ancestors but the absence of such gestures in our own society that calls for special explanation.

Just as I would deprecate automatic suspicion attaching to friendship, so on the other side I cannot but believe that those who are obsessive about so-called gay rights contribute to this unhealthy atmosphere.

I have no doubt that people will refer to the matter of clergy discipline. Well, one of my rule of thumb tests for ordination would be if a man was so obsessive a campaigner on this subject that it made his ministry unavailable to the majority of Church people, then I would see no justification in ordaining him.

To deprecate the casual and unthinking talk about homosexuality does not mean that we should abandon any moral judgment on the subject altogether or accommodate ourselves to echo contemporary judgment. Our contemporaries are divided on the subject, and if we have anything to offer to the debate we must start from the Church's scriptures, its title deeds, and its traditional teaching.

The Church itself is not united in its viewpoint, and I should like briefly to sketch, as I see it, the four main points of view, indicating my own preference.

First, some people see homosexuality simply as a sin and make much of the Sodom story. Even those, however, who still think in this way have to learn not to judge other people's temptations.

Then some see homosexuality as sickness and feel it may be catching. Those who still think in that way must have the obligation of exercising compassion.

And then, third, it is possible to see homosexuality neither as sin nor sickness but as a handicap, a state with which people have to cope with limitations and hardships in which the fulfillment of heterosexual love and marriage is denied. If you take that view, to which I incline myself, it has a very important consequence for your attitude.

We are learning to treat the handicapped not with pity, but with deep respect and an awareness that often through their handicap they can obtain a degree of self-giving and compassion which are denied to those not similarly afflicted.

27 February 1981

T THE HEADQUARTERS OF THE PHAR-
MACEUTICAL SOCIETY NEAR LAMBETH
PALACE: It is easy to sneer from the outside about the
work of those who make and sell pills in our society.
Moralists are quick to lament the way in which pills are misused
instead of using them to approach the more fundamental problems
of health and healing. Few need die in pain or suffer the torments
that every previous generation has suffered. Those who sigh for the
tranquil idyll of the 18th century often forget the agonies which did
not spare any class of society and from which modern pharmaceutical
science has largely delivered us.

It is easy, too, to be cynical about your retailing. I heard recently
of a shop that displayed the ambiguous and somewhat worrying notice, "J. Ohm & Sons, Chemists: We Dispense With Accuracy."
The fact that we can laugh is a measure of the success your Society
has had in promoting high standards of safety and service.

Moreover, during the last decade there has been a growing
realization that we must go into partnership if healing at the profoundest level is to be achieved. There has been a lingering idea that
patients are infected by some kind of alien disease that is then com-
batted by able and highly trained technologists without the patient
having a very active role. But such a view has yielded to the recognition that, although we deal with symptoms, notably with pain
and specific disorders, true healing occurs when the picture is related
to a wider understanding of how a man becomes sick if his relations
with himself, family, or society are wrong and if the therapeutic
structure of the community itself is crumbling. The accent of the
new approach to healing is not only how to cure disease or defer
death but to achieve real health.

8 March 1981

AT WESTMINSTER ABBEY, LENTEN ADDRESS: Just over 50 years ago the Bishops of the Anglican Communion saw little hope of unity with Rome. They regretted that Pius XI appeared to contemplate "complete absorption" in his encyclical *Mortalium Animos* of 1928 as the only method of achieving unity. . . .

At the penultimate Malines Conversation in 1925, Cardinal Mercier read *'L'Eglise Anglicane Unie non Absorbee*. It had been prepared by "an anonymous canonist," now known to have been Dom Lambert Beauduin. It seems rather fanciful today: his stress on the pallium — a woollen stole blessed by the Pope that caused no end of prelatical rivalry in the Middle Ages; also his contention that progress towards unity would be wrecked over the question of precedence of Archbishops of Canterbury over Cardinals or vice versa. Well, Cardinal Hume and I will not lose much sleep over such matters! Nor did the Canon take seriously enough the indigenous English Roman Catholic tradition: on his view the new Sees created after the restoration of the Roman Catholic hierarchy in 1850 would simply be suppressed. Yet in spite of serious flaws, the paper remains significant because it is the first clear recognition that the Churches of the Anglican Communion are bound to seek a unity which respects their autonomous tradition. It is an initial systematic essay on the *kind* of unity Rome and Canterbury seek. . . .

In spite of oversimplifications, Beauduin's essay makes its point: we can't tolerate an Anglican Church *absorbed* by Rome: the Anglican Church, united not absorbed. However, once it is admitted as a fruitful approach (and such an approach was more than once publicly endorsed by Paul VI) an immediate question arises: what range of diversity is compatible with unity, or to put the matter another way, what are the limits of acceptable diversity? The question has to be asked in *any* ecumenical discussion. It is a particularly pressing question for any Church in dialogue with Rome because of the Roman tendency towards an authoritarian centralization and uniformity. Forgive me for making this point somewhat crudely. The character and model of the Church in the dominant Roman tradition owe a great deal to its origin and location in the center of a great Empire. Many of the detailed administrative practices, legal systems, and even archives survived to mould the minds of the architects of the original Papal monarch. The tendency of such an order is to favor a stable ideology, both communicated and enforced by a bureaucracy functioning according to juridical models. The precondition of the system was the Latin language, which became even more useful to the Roman Curia after it had died as a living language. An ideological stability is easier to maintain through the medium of a fixed language. The changes in living languages are always subversive to unchanging theological definitions — words not only change their meaning in a living language, they change their resonances and their place in a cultural economy. The collapse of the Latin culture over the past two decades, the liturgical changes within the Roman Catholic Church, the new confidence of the non-European cultures into whose languages Christian truth needs to be baptized — all mean that the problem of perceiving unity in inescapable diversity is now a pressing one for the Roman Church, which for so long has been able to fend off the difficulty by reducing diversity to matters of ornament and detail. The Anglican Church has to face problems of serious diversity — but the Roman Church has to face problems of unity. Not surprisingly we have both been having a hard look at the New Testament and the Early Church. . . .

When we turn to the Early Church we have the impression that instead of looking for unity in diversity we are now looking for diversity in unity. . . .

In now going on to speak of Anglican comprehensiveness I do not wish to insinuate that the Anglican tradition is the direct or only heir to the Primitive Church. Nor do I want to suggest that Anglican comprehensiveness is the only possible way of achieving unity in diversity today. I do want to suggest, however, that the unity and diversity presented to us by the Church of the New Testament and the Fathers may put Anglican comprehensiveness, when rightly understood, in a more favorable light, as well as indicating the range of diversity feasible in any Anglican/Roman Catholic union. . . .

Where is the line to be drawn? At the close of the 16th century and during the 17th century, in the polemic with both Puritans and Recusants, the classical Anglican answer emerged. It gave Anglicanism its distinctive ethos. First, that the common Reformed appeal to scripture was tempered by the role of tradition, not, of course, as an additional source of revelation, but as a sure guide to the uncertainties of scriptural interpretation. . . . Eventually the doctrine of the Incarnation became more central to mainstream Anglicanism than justification by faith. Next, there was an appeal to reason which reflected the assurance of Renaissance Humanism. . . . Finally, that doctrine was presented in the liturgical worship of the Church. The *lex orandi* was the guide to the *lex credendi*. Unlike other Reformed Churches the Anglicans used the Prayer Book as a formula of faith. Now these three characteristics were and are by no means exclusively Anglican, but their particular combination gave Anglican theology, spirituality, and pastoral practice its distinctive stamp. . . .

We are now at the stage of dialogue where the hard questions need to be put — and Rome will have some tough questions to put to Anglicans as well. In this exchange both traditions will be purified and renewed. Both will have something to give to the other.

11 March 1981

Westminster Abbey

EDITATIONS FOR MAKING THE WAY OF THE CROSS WITH YOUNG PEOPLE IN LONDON'S NOTTING HILL AREA: If this were an ordinary story, its climax and victorious ending would have come with Jesus riding into Jerusalem amid the cheers of the crowd. But it is at that point that our strange and wondrous story begins. We are going to follow Jesus through the streets, through betrayal, judgment, pain, and death, and after that we are going to see a different kind of climax and victory, a strange victory.

As we walk with Jesus through these next hours, it isn't necessary for us to alert ourselves to religious thinking. The thing to do is to be attentive and relaxed and let the story speak to us. We are all here from many different Churches after hundreds of years of being divided from one another and even sometimes hating one another, but we are all here because this Easter story is *the* Christian story. It transpired before there were divisions among Christians. Now, these many years later, real unity and friendship between Christians comes, not when we are gazing at one another, but when we look together in the same direction at Jesus Christ. It is while retracing His steps that we discover each other as brothers and sisters and not as Methodists or Roman Catholics or Anglicans. Let us begin our walk by saying together the prayer Jesus Himself taught us.

II. MEDITATION, AT THE WHETSTONE ROAD OPEN SPACE: Judges, police, crowds — we often think of them as very different and opposed to one another, but here they are all on the same side. Let us not despise any of them, for they are closer to our positions than we may care to think. They all wanted a better world and they thought that the way to get that world was by power and force. The police, by keeping people in order, dividing the law-abiding from those who break the law; the crowd, hoping to achieve their better world by overthrowing the foreign government and dividing people into patriots and traitors. The crowd, the judges, and the police — they believe in different worlds but their way of getting there is the same: power, violence, the clenched fist. It was by a clenched fist that Roman soldiers saluted their officers, and perhaps we shall see them doing that as they march along the road. It is what most of us stand for — hitting back, being tough, getting our way, if necessary by trampling over people. But violence breeds violence; martyrs produce martyrs. Down the centuries, it is that iron law that has made men miserable and wretched.

But look now at Jesus: He follows a different way. It is easy to hold him in contempt, and probably, if we had been there that first Good Friday, we would have thought Him pitiable and contemptibly weak. But Jesus' way is the hard way of a really strong man, strong enough to love even His enemies who beat Him and were going to execute Him. It is a love that changes people deeply when they are crushed or silenced by violence. At the same time we recall that there was a Roman centurion in the Easter story who, as a man of power and war, recognized that the love of Jesus showed that Easter was not weakness but strength beyond most of us. He saw the way Jesus suffered and did not hit back or curse, and so the Centurion said, "Truly here is the Son of God."

But this way we shall be following, now that Jesus has His Cross, becomes a very, very hard way. And if we have thought of the Easter story as something beautiful and magical and have not been afraid of it, we have not really understood it.

III. MEDITATION BENEATH THE WHETSTONE ROAD OVERPASS: We see Jesus meeting His mother, Mary, on the way to His crucifixion. Now, as then, there are plenty of reasons for mothers to be worried and anxious. We are concerned about the world in which our children will have to grow up and what will happen to them. Life sometimes seems to be extremely cruel and harsh with those whom we love. Words like violence, unemployment, and sickness suggest those things in life that can crush the individual. Here we are standing near a road built for the convenience of people who want to be somewhere else other than this place. The highway's noise and domination mars the life and land-scape of the area. It is a good symbol of all those elements that threaten the local and the familiar — son, daughter, family. So Jesus

encounters His mother at the roadside, and you can understand why she, like so many modern mothers, is anxious and distressed.

The picture, however, is not all dark. In a world where all kinds of forces beyond our control threaten those we love and seem to overwhelm the places we love, there is still a flourishing of love. Even in the worst circumstances, even in the camps of Nazi Germany or the hunger of an African village, love flourishes and nothing can root it out. We can sympathize with Mary in her pain but we can also give thanks for her love, the love of all mothers, the love that is part of nature and that nothing in all creation can or will destroy.

IV. MEDITATION FROM THE ILLUMINATED BALCONY OF A NEIGHBORHOOD HOME:

There is much to be derived from the scene of one thief who is impenitent and another who kneels at the feet of Jesus. Both are thieves and are being brought to justice; they will share the same form of execution as Jesus. But for Christians, the story does not stop at that point. The thieves have been judged and sentenced, but for Jesus Christ the real test follows in accepting human judging and sentencing. Granted that the thieves and all of us, in one way or another, have spoiled our lives, failed, done things of which we are ashamed, the question remains for the thieves and for us: what are we going to do with the broken bits of our lives? There is a choice: either we retreat further into isolation or bitterness, like the impenitent thief who is to curse Jesus on the Cross, or we take the broken bits of our lives, we see them without illusion, we see through them how much we need to be forgiven, and so we come to Jesus. The man who sees, in the broken bits of his life, his own need for forgiveness, is the man who in his turn has the power to forgive others. It is a power that can bring a fresh start and new hope out of all the brokenness of life. People who have come in that way to a knowledge of themselves as broken people and who have learned to forgive and to be forgiven are those who can help us deeply in our greatest hour of need. The hard-boiled, the successful, the virtuous who have never gone off the rails, who have never been forgiven, who have never understood that they need forgiveness, often become the hard and severe people Jesus met so often during His earthly life. The choice is before us: what do we do with the broken bits of our lives?

V. MEDITATION AT THE CORNER OF LEDBURY ROAD WHERE JESUS MEETS SIMON OF CYRENE:

Jesus has been beaten and ill-treated. He has walked a long distance carrying a heavy cross and is hardly capable of going on unaided. Simon of Cyrene was probably one of the early Christians; he is a well-known figure, described as the father of Alexander and Rufus. He demonstrates, in the most practical and moving way, what life in the Church and for the Christian believer is supposed to be. In every sense, we are meant to bear each other's burdens. We are intended to be alive to the needs of all those around us. We ought to concentrate on building up and making sure that our lives are not full of the kind of criticism and hatred that is so easy to fall into and is so destructive. The Christian attitude to other people, whether they are Christians or not, is that they are brothers and that we must share their burdens. There is room in the Church for repentant prostitutes such as Mary Magdalene, thieves who are sorry, and for reformed characters like Matthew the tax-gatherer. But there is no room in the Church for those who live their lives passing by on the other side of the road and refusing to get involved in helping to bear the burdens of others.

Simon is given the privilege of helping Our Lord, and he shows us a picture of what Jesus has been doing all the way through the march, what He will do to the end of His earthly life, and what He does for us now. He is walking that tormented path because He desired to share our burdens, and, even now, if we will let Him help, He is present with us to help us with whatever our burden in life might be.

VI. MEDITATION AT BRUNEL ESTATE GREEN: The Archbishop reads a passage beginning with Luke 23:33, "When they reached the place called The Skull. . . ."

FINAL MEDITATION:

We have seen Jesus on the Cross, but for the Christian the story does not end even with that tragedy. We have experienced the power of the Spirit of God to bring new life into a world that seems to be all negative, all barren, all in love with death and violence. We are standing in a place by the canal, and it is in itself a wonderful picture of what I am talking about. The present reality is rather bare and sparse, but there is hope — there is the Meanwhile Gardens Community Association. They have a vision and a hope of turning this place into a beautiful garden by the canal. There could be no better place for celebrating the power that God has to turn what we wearily call "present reality" into a future that is more full of life and sap. Here, then, we wait for Him to do His work. But the waiting would be no use if there were not also hope and a willingness to see Him. Here we wait in what will be a garden transformed by a vision. We could not wait or hope in a better place.

Holy Week, 1981

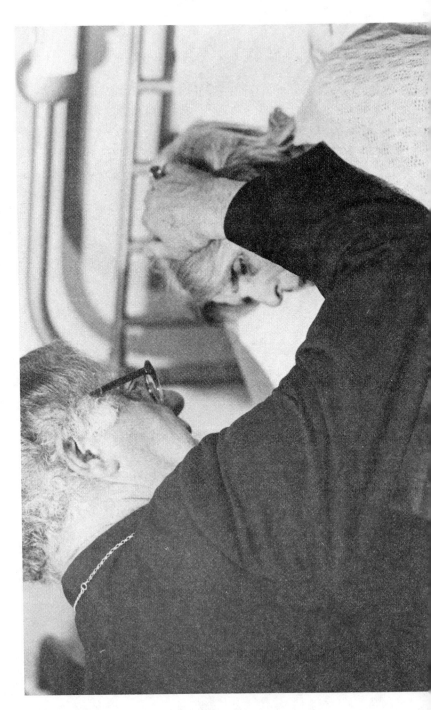

AT CANTERBURY CATHEDRAL'S MAUNDY THURSDAY LITURGY OF THE BLESSING OF THE OIL: Many customs are associated with Maundy Thursday. The name of the day comes from the Latin word *mandatum* which means "commandment." It is the day of the new commandment, "That you love one another."

Most of us think of the Last Supper, the Eucharist, as a sign of our communion with the Lord of love and with each other. Another event of the Last Supper is the feet washing as an illustration of loving service in the Name of Christ. And on this day there is still another ancient custom — the blessing of oil that is a sign of the healing ministry of the Church.

We have good news for human ills, and so a part of the customs of the day is the tradition of priests gathering around their bishops as a sign that we are at one in the ministry of healing. In the words of the Psalmist, "Behold, how good and joyful a thing it is to dwell together in unity! It is like the oil . . ." — oil of healing, oil of harmony.

The symbolism of oil in the ministry is a very simple one. Oil is a medicine, an emollient. It soothes what is sore and moistens what is dry, for such is the kind of healing Christ can bring to His people. He banishes soreness and dryness of body and spirit.

Throughout the Catholic world — Roman, Orthodox, and Anglican — there is always a special celebration of the Eucharist on this day to express joy in the healing that comes from God, to express our unity in the sacraments, which are a sign and vehicle of the healing ministry.

In the Armenian Church, all of the oil that is used by Armenian communities all over the world is blessed at a holy place called

---

← The Archbishop anoints a woman patient during a Holy Week visit to St. Joseph's Hospice near London. Press Association Ltd.

Etchmiadzin in the Soviet sector. It is indeed a sign of unity among that ancient Christian people.

I have been to Etchmiadzin during Holy Week. On the first day they collect herbs. On the second day they make the oil, and on the third day of Holy Week they boil it. And on Thursday, of course, the oil is blessed. Now that the new Prayer Book provides an order for such a blessing, I thought we should bring that small ceremony out into the open and arrange a service in the Cathedral at a time when the clergy, as well as some of the laity, are free.

Of course you will have the Eucharist in your parish services this evening; this is a day when, by tradition, it is appropriate to take Communion for a second time.

The service in the Cathedral means that, at the heart of the diocese in Holy Week, we are giving thanks that all healing flows from God — and we are giving thanks, too, for the sacramental signs of that healing. It means that we can give thanks for our priesthood and pray for the unity of our ministry together. It is also an opportunity to pray that those who celebrate the Easter mysteries may be fortified and directed aright.

Often in the course of a year, diocesan administration may seem distant, impersonal, and remote. Archbishops and bishops seem authority figures, far removed from the cares and concerns of ordinary priests in the ordinary parish or the chaplains in the hospitals. Here is a chance to share as brethren together at the simplest level in what our work is all about. We share in the Gospel and we share in the sacrament that brings the Gospel into the present.

Two thoughts about sacraments have influenced me greatly:

1) A book by Oliver Quick on the sacraments says that they represent a truth of the Gospel and are instrumental in achieving the truth. So, for example, God is someone who wills our healing. When we anoint a person we not only represent and declare that truth but we also change the situation. I wish that the custom of anointing to declare and assist might be more commonly used; sacraments are real but they are not magic.

2) There is a statement from Father Kelley, the founder of the Anglican Society of the Sacred Mission, in which he defends the objectivity of sacraments against the heresy that their actions depend upon our degree of worthiness. The position I am trying to explain,

he wrote, can only be expressed in the words *I want Christ*. And I mean that in the same sense as a child crying in the night, *I want Mother*.

Adults may believe, and the child may learn, that although Mother has gone away she is not far off. But we shall not persuade ourselves and we shall not persuade the child's trenchant truthfulness that it is the same thing. It is hard enough for me, and more than I deserve, that I may find my Lord at all — and if even that depends on any capacity of my own or depends in any degree on my spiritual state or force — that, may God help me, I will not believe.

It is difficult for me to make any response to Christ, to find the energy to worship Him, or the faith to believe in Him when He comes. If *I* am to find the energy and faith to fetch Him, I must give it up.

All of these factors that I have mentioned combine to justify our Maundy Thursday blessing of the oil. Remember above all that it is the day of the Lord's giving. We may reject His gifts. We may distort or evade them. But they are always generously available to us.

Christ gives the new commandment. He gives the Eucharist. He gives our partnership in the Ministry of the Gospel and sacraments.

In all of this, the Lord wills our wholeness, our unity as priests and as Christian people. "Behold, how good and joyful a thing it is, brethren, to dwell together in unity! It is like the oil. . . ." Thanks be to God!

16 April 1981

T CANTERBURY CATHEDRAL FOR EASTER, 1981: Last Monday I took part in a procession through the streets of Notting Hill in London. In well-chosen places the events of the first Holy Week were acted out with vigor and conviction by a large cast of locals. It was not a pale, pious production. There must have been about 3,000 persons drawn into the procession. It was an event in which all the local churches cooperated — Roman Catholics, Anglicans, Methodists, Pentecostals, and with a Salvation Army band for the music. It was not what is sometimes sneered at as "bland ecumenism." We were eager to get beyond the day of division to the experiences of the first Holy Week. It meant that different sorts of Christians were not looking at each other thinking the other's practices and customs were strange or odd. We were together turned towards Jesus Christ — His suffering, His resolution to do the Father's will, His death on the Cross, His demonstration of God's love for us.

But there was something more. We were of very mixed race and color. The Christ figure was black, a local youth leader. He joined us as we mingled with Spanish, West Indians, Irish, and Italians, and rubbed shoulders with Cockney and a dash of Kensington. Of course the police were there, but they were recognized as familiar locals, too, and without their coping with the traffic and keeping an eye on us we could not have managed.

At one point we stopped to watch the scene of the betrayal and arrest on the very spot where some years ago the Notting Hill Carnival had been disfigured by violence and riot.

Later, after a moving Crucifixion scene and meditation amidst a high-rise block, with residents viewing it from every balcony, we came to the final scene where some dreary wasteland beside a canal is being slowly transformed into a garden.

There in the dark, apart from the glow of torches, the Resurrection story was read, and the shouts of triumph, rockets, and fireworks went off, and one of those firework set pieces — the kind that usually don't work — spelt out in glowing lights, "Christ is Risen." And the whole crowd burst into an Easter hymn.

I tell you this story at some length because it was for me an Easter experience and a reward for the reconciliation that has been worked at for years in that area.

Yet the event had small press coverage. There were no scuffles. There was no bad news. Apparently the assembling of 3,000 people of mixed race in good-humored cooperation was not of sufficient interest in the week of the Brixton riots. I expect the first Good Friday would have made the news, but the Resurrection was hushed up.

Although we live in grim times, we are in some danger of poisoning ourselves with bad news that ranges from international tension to the failure of pandas to mate. The bad news is sometimes projected in such exaggerated and aggressive language that the voice of moderation cannot be heard.

Anglicanism's South African Bishop Tutu recently spoke at a meeting in England over which I presided. He sounded like a man with constructive suggestions at the eleventh hour for peaceful changes in his country. It was amazing to find the same speech reported in the South African press as if he was simply a bloody revolutionary.

I believe there are plenty of signs of the Resurrection and new life in the Church and in the world. You need the eyes to see them and the courage to cherish them, and you must never lose the capacity to be astonished by the mystery of death and resurrection. Good springs out of evil in the most unlikely places. The solemn, the cynical, the know-all, the "You can't change human nature" brigade will always be at odds with Easter and so at odds with Christianity, which is wholly based on the Easter miracle and the Easter experience.

But the Bible warns us against those who cry too easily for peace where there is no peace. Consequently, my experience in Notting Hill did not separate Good Friday from Easter Day. The Resurrection moment in the wasted place transformed into a garden pointed back to the Way of the Cross and declared it to be a victory.

The Resurrection does not cancel out the Cross like a divine "abracadabra," but in its sign and its gift of the Spirit we discover that His way can be our way. Instead of hitting back, you can so absorb and handle the negative and destructive forces in life — the forces of cruelty, conflict, sickness, even death itself — that they increase the total output of goodness in the world. It is not sentimentality. Of course suffering is evil, and of course it can and does degrade and crush people. But there is the difference between them and those who find themselves able to grow, to forgive, to trust in their trials. That is what is meant by saying there is no tragedy that cannot be redeemed with the strength Christ gives. Moreover, you will notice that the Risen Lord did not appear to Caiaphas or to Pilate, the soldiers or the mob. He appeared to the men and women who had kept company with Him and watched it all.

The Christian faith in a Living Lord is always part of a long discipleship. Thomas could not have said, "My Lord and my God!" after Easter if he had not said earlier, "Let us go with Him, that we may also die with Him." If you have walked with Him in Galilee, in the ordinary workaday world, and if you have in some sense died with Him on Calvary, and kept trust in the long, dark shadows of life, then you can accept the end of the Gospel story, too. If you have seen Jesus taking the sting out of death, then the completion and proclamation of that conquest over death at that first Easter are not incredible. Without these experiences, men and women will always laugh at Jesus and the Resurrection as did the sophisticated Athenian of old. With these experiences Easter Day wins conviction but never loses its wonder and power to astonish us.

I have heard many Easter sermons. Sometimes I have been troubled because they left me so cold. I believe the reason is that they sound too dogmatic; they seem to have strained away the mystery in a smooth confidence of assertion. I remember walking away from a memorial service with a friend in Cambridge. He was a highly intelligent agnostic and scientist. He said to me, "You know I would be delighted and astonished there was an after-life" — a remark that I have never forgotten because in many ways he was not far from the Kingdom of Heaven.

I am sure that any presentation of the Resurrection that simply scales it down to human understanding is false and futile. Our hope must come from outside ourselves or it is in vain.

In the procession at Notting Hill, in that celebration of Cross and Resurrection, we were witnessing that there was nothing inevitable about Church divisions. More importantly, there is nothing inevitable about racial conflict. And that is the deepest truth of Easter — we have spiritual resources with which to challenge the fatalists.

I never tire of quoting the Welsh preacher, Hugh Pryce Jones, "If anyone says that war is inevitable, poverty is inevitable, unemployment is inevitable, I shout out 'Thank God that's a lie.' Jesus Christ lives and His Kingdom will come."

That is what Easter means. It means that if the first disciples were to broadcast today they would not do so at 8:45 a.m., the time for the "Week's Good Cause," but at 9 or 10 at night, for what they have to proclaim is news. It is *good* news, and we are Christians insofar as we respond to and act on that news with confidence and with joy.

19 April 1981

T A DINNER GIVEN BY TRUSTEES OF THE UNIVERSITY OF THE SOUTH, SEWANEE, TENNESSEE: Links between Archbishops of Canterbury and this University go back to the very beginnings of this institution. As Bishop Quintard of Tennessee said in 1869, "The University stands today, a witness before the world of the unbroken unity of our Church, and an enduring memorial of the first Lambeth Conference." . . .

I very much admire the pattern of education to be found here — a seminary at the heart of a thriving university and, at the heart of both, the Chapel. You have laid out a characteristically Anglican approach to questions of truth and knowledge. The seminary would be impoverished without the other faculties . . . but I believe also that the other faculties would be the poorer if they did not have a seminary in their midst, [for] all learning should be yoked to its proper end, which is glorifying God. . . .

In the West, information is so easy to come by that the flow has reached a chronic state of congestion and distraction. I have met not a few cases of cultural indigestion. We are deluged with words, including theological words, most of which are said without cost or constraint, with the result that they have little value. Words regain their potency, however, when we come to them from prayer and the reverent worship of God, rekindling wonder and enabling us to see the world with fresh eyes. Hence the Chapel is absolutely central — a characteristic although not, of course, an exclusively Anglican insight. Worship is at the very center of our lives, and, as we are drawn further into the life of God and into His way of seeing, it changes our perception of everything around us. Worship opens the eyes through thanksgiving and by rehearsing the fundamental affirmation of the Faith, the Creeds, Canticles, the Lord's Prayer, and Psalter. It is our way to that deeper knowledge in which information is transformed into thanksgiving and wonder, and that can daily bring us closer to God. . . .

In England the Reformation did not produce a Church as determined on theological definition as the Lutheran and Calvinist Churches on the Continent. Instead attention was lavished on providing a Prayer Book, in English, which priest and people were required to use in Church and encouraged to follow in their own homes. You have recently spent much time debating about your liturgy, an activity that critics have tended to interpret as evidence of a Church bound up in its own parochial affairs, oblivious to the world of need beyond its ghetto. I profoundly disagree with such a negative view. While liturgical debates can be tedious, it is a matter of very great importance that the Church has an expressive liturgy, capable of nurturing a reverence for God and of steeping the Christian believer in Our Lord's way of seeing the world. It is only by such discipline and such worship that we shall become proof against the strident counter-conditioning of our contemporary materialistic dreams.

23 April 1981

T THE 350th ANNIVERSARY OF CHRIST
CHURCH, STEVENSVILLE, MD.: I am glad
that your theme is that of rededication to the missionary
task Our Lord assigns to all the members of His Church.
The phrase "missionary task" sounds a little daunting. It conjures a
picture of stridency and aggression and the sound of a tambourine,
but in reality the essence of the task is a longing that more and more
people should share and know the good things God has given us and
a willingness to be used by Christ, not necessarily in showy or spectacular ways, but by doing and saying things for Him and in His
Name in a way that draws others to Him. Aggressiveness about
religion can sometimes succeed in gaining scalps but is not faithful
to the way of Our Lord, which was to love the loveless into loving.

The missionary work we are called to do can be very different.
For a mother, it may be teaching her children by word and example
to grow up as men and women of integrity. Some may be led by
their God-given talents to a life of service, to the suffering or the
handicapped. Some may be called to speak of Our Lord more directly, as priests.

Whatever we do, however, we must have the disposition and the
willingness to be sent and to be used by Christ. Some tasks will not
be glamorous, or attract much attention, but the world is being
changed in its depths every time a believer willingly puts himself at
the service of God. We must be willing to be used but also willing
to be sent out. Christian communities do not thrive when members
are obsessively looking at their relationships with one another. But
if you look together in the same direction at your missionary task,
you will be imperceptibly united and you will grow into a truly
Christian fellowship.

25 April 1981

T THE FOLGER SHAKESPEARE LIBRARY, WASHINGTON, D.C., FOR THE RAMS-BOTHAM LECTURE ESTABLISHED TO HONOR A FORMER BRITISH AMBASSA-DOR TO THE UNITED STATES: The many modern pilgrims to Canterbury provide a vivid illustration of the rejuvenation of the Cathedral after centuries of snoozing in a tranquil backwater of life. It was in fact in Shakespeare's time, in the 16th century, that the Cathedrals were entering their period of long eclipse. The impulse to go on pilgrimages petered out in an orgy of satire and controversy. Spectacle took flight for the royal court and the theater, leaving Cathedral divines to sing their truncated offices as the splendid ornaments were sold to pay the bills.

As a backdrop to these developments, there lingered the memory of the Archbishops who had been martyred. None rivaled the fame of Thomas Becket, hewn down within the sacred precincts at Christmas 1170. By the year 1420 when a jubilee of St. Thomas was celebrated, 100,000 people visited his shrine during the fortnight of the festival. Then, in the next hundred years, the income of the shrine and the numbers of pilgrims declined to the point that Archbishop Wareham cancelled the jubilee when confronted with an exorbitant demand before plenary indulgences would be granted by the Pope then rebuilding St. Peter's. The end came in September, 1538, and the shrine, for so long a center of popular devotion, was broken up with remarkably little resistance, and Becket's bones were scattered.

Even if reverence for the remains of dead Archbishops was fading in the early 16th century, living Archbishops still kept court on a splendid scale. At a banquet marking Archbishop Wareham's enthronement in 1504 (on Passion Sunday of all days) the guests sat down to 236 different dishes consisting exclusively of fish—and all served at tables decorated with pastry representations of notable events in the Archbishop's life!

Nonetheless, enthronements provide a good index of the degree of pageantry and spectacle in Cathedral life. Their decline was lamentable. Their recent revival is cause for celebration.

In the ensuing years, it was Archbishop Cranmer who saw to the simplification of Cathedral worship in accord with new theological outlooks.

In other respects, however, the decline continued, and eventually there was a ten-year period when the voice of prayer and praise, heard daily for a millennium, fell silent. The great bell that had summoned the faithful to Matins and Evensong then tolled but once a week for the mundane announcement of the opening of the town market. Well past the 18th century a heavy torpor lay on the Cathedral's life, its traditions more often despised than honored by its guardians.

As for enthronements of the Archbishops, they became mean affairs conducted by proxies. During the 133 years from 1715 to 1848, no Archbishop at the outset of taking office even bothered to make the journey to Canterbury. The later years of the 19th century saw some quickening of tempo, but at Canterbury it was not until George Bell became Dean that color, spectacle, and drama flooded back into the Cathedral's life. Bell was later to be Bishop of Chichester, but long before that time, in 1928, he threw himself into organizing Cosmo Lang's enthronement as probably the most impressive and spectacular since Wareham's in 1504. Copes were reintroduced, and Anglican divines who had looked like magpies in their severe black and white were overnight transformed into birds of paradise. I like to think it was not simple vanity or exhibitionism. After the great, long, earnest Victorian gabfest, the English Church had become Word-saturated. The Reformation protest against the pictorial mode of instructing the faithful was understandable, granted that it had been used to accentuate the picturesque and to obscure the pure milk of the Gospel. Now pictures, color, and symbolism, after four centuries of fasting, were able to speak with matchless eloquence about the majesty and wonder of God.

George Bell was also a protagonist for religious drama for healing the divorce between theater and Church that had become absolute by Shakespeare's time. He persuaded T. S. Eliot to write a play for performance in Canterbury Cathedral, and the result was a drama describing the last days of Becket — *Murder in the Cathedral*. So we come full circle, and the play has contributed greatly to a resurgence of interest in the baffling figure of St. Thomas.

The Cathedral is now the home for a rich diversity of cultural life as it was before the Reformation — concerts, exhibitions, plays, special services for myriad causes. Like Washington National Cathedral, it is also a meeting place for all the arts. In both places, stonemasons as well as workers in stained glass, stone, and metal find their highest expression.

At the same time, in an age when millions can easily travel, Cathedrals once more attract vast numbers. At least one consistency remains: it was not easy in the Middle Ages to distinguish between pilgrims and holiday-makers, and it is not easy now. But in the contemporary search for meaning and vision, Cathedrals are places where many puzzled or honestly curious people can come to look and listen without being drawn into the premature commitments almost inescapable when undertaken in the small-scale, community church.

On the whole, Cathedrals minister to our generation's largely inarticulate craving for order and vision. It is no longer necessary to defend their usefulness. In fact, as an Archbishop, my main fear is that they have become too much the scene of frenetic activity. They were dignified and tranquil roosts for learned men whose main contribution to the life of the Church was writing books and enriching the stock of clerical anecdotes. Now, alas, the ideal Canon needs to combine the virtues of an oriental guru and a dynamic entrepreneur with little time to concentrate on recondite studies.

By the same standards, I would not counsel anyone who wanted to compose erudite lectures for the Folger Shakespeare Library to become Archbishop of Canterbury! In the 19th century it might have been done. The Archbishopric was considered a light job suitable for the older man who was not up to the number of evening engagements inescapable if you were, for instance, Bishop of Winchester. Now the story is different because Archbishops, like Cathedrals, have found — to their astonishment — new usefulness in a restless world of high mobility and deeply troubled pilgrims.

25 April 1981

T THE WASHINGTON CATHEDRAL SUN-
DAY EUCHARIST OPENING A WEEK-
LONG MEETING OF PRIMATES OF THE
ANGLICAN COMMUNION: The whole world
has been united in excitement and admiration for the American
achievement in successfully launching and recovering the space shuttle. It represents not only a superb feat of technology and personal
courage but also something that promises considerable benefits for
life in our global village. When the shuttle is fully operational it will
be able, without great expense, to carry into space communications
satellites of undreampt size — an important contribution to increasing
mutual understanding and thwarting the ambitions of those rulers
who would keep their countries isolated.

While we have come a long way over the last two decades since
the first manned space flight, the launching of the shuttle was also
the 20th anniversary of another event, the trial of mass murderer
Adolf Eichmann. In these simultaneous happenings we see a terrifying disparity between our technical achievements and our moral
progress. The terrifying aspect is that the space shuttle is being
discussed in terms of *military* potential. I sometimes think we are
children let loose in a laboratory full of dangerous chemicals and
substances. It is a thought that prompts me to declare the urgent
need to mature and educate that child in the peaceful uses of all he
has at his disposal.

Meanwhile, there are spectacular eruptions from inner space in
places like the Middle East; violence and fear are never very far
from the surface of any of our societies. For that reason the need to
explore *inner space* is just as urgent as our reaching into outer space.
In any such research, the first thing to establish is method. For

---

← *Washington Cathedral's stern verger, flanked by sterner prelates Runcie
(left) and John Allin, escorts Prince Charles to read the evening
lesson.* RNS

Christians the proper research method is reverence for the Word, for the love of truth that dispels illusion. In that respect, the Christian Church's first allegiance is reverence for the Word, respect for truth, and opposition to any attempt to stir up fear and violence by labeling or dividing humankind into devils and angels. . . .

Sensing such attempts, many good people are immobilized by fear. They are tempted to retreat into fanaticism, cults of unreason, or hidden indulgence in drugs or alcohol — all flights from responsibility.

It is a plight that returns us to the first Easter when the disciples were sitting in a locked room for fear of the Jews. When Jesus came to them, He said, "Peace be unto you" and in so doing gave them spirit and hope sufficient for them to emerge from their locked room. The demoralized disciples of a convicted blasphemer became a world-converting force. In His dying and resurrection, Jesus Christ has shown us that there is no situation so barren, so full of pain and suffering, that it can defeat God's power and love. It is that truth that we assert.

26 April 1981

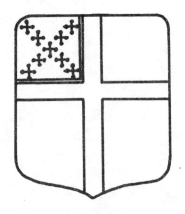

The Episcopal Church in the United States

T A LUNCHEON AT THE NATIONAL PRESS CLUB, WASHINGTON: The Archbishop of Canterbury may be associated with all kinds of picturesque situations, but in essence, his task, like that of Christ's apostles, is to communicate faith and hope, and to promote love in the world. In today's world, it means he must be serious about working with the media and conscious of their great potential for good.

The superior penetrating power of the Washington press corps was demonstrated when Cosmo Gordon Lang visited the city in 1918 as Archbishop of York. He was being photographed on the White House lawn when one of the cameramen, noticing that the Archbishop's pectoral Cross was caught in the sash of his cassock, ran up to him and flipped the Cross free, saying, "I guess you'd look a durn sight better if you showed your charm!" Well, I am attempting to show my charm, for Archbishops of Canterbury have been rather solemn figures in the past. They still have a place in English national life which would make too many capers undesirable. But I am attempting not to become a museum piece trapped by a history which stretches back to A.D. 597 when the first Archbishop of Canterbury was enthroned.

My job involves work at the local, national, and international levels. Unlike the Presiding Bishop of the American Church, I am also a diocesan bishop with direct pastoral responsibilities for the Diocese of Canterbury. It is vital because when one is promoted to the bureaucratic stratosphere, one can easily dry out and become a person who deals only in generalizations and platitudes. My travels around the Diocese put flesh on some of the themes that preoccupy me in my national work. I can better understand what it is like to be unemployed when I know people faced with the situation. When school problems or mental hospitals are discussed, I can relate the abstractions to institutions with which I have a pastoral connection. It is the Diocese of Canterbury that gives me roots.

As Primate of All England, I am obviously much concerned with the leadership of the Church of England and of its governing body, the General Synod, and most of my work is done from my London base, Lambeth Palace — home of the Archbishops of Canterbury since 1200 although it has changed a bit since then.

The Archbishop is also regarded as some kind of national oracle, called upon to speak on great occasions. Although he is expected to address himself only to Church people, he must not be narrow in his sympathies, for he must appeal to and speak for the national family as a whole. The wedding of Prince Charles and Lady Diana Spencer is such an occasion, which not only unites us in enthusiasm for the young couple, but enables us to celebrate the Christian values of home, family, and the stability of marriage.

As in every country, there is some cynicism in England about official life, but the monarchy is more popular today and regarded with even greater affection than in Queen Victoria's era. In those days there was a flourishing Republican movement in England, whereas now not even the minuscule Communist Party advocates abolishing the monarchy.

The Archbishop of Canterbury also has some political duties as a member of the House of Lords. Moreover, he has local and national responsibilities to reckon with; in days of personalized leadership, the microphone tends to be put in front of *one* man.

As spiritual head of the Angelican Communion, the Archbishop finds himself a focus of loyalty and affection for Anglicans worldwide. The Church has spread in the wake of the British Empire. It has not only survived the Empire's dissolution but has put down roots in local cultures all over the world and is today, after the Roman Catholics, the second most widely distributed Christian body. Its leadership and inspiration are no longer exclusively English-speaking. For the majority of its members, English is the second language.

The Anglican Communion is no longer the Church of England and her dependencies, but a family of Churches united by a common vision and enriched by a variety of national cultures and temperaments. Hence it is insightful to examine our emphasis.

We begin with worship. The attempt in England to recover a less cluttered Catholicism began with the Anglican Fathers devising an English Prayer Book and enforcing its use. What they accomplished in the Prayer Book is central to Anglicans everywhere. It aims, through the fundamental texts of the faith, to steep the believer in our Lord's way of looking at the world. It admits very little to public worship that does not belong to the stratum of the essential catholic expressions of the faith as honored by all Christians.

. . . I frequently encounter people who tell me that the truths taught by the Bible are self-evident. "Let the Bible speak for itself," they say. Alas, it is a very short step from that demand to the point where the Bible means what we want it to mean.

Throughout its history, Anglicanism has been anxious to keep its lines of communication open with the contemporary world, to celebrate and support social unity rather than draw rigid distinctions between the damned and the saved. I should like to think that Anglicans continue to care for the health of the national community rather than being obsessed with the affairs of their own Church. . . . Recently we have had to learn, in places like South Africa and Uganda, that sometimes loyalty to Jesus Christ and a concern for the national community demand opposition to the government. For instance, as Anglican Primates, we are united in our support for Bishop Desmond Tutu who has recently had his passport withdrawn by the South African government.

The larger framework of international issues includes, of course, the dread possibility of nuclear war. The individual has lived with an awareness of his own individual death since the beginning of history, but only since 1945 has he acknowledged the possibility that the whole species could be obliterated. . . . Without playing on the full registry of horrors that would attend a nuclear war, I must say with all the force at my command that we are exposed to a peril almost too ghastly to contemplate. We are capable of unbinding the forces which lie at the heart of creation and of destroying that civilization. We have made great advances in technology without a corresponding advance in moral sense. The challenge is before us to conquer the destructive impulses in man which could blot out his name from the universe. The Church cannot merely lament that evil possibility, it must fight against all callous acceptance of it as a normal situation and urgently work for a new way to prevent it, and must be concerned that the evil of nuclear weapons be constantly underlined.

Behind the mild facade of "flexible response" lies the terrifying

possibility that our political leaders may be the first to unleash nuclear weapons against another country. It is vital that we see nuclear weapons for what they are—evidence of madness.

As a Christian body our chief effort has to be directed against the lies and prejudices which are the soil and seed of violence. . . . The Christian Church is in business to cultivate the seeds of a better world. It is a long haul and there are no short cuts.

28 April 1981

← *The Archbishop addressing the National Press Club, Washington, D.C.*   UPI

T EVENSONG AT GRACE CHURCH CA-
THEDRAL, SAN FRANCISCO: I had a mother
who, as a romantic, visited and fell in love with San
Francisco. Thus I was brought up in drizzly Liverpool
to dream of sunny California. I now have a son who, as a 20-year-
old student from Cambridge University, spent last summer here and
told me I had not lived until I had been here. So, in at least two
ways, this part of my visit to the United States is a fulfillment of a
dream.

Before I met your Bishop I had read an article with a headline
that proclaimed "The Easy Riding Style of Bishop Swing." I expected
to find the Bishop's throne had been replaced by a hammock! Imagine
my surprise to discover an energetic man who aims to do more
pushups in a day than I have done in a lifetime and who shows equal
vigor in promoting his "Dream for California" — a good title for a
serious program of mission. He knows that this is a place where
people come from all over the world because they have their private
dreams. He knows that such dreams can degenerate into self-indulgence. Therefore he has said that his "Dream for California," a
Christian mission, needs to be held steady in the heart of the worship
of this Cathedral. It should be its heartbeat.

3 May 1981

Seal of Grace Cathedral

84

T A LUNCHEON OF THE WORLD AF-
FAIRS COUNCIL OF LOS ANGELES: The tra-
dition of human rights is venerable. It was already ancient
when it occupied the center of the world of John Locke,
one of the philosophers who most influenced the American Revolution. If I may paraphrase Locke's view with outrageous simplicity,
it is that justice requires that certain natural rights that belong to
individuals should be respected at all costs. Injustice can be defined
as the denial of those rights.

Such passionate emphasis on the inalienable rights of the individual as being at the very center of what it is to act justly and
morally has widened our moral horizons and helped to change the
world. For example, in his *Essay on Toleration*, Locke used that
emphasis on the inalienable natural rights of the individual to provide
a theoretical basis for the liberty of the individual conscience to
dissent from the religious establishment. It became one of the most
cherished rights of both England and America. Barely 150 years
before Locke's time it was inconceivable that anyone could claim the
right to dissent in religious matters. It was believed that to admit
such a right would be immoral because it would destroy social cohesion since a kingdom divided against itself cannot stand. However
strong the belief, it proved not to be the case and the consolidation
of a right to religious dissent has enriched the life of our country
and of yours.

Locke also insisted that the rights of individuals over and against
tyrannical governments should be at the center of political morality.
His was an important notion incorporated in the Declaration of Independence and reiterated in the guarantees of the Constitution of the
United States.

Nowadays the tradition of putting individual inalienable rights
at the heart of justice and political morality has so colored our thought
that it would be easy to underestimate its creativity and the radical

character of the changes in the world that have flowed from its widespread adoption.

The creativity of the tradition, for example, is still not exhausted, particularly in the field of women's rights. Between 1850 and 1950 women came of age, in the sight of the law and social attitudes. Their status changed drastically. Women are now deemed to have wits as well as wombs. For the first time in our history a woman can be torn between her desire to be a mother, partner to her husband, or a tinker, tailor, soldier, or sailor.

However, the tradition of inalienable rights as the centerpiece and touchstone of political morality has been challenged over the last two centuries — and creatively so, I believe. . . . The sense of brotherhood that began as a religious vision is now being substantiated by some very significant contemporary developments. The photograph of our beautiful planet from the moon is both itself sinking deeply into our consciousness and also a symbol of how developments of technology and economics are propelling us into a new global consciousness. In addition, the speed of modern communications means that the fate of a young man in an Irish prison thousands of miles away impinges on the consciousness of millions. . . . I really believe, in the words of Benjamin Franklin, that if we do not hang together we are in danger of hanging separately.

5 May 1981

T A DINNER GIVEN BY THE DIOCESE OF LOS ANGELES: I understand your present Bishop is only the fourth Diocesan you have had in Los Angeles since 1895. You certainly know how to look after Bishops, and now I can testify that you know how to look after Archbishops as well. Although I must confess that I had my doubts this morning as I flew into downtown Burbank — well known to me for Rowan and Martin's *Laugh-In* — only to find that the good Bishop and a welcoming party were waiting to receive me at the Los Angeles Airport. Typical downbeat humour!

But I have discovered that hospitality is indeed one of the keynotes of the Episcopal Church. It goes wider than visiting Archbishops. At a time when Los Angeles has become the second largest Mexican city in the world and when also you have received successive waves of refugees, particularly from Southeast Asia, I know that you have not shirked making a creative response.

For Christians, welcoming and working for the well-being of the stranger within our gates is indeed a sacred duty. It has been a duty laid upon those who would obey God from the earliest period. The Book of Leviticus says that when a stranger sojourns with you in your land, you shall not do him wrong, you shall love him as yourself.

You have been translating this unambiguous biblical command into programs and practise. Individual parishes have sponsored hundreds of refugees, helping them to feel welcome and to establish themselves in this country. You have helped immigrants also to become aware of the American way of doing things to insure that they also feel at home and can play their full social and political part in American-style democracy.

But while equipping people to participate and share in the new, it is no part of the Christian duty of loving the stranger, to persuade him to abandon his traditional culture. I am delighted to be going tomorrow to the Cinco de Mayo celebrations in the Church of the

Epiphany where Anglicanism is being enriched by being adopted by an exuberant Spanish-speaking culture. I am proud to belong to a Church which has shown so much energy! . . .

With all these windows on the world, you have an opportunity which I know from your record you will not refuse to articulate and to spread a global consciousness that is appropriate and needed in today's world. The Church is in the front line [although] we are often criticized as Anglicans for being an Establishment Church. There is, of course, some truth in it. I have just discovered that one in every nine Congressmen in the United States is an Episcopalian, but that need not necessarily mean that our Church is a community of the comfortable and complacent. . . .

But we shall not make our full contribution if we are just people of promiscuous benevolence. We must have a clear vision of the community we wish to build, a clear vision to offer to the city, the Diocese, and the country, one that will guide our actions, giving creative dissatisfaction with present reality. We do not want to be people with endless critical indignation but the architects of something better and finer.

5 May 1981

O AN ECUMENICAL EUCHARIST AT
AMES, IOWA: Our thanksgivings today are not just
for the Church. They are for the whole community, for
the land, the rain, and the sun, all God's gifts. . . .

Thanksgiving, however, is not just a way of cancelling a debt.
It changes the way we look at the world. If you take things for
granted, you act out the lie that you were made to be the center of
the world and have a right to enjoy everything going. If you take
things with gratitude, you refer them to the giver.

As we are doing in this Eucharist, you hold up the elements of
life — bread and wine and everything that goes into them: rain, sun,
earth, and human labor, to God the author of life. In the process of
giving thanks you begin to see bread and wine and life itself for the
wonderful things they are — expressions of God's love for us. So
when we eat bread and drink wine after giving thanks over them,
we receive more than food for the body, we receive food for the
spirit as well because we can taste and see the depth and richness of
God's love for us.

We must cultivate the habit of thanksgiving, not just in Church
but throughout the whole of life: before a meal, after work, before
reading, while playing with the children. If you cultivate this attitude
to life, you are growing as a follower of Jesus Christ, who took bread
and first gave thanks. If you are a Christian, you are a person who
has a growing sense of life as a gift.

When we understand, through the sacrament, how richly we
have received, then, if we are to progress still further as followers
of Christ, we must learn in our turn to be generous givers. He took
bread, gave thanks, and then gave it to His disciples. First thanksgiving, then distribution. . . . Be ready to give away and to share,
and so acquire a treasure which will form a good foundation for the
future.

8 May 1981

T THE CATHEDRAL CHURCH OF ST. JAMES, CHICAGO: I am particularly glad that you have chosen to make a beautifully constructed and inspiring Eucharist the climax of my visit. It allows me to give thanks that the Church is active and energetically involved in the problems and opportunities of the city, in promoting racial harmony, in struggling to improve housing and educational facilities, and in much else.

It is of vital importance in whose Name these activities are undertaken. If they are used to enhance the power and prestige of our Church or minister to our sense of self-importance, then we shall be like a character described by C. S. Lewis, "She's a woman who lives for others and you can tell the others by the hunted look in their faces." It matters greatly that our social activity is part of the worship we offer to the God and Father of our Lord Jesus Christ, the image of the invisible God, and not part of worship directed at some other God such as our ego or our hope of social advancement.

Men and women are natural worshippers. Everyone is engaged in worship every day because human beings have so evolved that they constantly look beyond themselves to refer what they are and what they are doing to something or someone they regard as fearsome or attractive. But, of course, the gods people worship are varied. The most popular gods are abstract — success, security, power, wealth. They are abstract but not impotent. They exert a powerful influence on how we behave, how we choose our friends, whom we invite to dinner, how we spend our money.

In worship, there should be no question for us. We worship the Father as we see Him in Jesus Christ, "for in Him the fulness of God was pleased to dwell." The Father is our point of reference for all that we do and for all that we are becoming. Granted that worship is inescapable, it is clearly of very great importance for us to ask these questions: What am I worshipping? What is my dominant point of reference? You cannot help giving away, often unconsciously to others, the name of the God you worship.

The dominant influence on your life is going to leave a mark on you. It shows in our behavior and our faces. We have all registered the serene beauty of the faces of those who have devoted themselves to the worship of God. Perhaps the face of a nun comes to mind. In contrast, we have also noticed the strained and avid faces of those who really worship money or power, whatever formal religious allegiance they may profess. The truth is that after the age of 40 we are in large measure responsible for our faces. . . .

There is a danger of reducing God to something of a buddy and ignoring the harder demands of His Word, which insists on our being just and truthful and moral whatever our likes and dislikes. The neighborhood god, jogging with us through life's way, is not the whole truth about our object of worship but only a fashionable puppet who fails our imagination as soon as we look into the vastness of space, face the mystery of creation, or encounter the intractable tragedies of the city.

9 May 1981

T A EUCHARIST AT THE EPISCOPAL CHURCH CENTER IN NEW YORK: Your Presiding Bishop has been a thoughtful and relaxed guide. That's important for a visitor who gets a bit frantic about the next thing he should say, or what he may be expected to wear, or where his staff happens to be at a particular moment. I would like to thank the staff of 815 Second Avenue because I know how much the Presiding Bishop depends on all that is done here. In that connection, I want to quote Edmund Blake who said that "if anyone would love, he must serve in *minute particulars.*" We often are engaged in separating the pastoral and mission dimension of the work of Christ's Church from the administrative. But the administrative is part of responsible love and *of minute particulars.*

It has become almost a matter of principle in the Church of England that the office should be separate from where a bishop or archbishop lives. I don't believe there is a bishop in England who actually has a desk in his diocesan office. When I was Bishop of St. Alban's, I thought of moving into the office but they said, "Oh, no, because, you see, people always have grouches, and they like to have something to complain about and the office makes a target. And they mustn't be complaining about the Bishop, they must love you. But the office provides opportunities for indignation."

For instance, I remember a vestryman who said, "Bishop, we're having a lot of trouble with the Diocese."

"Oh yes?" I replied.

"Yes, we can't get a reply out of them about voting procedures," he said.

"Oh," I said, "you're having trouble with the office. *I'm* the Diocese."

"Oh no," he said. "It has nothing to do with you, Bishop!"

When a computer was reportedly installed in the Diocesan Office, a very old parish priest [Canon Bernard Pawley] went to the clergyman next door and said, "You have now a computer in the

Diocesan Office: now is our Salvation nearer than when we first began!"

Whatever the case, the work of administration is very important. All of it is part of the mission of following the Gospel.

11 May 1981

Cathedral Church of St. John the Divine, Diocese of New York

T A DINNER OF THE ENGLISH-SPEAKING UNION AND THE CHURCH CLUB OF NEW YORK: Quite frankly I've been astonished by the amount of interest generated by my visit, in particular by my harmless hobby of hog-raising, which led to an extremely joyful spell in Iowa. While breeding Berkshire hogs is a very minor part of my life, it assumed great proportions in Iowa and as a climax to the whole celebration I was presented with a pig of great pedigree, whose manners, I thought, were so impeccable I was able to hold her up to the camera. That, of course, became *the* picture. I wonder whether anybody in England will ever take me seriously again?

On a more serious note, I have been greatly impressed by the vitality and ubiquity in the Church life I have seen. I remember the welcome given me at the University of the South where theological students talked to me about the need for renewal. They are upholding the finest traditions of Anglican scholarship, especially the respect for truth and excellence which is very much a part of the Anglican tradition and is to be cherished at this time of all times.

I don't think people always realize that one of the great problems of modern times is that with the rapid expansion of knowledge it is much more difficult to believe in the way in which people believed in the past. Anglicanism has something rather special in its readiness to listen to the voice of God speaking not only through the tradition but through the best thought of the day.

I shall also remember the Mission of the Good Samaritan in San Francisco and its very lively congregation of French, Haitian, Spanish, and English ingredients. I shall not forget the St. Anselm of Canterbury Refugee Center in Garden Grove near Los Angeles where there is such a magnificent work being done in receiving and settling Haitian refugees. It made abstract generalizations that I have to deal with in public speaking so much more immediate and personal. We know about all the urban mission work in Chicago, and the character of the service at St. Philip's in Harlem will long remain with me.

Indeed, the quality of worship I have encountered on formal and ceremonial occasions has been of a very high standard — from Kent Island in Maryland to yesterday's Evensong in the Cathedral here in New York. I'm glad mention has already been made of the architect of that service because I know a great deal is owed to the man I regard as the *diaghilev* of the Episcopal Church, Canon Edward N. West.

I personally learned so much from the Episcopal Church. It has confirmed the wisdom of calling together the Primates of the Anglican Communion. In turn, the Primates' meeting in Washington and my visit to your Church have left me more convinced of the vital contribution Anglicanism has to make to world Christianity. As I have said before, we do not claim to be *the* Church but we *do* claim to be a part of the One, Holy, Catholic, and Apostolic Church, and our insistence on reverence for scripture and tradition and on respect for truth and for reason is even more vital at a time when people are tempted to retreat into a narrowly based fanaticism, in a world in which fear and anxiety nourish the irrational and the stridently exclusive.

In the Anglican Communion, not least in the Church of England, we are, I believe, growing into a vision of a worldwide Church where all the parts and members have something special to contribute, and where we would be poorer if left with just our partial national visions. I have also been encouraged by my encounters with leaders of other Churches. So there has been an Anglican dimension and an ecumemical dimension, and the opportunity to consider together some of the most pressing problems of our day. . . .

It is wonderful and worthwhile to be a pilgrim for Christ in today's world.

11 May 1981

HIS GRACE ABOUNDING

"THE new Archbishop of Canterbury is a really *thoughtful* man!" exclaimed an American who had briefly renewed acquaintance with Robert Runcie during his U.S. tour, 21 April to 12 May 1981.

Why such effusiveness for a prelate miles away, geographically and ecclesiastically?

"Well," said the woman, "I was in Canterbury on the Feast of Thomas Becket when there's a procession to the martyr's shrine. The Archbishop saw that someone's candle had gone out, so he reached over from the aisle and lit it from his own."

It was small, similar considerations that people noticed repeatedly during Archbishop Runcie's coast-to-coast travels — joyfully giving the deaf the sign of peace at Ames in the Diocese of Iowa; patting a child's head later the same day as he approached the altar at Seabury-Western Seminary. (It had been, in fact, on the morning of that incredibly crowded day that he had stood amid bales of hay addressing a group of Iowa farmers and, speaking of the young, had mentioned his own son and then, with tears suddenly glistening in his eyes, had remembered aloud, "who is twenty-one today.")

To know the Archbishop "in the round," as his sculptor Nigel Boonham says, is to see him poised but warmly human in a variety of situations that punctuated his sometimes helter-skelter, three-week journey.

In Easton, Maryland, Dr. Runcie clambered from a plane to shake hands with a woman from the Standing Committee of the small diocese on Maryland's Eastern Shore. News photos show him giving her complete attention and she is beaming as the Primate says, "I'm always glad to see women given positions of responsibility in the Church." It was a remark he made often and if it seemed an advance attempt to ward off questions on women's ordination, it was nonetheless sincere. It is perhaps germane to remember that in effect he "reports" to three women: wife Lindy who has a loquaciousness that Lambeth Palace has never previously seen; most formally and quite frequently to Her Majesty the Queen; and often to the woman who forwarded his name to the Crown, Prime Minister Margaret Thatcher. Of the latter, it is easy to believe that they were Margaret and Bob when involved in undergraduate politics in the Oxford Union.

It was in such an academic setting, when Runcie went to Cambridge for theological training, that he met his future wife. A slim, alert woman, Lindy Runcie joined her husband for the Los Angeles and New York portions of his trip. Jet lag after her arrival on the West Coast caused her to lean briefly against a pillar of the Biltmore Hotel ballroom. She was at that moment in a receiving line so long it had eventually to be cut short so that the several hundred guests could go in to dinner. Even as they shook hands with dozens of people they were told that Bobby Sands had died from his hunger strike in Ireland. They knew instantly that the Archbishop would be expected to comment.

Publicly, the Runcies have a kidding relationship reminiscent of the Lambeth residents of twenty years ago. In the early 1960s at a dinner in New York's Hotel Pierre, Lord Fisher pretended to shield his face from being slapped when he openly joked of his wife's alleged eccentricities.

In comparison, the Runcies are more forthright and amusingly caustic.

"Thank you for this lovely tray," Lindy responded on receiving a gift from Janice Rusack, wife of the Bishop of Los Angeles. "Its durability will be appreciated because my husband is such a messy eater!"

Moments later, presented with a Steuben vase, Runcie observed that "it seems sturdy enough for even my wife's enormous capacity for breaking things."

Archbishop Runcie, as primate and metropolitan, is usually seen in the familiar purple cassock of bishops or in ornate cope and miter: those are the public views of an amazingly agile, athletic figure. An impression far less widely seen is that of Runcie as man's man, especially that chilly spring morning in Iowa when he wore white overalls zippered to the neck, yellow boots, and a yellow visored cap. He readily traded hog-talk with a savvy group of breeders, looking every inch the knowledgeable knockabout gentleman farmer perfectly capable of turning a good profit on sending pigs to market. It is in those moments that one sees the World War II tank commander beneath the facade of Lord Archbishop. And it is when he is in the pulpit or at the altar that one senses the caring for others that prompted him, under fire, to pull a comrade to safety from a burning tank.

Runcie is an able pulpit orator, shifting easily from an extemporaneous introduction to prepared remarks. He tends to belabor his manuscripts until the last moment like a student with a reluctantly relinquished essay. Even press releases of the Church Information Office often bear careful editing in his own hand.

Yet for all his capabilities as preacher in great places, as celebrant in intricate and hastily rehearsed liturgies, or as an almost unexcelled after-dinner speaker, Dr. Runcie is at his best in one-to-one relationships—whether with the newest member of a ship's crew (he recently made his first official visit to the Royal Navy) or the president of the World Bank at a Washington luncheon table. It was, incidentally, the visit with such men as Robert McNamara and Caspar Weinberger, himself an Episcopalian, that Runcie savored and referred to in subsequent addresses. His mind is that of the practical theologian who readily connects the Gospel with the complexities of international needs.

The one-to-one relationship—the tutor in his study—that is the true Runcie discerned by most observers. He is forever referring to former teaching posts and students. The very sight of them—alert, questioning, responsive—makes it obvious that the groves of academe are where the Archbishop longs to linger.

Nearing his sixtieth birthday on 2 October 1981, he took his 7,000-mile American trip in stride. He'd mapped out most of the schedule and he stuck to it cheerfully, spared only now and then by the Presiding Bishop or others who would quietly cancel a meeting or extra visit when exhaustion seemed near at hand. Still, Runcie kept to a killing pace, always in good humor and always diplomatically answering even the most loaded questions.

Seemingly unselfconscious, he was never unforgetful of the dignity and reasoned thought expected of the holder of the office that is at the center of the Anglican Communion.

The final fatigue, stretching out on the Concorde after the last good-bye to the Presiding Bishop, must have been an encompassing weariness — something that the PB himself would have well understood. Somewhere aboard the plane, amongst the trunkful of trinkets and trophies acquired by the Runcie entourage, was what the English call a "press cutting" from the *Washington Post*. It was the story that appeared with a huge headline on the final day of his Washington visit: THE VERY MODEL OF A MODERN ARCHBISHOP.

Yes, indeed!

T ST. MARY'S, BREDIN, TO LAYREADERS OF THE DIOCESE OF CANTERBURY: In you as Readers we have a body of trained men and women who are a great resource for the Church and one that ought to be used more creatively. Yours is a venerable institution. You receive an honorable mention in St. Justin. You flowered again briefly as an answer to the pastoral crisis in the Elizabethan Church, but your modern history dates from 1866. Your role in the worship and life of the Church has developed from assisting in the conduct of services to a wide range of pastoral, educational, and liturgical work.

First, you *are* Readers. It is a designation that developed from your *public* reading of the services and of scripture. It is not mechanical, it is a profoundly sacramental act. As we read the Bible in public, so we are giving voice to our Lord and to the Spirit.

It is important that we not give voice as a parrot, who knows the words only, but with the deep understanding that comes with prayer and reverence and study. Indeed, study is inextricably bound up with your first obligation, for to be *readers in public* you must fulfill the duty of being *readers in private*. There is a great need for more theological sophistication. I do not mean pseudo-academic, technical talk. I mean men and women who are capable of looking at their jobs, politics, social problems, in a theologically instructed way. And if our theological perception is not deepened as a Church, we shall dissolve into an institution which offers nothing more than promiscuous benevolence and which is an easy prey to fanatics who flourish in times of tension and anxiety. So I would see all Readers as students of the Word — lay theologians with an increasing involvement in the vital work of adult education in the Church.

How, then, are you to be distinguished from the clergy? There is some desire for a more clerical role — for Readers to be licensed to be in charge of parishes or licensed to baptise. I would be sorry to forward these developments. All laymen can baptise in cases of emergency, and I think a more clerical role would undermine the second great principle of your ministry if we were to agree to any change. You are *lay* theologians. The Church for centuries has been bedeviled by a false equation of leadership that argues that if you are a believer you should become a clergyman, for the clergy are the officers of the Church Militant and Readers perhaps qualify as NCOs! That is not how I see it at all. The leadership of the clergy is of a very particular kind. Their education and their circumstances in life do not, for the most part, qualify them to understand the real day-to-day, intimate pressures of the school, the factory, the Social Services Department, the police station. The primary function of the clergy is to insure that the demands of the Gospel remain sharp and are not accommodated to mere fashion. The lay theologian has a distinct but vital task — to insure that the Church is addressing itself to the questions actually being asked in the community as a whole, where the Reader lives and works. We have here two distinct kinds of leadership which ought to be in fruitful dialogue to produce in the Church's life a ferment rather than a stodgy pseudo-consensus that masquerades for the peace of Christ in some of our communities. . . .

There is a rightful tension between those whose leadership consists in insisting on the demands of "the Faith once delivered to the Saints" and those whose leadership consists in informing the presentation of the Gospel with the realism which can only come from living among the mundane realities of work and home. These are two simple ideas — that you be both Readers *and* students of the Word — and I advance them knowing that you presently are not all being used in such a way and are not able to fully express the fullest ministry. But I hope I have said enough to provoke a constructive discussion or perhaps even a howl of rage.

22 May 1981

T HILLSIDE FRIARY, DORSET, FOR THE
INTERNATIONAL CHAPTER OF ANGLI-
CAN FRANCISCANS: This is the age of the conference and the consultation. Very naturally, in a time of
rapid change and expanding moral and social horizons, people wish
to come together to pool their experiences and to check their strate-
gies, one against another. I am delighted that you have asked me to
participate in this consultation that brings together the leaders of one
of the most vigorous and hopeful movements, not only in our Church
but in the whole of the contemporary catholic Church. One of the
searing things, however, about your tradition is the absolute and
uncompromising way in which St. Francis himself embraced the
Gospel as peculiarly vivid for him and how he hastened to put it into
practice.

Following in his footsteps and reflecting on the Gospel, you, as
Franciscans, can hardly fail to be influenced by St. Matthew X:7-19
and the Gospel call contained in that passage — to share the life of
the poor, of those who are excluded from the safety and security of
prosperous society, and to discover, in that way of poverty, a royal
road to sharing the very life of Christ Himself, understanding His
way, and conforming ourselves to His demands.

It seems to me that the way of poverty associated with that moving and disturbing passage in St. Matthew's Gospel is still so powerful that it cannot be handled or considered without a painful
awareness of how far we have all fallen short.

I wish to consider the way of poverty as a response to the Gospel
and a way of following Our Lord at three levels of experience: the
personal, the social, and the global.

The first two were intertwined in Francis's own experience at the
beginning of his mission. . . . It is impossible to disentangle them.

The co-mingling of the person and the social is identifiable
throughout the history of Anglican Franciscans. In England, for
example, one of the influences behind the Franciscan revival was the

desire to help the unemployed on the tramp. The movement also exhibited the ambivalence of Christian talk about poverty. The poor were to be relieved but part of the relief was in saying that poverty of spirit, unless it is to be hopelessly sentimentalized, must be associated with a measure of actual poverty. Thus was established the condition of really seeing profoundly the nature of Our Lord's Kingdom and identifying ourselves with His work for it.

In personal terms, the need for such insight in our own social life is evident. We are born into a world of distraction and congestion. We are choked by so many good things that we are able to savour very few of them. We have much to live with and little to live for. We are not heart-whole, and our energy is turned from us by the pursuit of a mass of conflicting desires. Fasting from the excess that causes congestion and distraction, embracing a simplicity and austerity of life — those two resolute actions are indispensable if we wish to recover our taste buds and our zest for living.

The abandoned life Our Lord talks of, which can be enjoyed in His company, is so different from the death deferral to which so many of our energies are directed. The passage from congested and distracted living to Our Lord's simplicity and enthusiasm can, I believe, only come with the revival of a joyful asceticism, and in that the tradition of Franciscan poverty has much to teach us.

Socially, also, one of the consequences of the tradition of poverty is that Franciscans have always travelled light and been able to enter realms and areas of society barred to the plump and well-meaning. . . .

In view of your tradition and the present need, I was interested to see where Franciscans are currently deployed. I confess that part of my reason for coming here is in looking for reassurance that your heroic efforts in Plaistow, Belfast, Liverpool are going to be the shape of things to come, and not front-line positions that will be abandoned.

In this beautiful place, you enjoy freedom and tranquility that, in the modern world, are almost beyond purchase for most people. You are active in the universities and large numbers of suburban parishes, and that activity is good. But it would be tragic if you were to direct your chief efforts in England and worldwide to areas where the contemporary Church is actually rather well organized and deployed. To be true to St. Francis's understanding of the Gospel, we would expect Franciscans to be found with the sick. We look for them, too, with the lepers of our society, the outsiders, and particularly with the homeless and the mentally ill.

Even in St. Francis's day, however, it rapidly became clear that the global implications of the social and personal living out of the Gospel were staggering. Franciscans rapidly moved into universities because you have a theory of knowledge and a way of learning that have implications as radical as Marxism for the understanding of the world of knowledge. Indeed, it seems to me that your particular association with the poor and the expansion of your Order throughout the world give you a good opportunity to build on the important work you have already done in increasing awareness in the Church. We must see ourselves as world citizens with no limits to our concept of brotherhood and no geographical boundary to the responsibilities Christ calls upon us to shoulder on behalf of our neighbors.

As you reflect on the life of your Society over the next few years, I hope and pray that you will be as anxious as you have been in the past to *balance* the personal, the social, and the global implications of embracing the way of poverty as a response to the Gospel of Our Lord Jesus Christ.

May 1982

Anglican Franciscans

T THE 900th ANNIVERSARY OF ELY CA-
THEDRAL: . . . Today we look back on nine centuries of achievement written in the fabric of this beautiful
cathedral. As we try to peer into our own future, our
thanksgivings for the past take on a particular urgency. Beyond our
proper gratitude for finely wrought stone and ingenious architecture,
for a tradition of learning and noble worship, is there a story here
that can give us hope and inspiration as we seek to build for generations yet to come? Those who built here possessed a single-minded
devotion to God which puts most of us to shame. Double-mindedness
is not a new phenomenon, but it is one which can cost us some of
our best energies. There is the spectator who finds much to interest
him but whose loyalties are not engaged by anything in particular. . . .

Others have loyalties: they believe, but live their lives in com-
partments. Religious practice is a Sunday secret whereas weekdays
are governed by a different logic of getting and spending, and God
is only an occasional asset. I suspect that few of us here are free from
that species of double-mindedness which may sometimes be unconscious but which can also express itself in exhausting internal conflicts
between mutually contradictory world views. . . .

If we are single-minded in our devotion to God and His Will,
our devotion will overflow in great energy for what ought to concern
us in our daily lives. . . .

Divine single-mindedness is given in prayer when a human
being is united with the true meaning and end of his life and when
he is weaned away from the temptation to distort himself by pursuing
some self-selected ambition. . . .

The existence of this great body of stone is another, more pal-
pable image. . . .

If the future is to be marked by the like promise and fruit of
those who built here, then we must be as faithful and single-minded
as they were in prayer and work, seeking the Kingdom of God above
all else.

1 June 1981

T THE DEDICATION OF ST. ANNE'S CA-
THEDRAL, BELFAST: In the eye of the storm created by violence, you have continued to build. Why is
this? Because the Christian Church, of whatever designation, has the privilege of holding up the vision of perfection and
God's love. . . .

Even the violence can be of help. While it would be dreadful
to sentimentalize the suffering which so many have had to endure as
a result of the troubles, I have been astonished and moved by ways
in which tragedy has produced clearer vision and a determination to
build Christian love and forgiveness. Any other response to tragedy
is simply colluding with the hostility of life and to love which lies
at the root of violence. . . .

There is no alternative to patient, small-scale, local, and personal
attempts to bridge the divide and to build a new community in a
shared love for Jesus Christ.

2 June 1981

T THE PRESBYTERIAN ASSEMBLY IN BELFAST: I remember very clearly a godly Presbyterian relative who, on seeing a photograph in a paper of what seemed to be ecclesiastical capers, shook his head so solemnly and said, "What has this to do with Jesus of Nazareth?" I remember the incident as a simple and necessary appeal to the dead rock of faith without which we get lost in merely picturesque and pious trivia. I remember also the care with which the same relative prepared for his quarterly Communion with spats and a flower in a buttonhole as the outward and visible signs of an inward preparedness and devotion. The way in which he always called it "the occasion" has been a cautionary note for me as I stand in a tradition of more regular and frequent Communion. . . .

Well, many people are saying that the ecumenical climate at present is cold. I don't believe it. On narrow fronts we have struck some serious obstacles. Some of our old methods may have had their day. But if we are serious about our mission to the world, then I believe that we shall discover each other more and more profoundly as brothers and sisters in the faith of Jesus Christ. If we hold on to this truth and build up our opportunities for personal trust and keep in touch in every possible way, then I believe that there will be some surprises in store for the ecumenical cynics.

3 June 1981

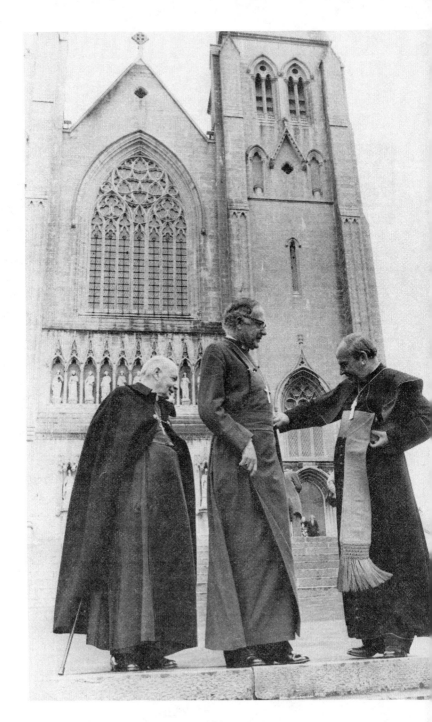

T ST. PATRICK'S ANGLICAN CATHEDRAL, DUBLIN: This year is the 800th anniversary of the consecration by the Archbishop of Canterbury of John Comyn as Archbishop of Dublin. He played an important part in the evolution of this Cathedral Church, but the very name of St. Patrick is a reminder that Comyn was building on foundations that were already old, and older than those of the Church of England. I am visiting it as something of an ecclesiastical Johnny-come-lately since the first occupant of my office did not reach Kent before 597 when the See of Armagh had been flourishing for more than 150 years. . . .

It is always easier to point the finger at others, so I only want to be specific, acknowledging the share the English Church and people have had in injustices and oppressions. The "saeva indignatio" of Jonathan Swift, Dean here for many years, has been one of the ways in which I have come to a realization of what London policies have sometimes meant for this island.

A sense of God's judgment, however, is intended to be creative. . . . It is not meant to annihilate but to nourish in us the determination to change our ways. . . . The Church of England, as you know, did attempt to set up a religious monopoly. . . . but despite all the laws could do, other Christian bodies have flourished and made great contributions to our tradition as a whole. . . .

[Yet] I would find it difficult to be anything but an Anglican. I find nourishment and challenge in the tradition we share with the Church of Ireland, and I firmly believe in the words of the 1878 Preface to the Irish Prayer Book that the Anglican tradition, established in successive Books of Common Prayer, contains "the true doctrine of Christ and a pure manner and order of Divine Service

---

← *Standing in front of St. Patrick's Anglican Cathedral at Armagh are, left to right, John Armstrong, Anglican Primate of All Ireland; the Archbishop; and the Roman Catholic Primate.* Press Association Ltd.

according to the Holy Scriptures and the practice of the Primitive Church." . . . It is only if we regard our own tradition and our own Church as our possessions rather than as a means to live in His way that we shall be fearful of seeing truth from another standpoint and learning from one another. . . .

The real enemy is the worship of appetite which provides everything for man to live with and little to live for. Some consumer religion, so different from the religion of Christ the Giver, is engulfing every country, driving out wonder and awe. . . .

It takes courage to make positive gestures in the present climate of harsh and sometimes historical rhetoric. . . . [Yet] if we have our eyes on Him, then anything is possible.

June 1981

T THE CENTENARY CELEBRATION OF WESTCOTT HOUSE, CAMBRIDGE: After centuries of producing the clerical leadership of the Church of England, the Universities of Oxford and Cambridge by the mid-19th century had become widely suspect. Many believed that they had succumbed to the forces of "Germanization and secularization," as Keble expressed it, and no longer provided wholesome incubators for future clergy.

A search began, therefore, for alternative ways of training ordinands. Some favored a withdrawal from the temptations of the University to places where a good "clerical tone" could be developed far from the jarring disputes of secular academics.

Such was not the vision of Brooke Foss Westcott. He was determined to preserve the link between the best in modern scholarship and training for the ministry. So in 1881 he established a Clergy Training School right at the heart of Cambridge. There were nine students who at first met at 20 King's Parade. Until I uncovered that fact, I had been wondering why I had been selected to preach on this festival occasion, but as soon as I came across the reference to 20 King's Parade, where I began my married life in a top-floor flat with Lindy, I understood all!

B. F. Westcott stood in a venerable Anglican tradition that holds that sound learning and a rigorous training of the mind are essential to the Christian ministry. In some reminiscences of the older Westcott, I was told by one of his former pupils of how he had seen the Bishop pounce on a copy of Liddell and Scott's *Greek Lexicon* with the cry, "Ah, this is the true beginning of all knowledge." He was devoted to the Gospel faith but convinced also that the faith is best illuminated and commended by sound learning.

Not everyone was sympathetic to that conviction, then or now. In every age there have been Christian enthusiasts deeply suspicious of learning and the intellect. I understand those who cry, "Do not quench the Spirit and do not despise prophesying." It is too easy for theologians of all kinds — those who teach in universities as well as those who seek to interpret faith and experience from the pulpit — to become like scribes chewing over other men's experiences and having their faith at second hand. Our Lord, unlike the scribes, astonished His hearers by speaking with authority from the heart of His union with the Father. There are, however, many grave dangers in refusing to apply our minds to the statements of the Christian tradition and to the scriptures themselves.

Sober analysis and scholarship, not only in the lecture hall but in the study while preparing sermons, and in lay-training courses, is an essential part of showing our reverence and respect for those who wrote the Holy Scriptures. They wrote in a world with different assumptions and their minds were stored with different mental furniture. We show them honor as scholars and ministers of the Word by trying to enter into their minds rather than grasping at what is most immediate and attractive about their writings, granted *our* presuppositions.

The theological enterprise, of course, goes beyond biblical study and certainly includes the history of the Christian tradition. The primacy of scripture has always been asserted in Anglicanism, but, as Lancelot Andrewes remarked, "We learn by the Bible chiefly, but in good part also by the books of the Ancient Fathers and lights of the Church in whom the scent of this ointment was fresh."

We ought also to apply ourselves to some study of Christian history or else we shall deserve to be bound hand and foot by the enthusiasms that do not know that they have flourished before nor the reasons for their speedy disintegration. A mind that is stored with a sense of the perennial temptations to which the Christian Church has been exposed may be spared the punishment of repeating the errors of Christian history over and over again.

We do not, of course, only study the history of our tradition to avoid error but also for inspiration and to receive fresh insight and consolation when present realities obscure what we can be and what we have been. To paraphrase Edmund Burke, "I would not put a man to live and trade each on his own private store of wisdom because I believed that store to be small and limited by a man's experience in one time and one place, but I would have him avail himself of the general bank and capital of all nations and of all ages." The study of Church History makes us inheritors of all the centuries of the Christian Church and rescues us from being merely provincial both in time and in place.

There is much spiritual benefit to be had from the scholarly disciplines of using words and language with precision and sobriety. . . . Care in our use of words and about the accuracy of our expression is a preparation for the attentiveness that is at the heart of contemplative prayer. It also fortifies us in our resistance to the wild and extravagant talk that is becoming more prevalent in our Western societies. The telegraphic speeds at which our public communication systems work do not encourage subtlety or balance or time for doing justice to the complexities of problems. They do encourage sloganizing and the simplistic explanations that can contribute to a climate of thought in society that is dangerously glib and immature. As Dag Hammarskjöld said, "Respect for the word is the first commandment in a discipline by which a man can be educated to maturity, intellectual, emotional, and moral."

The discipline of careful speech, learning, and study, is, of course, very hard work, requiring more strength and perseverance than are involved in the facile generalization or the general assertion. The dogmatist may carry the day for the moment with his show of certitude, but that kind of success is brittle. Certainty that does not realize that we are always being schooled by God to see a greater and more generous vision of the truth quickly becomes stale. In the words of a popular hymn, "New occasions teach new duties; time makes ancient good uncouth; they must upwards still and onwards; who would keep abreast of truth."

In our concern to train the mind to "test everything," we must not be narrow or merely ecclesiastical in our interests. Westcott commended a "holy worldliness" rooted in a sympathy for all sorts and conditions of men. We need to keep the channels open to our contemporaries. We need to listen to their language and to their way of describing the world. The Spirit is speaking through them as well. It would be arrogance to deny that, and we must not quench the Spirit.

We must also take the responsibility laid upon us by Our Lord of representing Him in contemporary debates. If our notions are not informed by a reverent study of our tradition, then we shall have nothing to offer except promiscuous benevolence and a dull echo of the currently fashionable liberal consensus.

12 June 1981

Cambridge University

AT THE GENERAL SYNOD'S DEBATE ON THE FILIOQUE CLAUSE: At his enthronement an Archbishop of Canterbury has even more liturgical initiative than when he uses the new Prayer Book. It will be remembered that I exercised that privilege by restoring the Nicene Creed to its original form to enable those gathered from all over the world, Orthodox and other Christians, to proclaim their faith together.

. . . I know some of you do believe that the filioque clause — "and the Son" — points to an important theological truth that you do not want to jeopardize by removing it on purely historical or theological grounds. . . . However, to restore the Creed to its original form is not to deny that the Holy Spirit comes to the world from and through the Son in the context of history; it is only to affirm that in the external relations of the Trinity, the Holy Spirit has His origin in the Father. To retain the filioque is to threaten the legitimacy of the Eastern Trinitarian tradition because as part of the Creed it raises the Western tradition's account of the eternal relations of the Trinity into dogma. In so doing we unconsciously impose a Western concept of the Trinity upon the East. . . . The resentment and hurt such imposition causes will give some impression of how the Orthodox feel about the matter and will explain why it is so important to them. It is the function of a Primate to take the initiative not as a threat but as a promise that it will be given the opportunity of righting an ancient wrong; of making a generous ecumenical gesture as a Synod, not unfounded in history, by removing the words that have divided Christendom.

1 July 1981

N ORDINATION SERMON ON THE CHARACTER OF THE PRIEST: The Eastern Church continues to employ a way of defining truth that goes back to the early Fathers. It is called the apophatic way. It means proceeding by the method of eliminating what is not quite the case.

Let us apply it to the character of a priest.

1) A priest is not a social worker. Social workers deal with people's practical problems of living — things like housing, old people's welfare, child-care difficulties, and the misfits of life. But while a priest is not a social worker, he will be bound to find himself having to do something about some or all of those things. He must be aware of what is available, always in touch, ready to do first aid when no one is around.

2) He is not a psychiatrist. He ought not to meddle with matters for which he is not qualified and where there is a danger he will do more harm than good. Having said that, a priest needs to be able to recognize mental upset and never forget that he is a physician of souls who is knowledgeable of the way in which spiritual illness always damages human well-being and that health concerns the whole person — mental, physical, and spiritual. The priest will follow a Lord who did not speak of the masses, mankind, or the multitude, but of a "certain man" or a "certain woman." He notices the small boy with his picnic lunch of rolls and sardines; the woman who gate-crashed a dinner party; and the dishonest rent collector up a tree. But even caring for individuals is not his whole work.

3) A priest is not an administrator or an organizer, whatever some would like him to be. Here especially are areas of what is often best left to lay ministry. But a priest has to be businesslike and efficient, and over a long period he will build up a respect for a proper sense of stewardship and for straight dealing.

4) A priest is not an establishment figure or someone who is

there to produce social or political respectability. It is his business to witness to the truth as seen in Jesus Christ, and that may be uncomfortable. A priest who is never a nuisance or never unpopular will hardly be doing the Lord's work. Having said that, in days of confusion about moral standards, a parish or a chaplaincy can well look to their priest and his family as an example of wholesome personal life.

5) A priest is not an autocrat or a dictator. He has no right to expect people to do this, that, or the other because he says so. The Church does not belong to him. He is no superior being in the eyes of God. He will be teaching and training Christians in a way that does not simply depend on services but on small groups of people whose faith and questions and growth in understanding must be shared. However, there will be times when he is called to give a lead, and a priest will not be able to give a lead unless it springs from a well-stocked mind and a praying heart. He must not dodge the responsibility that springs from the time he has spent in study nor delude himself that he knows all the answers.

We have cleared some of the ground for me to be able to tell you now what I think a priest *should* be.

He is concerned with other people for the sake of God and with God for the sake of other people. That is made clear by the celebration of Holy Communion which must be at the heart of his life. It makes it plain that he brings people with him to the Lord and he brings the gracious Lord to the people.

Others are concerned with people for their own sake, and that is a good life — social workers, teachers, administrators. Contemplative monks and nuns may be concerned with God for His own sake — and that is a good life and we need them.

But the priest must have the pastoral heart which is the blend of both. So I commend to you those who will try to serve their local community, to minister to individuals one by one, to promote responsible and efficient stewardship, to set something of an example in his personal life, and to give a lead in faith and prayer.

But it doesn't really matter if he sometimes fails, as we all must, in any of these, provided he has not lost the heart of the matter: *A desire and longing to be with other people for the sake of God and to be*

An unusually youthful picture of the Archbishop taken in one of his favorite roles as a counselor to ordination candidates. Press Association Ltd.

with God for the sake of other people. So long as that is there, we may never have any fears about the priesthood.

10 July 1981

T ST. PAUL'S AT THE WEDDING OF PRINCE CHARLES AND LADY DIANA SPENCER: Here is the stuff of which fairy tales are made: the Prince and Princess on their wedding day. But fairy tales usually end at that point with the simple phrase "They lived happily ever after." After all, fairy stories regard marriage as an anticlimax after the romance of courtship. But that is not the Christian view. Our faith sees the wedding day not as the place of arrival but the place where the adventure really begins.

There is an ancient Christian tradition that *every* bride and groom on their wedding day are regarded as a Royal Couple. To this day, in the marriage ceremonies of the Eastern Orthodox Church, crowns are held over the man and the woman to express the conviction that as husband and wife they are Kings and Queens of Creation. As it says of humankind in the Bible, "Thou crownest him with glory and honour, and didst set him over the work of thy hands."

On a wedding day it is made clear that God does not intend us to be puppets but chooses to work through us, and especially through our marriages, to create the future of His world.

Marriage is first of all a new creation for the partners themselves. As husband and wife live out their vows, loving and cherishing one another, sharing life's splendors and miseries, achievements and setbacks, they will be transformed in the process. A good marriage is a life, as the poet Edwin Muir says, "Where each asks from each/ What each most wants to give/ And each awakes in each/ What else would never be."

But any marriage which is turned in upon itself, in which the bride and groom simply gaze obsessively at one another, goes sour after a time.

A marriage that really works is one that works for others. Marriage has both a private face and a public importance. If we solved all our economic problems and failed to build loving families, it would profit us nothing, because the family is the place where the future is created good and full of love — or deformed.

Those who are married live happily ever after the wedding day if they persevere in the real adventure, which is the royal task of creating each other and creating a more loving world.

Such is true of every man and woman undertaking marriage. It must be specially true of this marriage in which are placed so many hopes.

Much of the world is in the grip of hopelessness. Many people seem to have surrendered to fatalism about the so-called inevitabilities of life: cruelty, injustice, poverty, bigotry, and war. Some have accepted a cynical view of marriage itself.

But all couples on their wedding day are "Royal Couples" and stand for the truth that we help to shape this world and are not just its victims. All of us are given the power to make the future more in God's image and to be "Kings and Queens" of love.

This is our prayer for Charles and Diana. May the burdens we lay on them be matched by the love with which we support them in the years to come. However long they live, may they always know that when they pledged themselves to each other before the altar of God they were surrounded and supported not by mere spectators but by the sincere affection and active prayer of millions of friends.

29 July 1981

Royal Arms

THE ARCHBISHOP'S REFLECTIONS ON THE WEDDING:* When I got up I felt curiously calm and relaxed. I'm afraid I'd often been grumpy when people said, "What is it going to be like, talking to 700-million people?" I tried to put that sort of thought out of mind. "Here I was cheerfully going to another wedding," I said to myself, "perhaps a bit dressier."

When we hit Fleet Street and I saw the immense crowds and heard a loud-hailer say, "And now here comes the Archbishop of Canterbury," I confess that my heart did sink a bit and my knees began to knock.

As we went up to St. Paul's I was aware of how much attention we were receiving, and I think I was more moved than I ever expected by the natural humanity of the whole occasion.

Then the arrival of the bride! I know that others have talked about the privilege and the anthems and so on, but I think that we all need special occasions in order to focus simple truths and make them memorable. I think that was true beyond all expectations when it came to the royal wedding — the picture of two people genuinely committed, nervous at the awesomeness of the occasion, and ready to be generous and selfless and hopeful about the future. It was a moving moment in its simplicity, dignified by a great occasion. [When the bride mixed up the name of the groom] my heart slightly missed a beat, but it was so real. It was the kind of thing that I've had at other weddings, and it added to the genuineness of the occasion. Then, because of the circumstances and above all the bride and groom themselves, you felt that you wanted to give of your best.

Afterwards you were a bit proud to have been a part of history. It's very easy to feel yourself acting a part. There is a sense in which, of course, you are put in a position where, for the sake of others, you have to act a part. You have to be the focal person of assured

*from BBC program, *Robert of Canterbury*

faith, and you have to appear as part of the stage property of some great occasion. You have to recognize that many people will see you. Most people will see you from a distance and will judge you from a distance. For that reason, you have to think of the effect you're going to have on the Christian cause and all sorts of intimate, personal levels where you would like to be but can never be.

Fall 1981

A T THE UNIVERSITY OF SUSSEX'S OPEN-
ING SESSION: I begin with a question, "For what
purpose does a University exist?" We are obsessed nowadays with so many management questions that we sometimes are not prepared to face some ultimate ones such as the reason
for a particular institution's existence. I want to argue that it exists
to give you your freedom. The point is made more clearly when put
in the form of a personal question, "What will you have to take away
from this place?"

My hope is that you will know more than you did about the life
and literature of this and other countries, about the development of
man's physical and social life, about the disconcerting habits of atoms
and neutrons. I hope, too, that what you will take away will be no
longer bulk without shape. You will have an increased power of
analysis. You will be able to distinguish what is more important from
what is less and thereby order what you know into some intelligible
pattern.

Increase in knowledge and the power of analysis is not the end
of the matter. They are not themselves the pearl of great price.
Rather they provide us with the currency to buy the pearl. The
buying has to continue throughout the whole of life.

Our knowledge, our powers of analysis and criticism, are the
means by which in life we receive our freedom, the ability to discover
for ourselves what is true and enjoy what is worthwhile. For that
task we are equipped at a university, but it will always remain a task
requiring effort—the effort, for instance, to resist the pressure of
mass opinion. While that is relatively easy to do in a university, it
becomes much more difficult as one settles down to a job and finds

---

← *The Archbishop engages in a spirited conversation with the cellist
Mstislav Rostropovich after a ceremony in which they received honorary
degrees. The topic: the difficulties of living with musicians.*

Press Association Ltd.

oneself surrounded by people who accept uncritically what is written in the more respectable and perhaps less respectable newspapers.

When I was first a student, there used to be a good number of eccentric people around propagating unusual views. I would be surprised if there are not still some tucked away in Sussex. Cultivate them. They will teach you to have an independent mind, and that is a great freedom.

Another pressure to be resisted is that of the latest fashion. It is the more insidious, for it has the superficial appearance of enlightenment. "What are you reading?" asks a character in one of Aldous Huxley's early novels. "Mary glanced at the book. 'Rather second-rate, isn't it?' Mary was accustomed in London to associate with first-rate people who liked first-rate things in the world, and they were mostly French."

It is not difficult to suppose that one is being original when in fact you are behaving like a parrot. The old adage remains true, even in opinions about a book, "He who is faithful in little will be faithful in much." The grandeur of the prophet — a Thomas More, a Kierkegaard, or a Solzhenitsyn — lies not so much in their opinions as in their readiness to stand against the trend and their heroic endurance in doing so.

Still another pressure to be resisted is that of oversimplification. An academic training that develops our critical faculties should make us aware of the complexity, of the need for critical analysis and qualification, cautious about those vast generalizations and blanket statements that people make.

Oversimplification was evidently in the mind of an American philosopher who would conclude lectures by asking his pupils, "Have you got that clear?" If they said it was clear he would murmur, "Gee, I guess you've got it wrong again."

If you can emerge from this place free from the pressure of mass opinion, or the latest vogue, and aware that things are never so simple as most people would like them to be, your life will consist of the appropriation of your freedom. It is, however, fraught with its own special dangers. St. Paul sums up the matter in a sentence, "You, my friends, are called to freedom. Only use not your freedom to indulge yourselves, but through love be servants one of another."

There is first the moral danger of using our freedom for self-assertion. It often leads to assertion of individual superiority. We are all familiar with the university student who begins to despise his parents or his background. Students of history and literature will know how the freedom of Renaissance man is indeed a menace to all if he has not learned to occupy his free energies in the service of all. If, when he has escaped all other bonds, he falls under the domination of self, the damage he will do is the greater, even if in our society as at present constituted it is mental rather than physical. There can be damage to family relationships, friendships, and to your own personality. Only by learning through love to be servants of one another will we prevent ourselves from misusing our freedom and thus perverting it and finally losing it.

. . . The second danger to our freedom is intellectual. Our freedom may lead us into cynicism. In the crucible of criticism all opinions are equally dissolved. Principles disappear. A number of points of view emerge. The character that should have been strong through freedom cultivates a detachment that makes him the least reliable of men. Look at what it did to Pontius Pilate. He wanted to evade his duty of administering justice to a Galilean peasant, and he found it in his freedom. "What is truth?" By ridiculing the question, he evaded the issue. But questions about the meaning of life, the existence of God, the destiny of man, are real questions, and we dodge them or sneer at them at our own peril.

Clever but selfish, clever but cynical. Are not these real threats to our freedom?

Discovering our freedom is the most human thing about us all.

10 August 1981

T GEOFFREY CHAUCER SCHOOL, CAN-
TERBURY, TO RELIGIOUS EDUCATORS:
A chaplain of my acquaintance attempted to attract if not
hold, the attention of his school by arranging to wave
a bony arm of a skeleton from the belfry in time with the chapel
bell! I sympathize with him because I know how difficult it is for
all of you to impart even most generalized religious values to children
in today's society. It must be approached as something more than
combatting the secular city and as more than a medicine that needs
a good dose of sugar before your pupils will swallow it. I am sure,
however, that we can never divorce religious education from the
society we have today nor particularly from its history. The background and the future of every nation are always profoundly influenced by the combination of traditions which have formed it and the
faith which sustains it. Understanding that, our children will see the
importance of religion *per se*.

One sentence in a recent report seems to summarize all that we
must try to achieve: "To explore the place and significance of religion
in human life and so make a distinctive contribution to each pupil's
search for a faith by which to live." I see it as part of a profound
curriculum which should underlie all school life and extend beyond
the limitations of classrooms and timetables. Yet those rather dry
words hide the simple and heartfelt need of every child to understand
his place in the world. From there he will be better able to compre-
hend that religion is not only man's search for God but God's search
for man.

What we must strive for in religious education is a curriculum
which can balance personal Christianity with the front-line influence
in shaping the nation, culture, and tradition. Religious education
must not just provide a handy pocket guide to do's and don't's nor
obscure the commitment of the teacher or others in the class. We
cannot allow our desire for so-called fair play to permit a child to

reach an entirely uninfluenced choice, meaning that we teach a "value-free curriculum." . . .

It seems quite right to include some introduction to comparative religion. In a multiracial society it is vital that children of every cultural background have the opportunity to understand each other's beliefs and fears. . . .

In this machine-dominated age, the individual must value himself and others as individuals. Such a sense of individual value can be as sharp and decisive a tool for human life as the well-honed chisel in the woodwork class. Our children need the tools, and it is up to religious education to supply it with spiritual value and everyday application.

3 October 1981

T THE ANNUAL MEETING OF THE MAG-
ISTRATES ASSOCIATION, LONDON: It is an
intimidating feeling to be summoned before the Magistrates, if only to preach to them prior to their Annual
Meeting. The most desperate felon does not have such a judicial
array weighing his every word. I derive some comfort, however,
from George Herbert who said, "Judge not the preacher, for he is
thy judge. . . . do not grudge to pick out treasures from an earthen
pot: the worst speaks something good; if all want sense God takes a
text and preacheth patience."

Today, then, preacher and congregation, we are all judges and
magistrates together, and in the Christian tradition that puts us all
in peril. Those who deal in laws and codes of judgments are essential
if some civilized order is to be maintained in the world, but they
run personal risks in doing their work, as a portion of St. Luke's
Gospel makes clear.

The dramatis personae in the story are a lawyer, some clergy,
a victim of robbery with violence, and a passerby — all familiar characters to you in your courtroom experience. But the story also reveals
some of Christ's profoundest teaching on the place of rules and laws
in living the good life. A lawyer approaches Our Lord and proposes
the question, "Master, what shall I do to inherit eternal life?" The
Bible goes on to say that "a certain lawyer tempted him, saying . . . ,"
and that sounds rather sinister. The verb translated by "tempted"
does not necessarily mean much more than testing him, trying out
the new teacher on a controversial question. Our Lord wisely asks
a question in his turn, and the lawyer gives a summary of the law
as love of God and love of neighbor. "This do and thou shalt live,"
says Jesus. The lawyer, however, is properly anxious to define his
terms — you would not tolerate slipshod generalities in Court — and
asks, "But who is my neighbor?"

His inquiry is not only relevant to first-century Judaism, but it
also illustrates a universal tendency. Of course, it is clearly common

sense to limit and define obligations in law and in contracts between people. Lives are usefully employed in attaining such precision, and you spend much of your time dispensing justice on the basis of the work of legal definition which has been done through the centuries. But this way of proceeding cannot be transferred to questions about our relations with God or our spiritual life. How do I inherit eternal life? How do I come to share in the life of God? Jesus tells the lawyer a story to show him that his customary ways of thinking, his attempt to establish limits to responsibility and to define obligations — such habits of thought are appropriate to life as a lawyer, or a magistrate, but could be the death of his soul if they are allowed to dominate the whole of his life.

With consummate tact, Our Lord points out the dangers of legalism by telling a story in which the clergy are the villains. In examining the story more closely, I recall that the road from Jerusalem to Jericho is still a lonely one, and, to this day, guides point out the khan where the Good Samaritan must have lodged the man he found naked and half dead. The emphasis St. Luke places on the man being half dead is probably intended to be significant and to give us a clue to the behavior of the priest and the Levite. By touching a corpse, both by contemporary notions would have been ritually polluted. It is therefore perhaps not so surprising that they passed by on the other side. Put in those terms, it is rather difficult for a modern man, even a priest, to put himself in the dock with the priest and the Levite. While fear of ritual pollution would seem to be at least one thing from which we are emancipated, I am not so sure. Survival — intellectually, emotionally, and even physically — seems to depend on limiting our area of response and responsibility, building walls to exclude when we are not strong enough to assimilate or control events or people. The lawyer's way of asking the question, "Who is my neighbor?" — in other words, where do my responsibilities end? — is clearly consonant with this deep psychological imperative. You open the doors at your peril, and the commonsense thing is to bar them against the unassimilable and the uncontrollable. Touching corpses may no longer bring us so threateningly close to being invaded by death itself, but there are other taboos. Contact with human derelicts or those who are on the fringe of respectable society, who make demands on us and awake self-doubts and fears, such contact is difficult for us all. We meet them in various places and guises — the bore at the party, the unattractive vandal and the drunks who come before you, the insane, the motorcycle gang, those who are deformed by loneliness. We are afraid to touch them. We feel we might not be able to cope and might even catch the disease. We construct a life in which such people are excluded, or put at a distance, or at least are always on the other side of the bench or pulpit. . . .

The modern equivalent of the priest and Levite would probably have an easier conscience: flashing past in his motorcar, he probably wouldn't be confronted by the figure at the roadside at all. We all have limits and frontiers of the kind I have been describing. We could not survive without them. I am just as much protected by comfort and privilege, perhaps more so, than anyone here, but the story of the Samaritan shows us that, if a share in God's life, eternal life, life without fear or end, is our goal, then the prudential, limiting logic which lies behind the question, "Who is my neighbor?" should not satisfy us.

The Samaritan was an outsider himself, despised by the Jews with the loathing reserved for a heretic and half-caste. Such people can often see with a clarity denied to those who are treated with respect in court and who have clubs and dinners and an ordered routine. "Whatsoever thou spendest more, when I come again I will repay thee," says the Samaritan. It is a practical act of charity, but there is something deeper.

If we want eternal life, the lawyer's original question, then the course we should follow is not setting limits to our duty but following up the invitations which occur in every life for going beyond the assured and taking a risk for the sake of compassion. The right question to ask, says Jesus, is not "Who is my neighbor?" but "To whom can I be a neighbor?" One posture is defensive and limiting, and the other seeks to enlarge the scope of our sympathy to an infinite degree. If we are really on the way to eternal life, then life now has to be marked by the willingness to come out from behind our castle walls, to meet new people and needs. The challenge of meeting and entering into suffering can draw unexpected depths of love and generosity from us, and we are enlarged by the experience. Follow the Levite's Highway Code and we are steadily diminished and shrivel, even in our enjoyment of the familiar. It is one of the terrible recurring patterns in the spiritual life: what begins as defence and fortification ends by being the instrument of our destruction. (I saw a striking image of the pattern in a Japanese film. A samurai in the period of the civil wars purchased a second-hand helmet. It proved to have been infected with leprosy, and what was designed to protect him became something which he could not remove and which in the end killed him.) "Whosoever will save his life shall lose it, but whosoever shall lose his life for my sake shall save it."

Luke again provides a fitting summary of what I am saying and also of the disquieting message of the New Testament. The Samaritan did not know whether the man was a decoy, or whether the robbers were still around. He did not count the cost; he moved forward, motivated by compassion. He is a man on the road to eternal life. The clergy in the story stay behind the ritual defences. They think they are playing safe, but it is the way that leads to death. There is much here for the clergy of today, and others, to ponder, especially one like myself, resident in a Palace but a professed follower of Him who had nowhere to lay His head. It is important to see that the work of defining obligations and responsibilities is not in the story condemned as such. It is work that brings a civilization out of bar-barism, and we have seen in our day a great extension of the law to protect the weak, the outsider, the vulnerable, even the fetus in the womb. Yet for a civilization to achieve spiritual maturity, to be on the road to eternal life, the limiting logic of law-making and limit-defining is never enough; it must be continually exceeded. You cannot dispense with the stage of codifying and refining the norms of social behavior, but you cannot rest content with that stage in either the life of an individual or of a society. The lawyer saw that and pointed to the man who took a risk and who showed mercy as the person and example to be followed. Jesus said to him, and to us, "Go, and do thou likewise."

9 October 1981

T THE ST. LUKESTIDE SERVICE OF THE
HOSPITAL OF ST. BARTHOLOMEW THE
GREAT: In the last 20 years I have only taken one
major medical precaution. I have made sure that my
doctor was trained at "Barts," and that means that I am entitled to
feel a member of the family at this gathering. I want to talk to you
first about St. Luke. Ernest Renan, no friend of the Christian religion, said that St. Luke's Gospel was the most beautiful book in the
world. Even more surprising is that on another occasion he acknowledged that there is hardly a cynic to be found who will not say,
"Thank God for St. Luke."

We have only to think of the shepherds at the manger, the Good
Samaritan, the Prodigal Son, Martha and Mary, the Penitent Thief
on the Cross, the walk to Emmaus — all of which are recounted by
St. Luke alone — to realize that these tributes are no exaggeration.
So the tradition that makes him a doctor and an artist probably
springs from the way in which he paints the story in which we find
healing for our sickness and imagination for our hopes in Jesus
Christ.

In one chapter Luke puts together the stories of the Lost Sheep,
the Lost Coin, and the Lost Son. The message is clear. If a shepherd
will go miles over the hills to recover the one sheep that has gone
astray; if a woman will search diligently for a lost coin; if a man
agonizes over the son who has made a mess of his life, how much
more will your Heavenly Father care for you. We are being told
that God is not a heavenly magistrate or celestial spy. He is the one
who values us, cares for us, yearns for us, and fundamentally is on
our side. That gives ultimate security.

There is another strand in St. Luke that is not so comforting.
It is severe. "When a man has been given much, much will be
required of him." Also note that "if anyone wants to be a follower
of mine, he will leave self behind, take up his Cross, and follow
me." Moreover, Luke observes "how hard it is for the wealthy to

enter the Kingdom of God." He also recounts the terrifying end of the one who didn't use his talents.

It is as if St. Luke wants the stories of Jesus to display the beauty, love, and hope of God, and then to ask, "Are you willing to pay the price these good things will cost us?"

In this unique mixture of gentleness, healing, sensitivity and toughness, discipline and endurance, we touch the heart of the Gospel. We are given the key to the Kingdom and a reason why we refer to a hospital such as Barts as a religious foundation.

First, any community worthy of the name needs to cultivate the homely virtues of acceptance, tolerance, welcome, companionship. They give people anchorage, security, and warmth, without which little thrives. The care for the sick, the misfits, the poor, the dying, is basic Christianity.

On the stairway of the Great Hall at Barts are two of Hogarth's finest paintings, *The Pool of Bethesda* and *The Good Samaritan*. They remind us that caring for people must mean more than just curing them. Rahere's first hospital, with the accent on compassion, in the absence of medical learning, was not so primitive. Some of your nurses in the 1930s recall how at Christmas there was drawn up a list of old patients who looked forward to admission not because they were ill but because they were lonely and poor.

A friend of mine was being rushed to a hospital after a car accident. Regaining consciousness, he asked the ambulance attendant why the siren wasn't going. The reply came, "It only worries the patient." We see a special sort of compassion coming from somebody in a job where cynicism could easily prevail. The warmth of the ambulance man, the nurse, and the porter are as essential as the skill of the surgeon. On the other hand, homey virtues on their own can be soft and flabby, keeping people in immaturity and dependence. We also need standards and discipline, a readiness to undertake tiresome duties and stick at them, the proper deployment of talents.

There are two other qualities that St. Luke brings to our notice, and again they are a contrast.

The first is loyalty. He emphasizes the command of Our Lord to His disciples to be a band of brothers and sisters and to go out as partners. At the Cross he alone records how His friends were gathered at a distance, as also the women who had accompanied Him from the beginning. Loyalty is another strand in Luke's story and another quality to make up the Kingdom.

Besides loyalty there is love. No community — whether it is a hospital, a regiment, or a country — will ever prosper unless it is loved. To believe Barts to be the best hospital in the world is a pardonable exaggeration, and such proper pride needs formal expression in a place where such excesses are seen in perspective. Hence this annual service.

But, again, loyalty can be narrow, exclusive, complacent. So we remember a final strand in St. Luke. Let's call it vision. It is a constant plea to open our eyes to a wider view of the Kingdom, to enlarge our sympathies. In the Emmaus story, Jesus made as if He would go further. He does lead us onward, never allowing us to be content with the achievements or insights of the present.

19 October 1981

T AN ALL SAINTS EUCHARIST, BRUS-
SELS: This festival of All Saints and this occasion, the
beginning of my visit to Brussels, conjures a host of
memories, some personal and some which all of us in
this Cathedral can share.

I remember Brussels well from the days of World War II when,
as a young Guards Officer, I received the kindest of welcomes here
and the most generous hospitality. But my visit to Archbishop Dan-
neels has echoes from a time well before the embraces and champagne
of 1944-45. The Malines conversations between Cardinal Mercier,
in whose chapel I shall have the privilege of celebrating tomorrow,
and Lord Halifax were part of a striving and a search for the faith
and vision which the Church throughout the whole of Europe once
shared in common. This occasion is evidence that those conversations
have already borne fruit in deeper respect and understanding between
Anglicans and Roman Catholics. We are here as the guests of the
Roman Catholic Church, and we are more than grateful for the
warm welcome and hospitality of the cathedral authorities.

All Saints tide is certainly a moment for remembering our immediate forbears like Cardinal Mercier and Lord Halifax, but also
we rejoice in our communion and unity with those who worship God
beyond the grave. And as we celebrate our unity with them, so we
look back to the time of the saints of the united Western Church,
who had experience of a Christian unity with their contemporaries.

In particular, I wish to propose a name which you may find
surprising for remembrance and thanksgiving. Sir Thomas More
spent a part of his childhood, some of his most formative years, in
the house in which I live in London—Lambeth Palace. He was a
pageboy to my predecessor, Cardinal Morton, and in the 1490s
learned how to conduct himself in public by watching the visitors
come and go in the Cardinal's audience chamber which still can be
seen above the great gate of Lambeth. Many years later, at his trial
just across the river in Westminster Hall, Thomas More made a

comment which I want to take for one of my texts: "And for the Kingdom, I have all other Christian realms." The old Europe was defined and inspired by the Christian faith and by a united Church. Thomas More was paying tribute to this ancient vision. The question for us is, can the Churches serve Europe now in its hour of need, or are they doomed to become ever more peripheral institutions, wasting energy on old quarrels and catering for a diminishing number who have a taste for the antique and a passion for the cultural achievements of the Christian centuries of the past?

I believe that Europe stands in need in three particular areas, which I wish to headline as Reconciliation, Compassion, and Meaning. I believe that in every one of these areas Christians have a vital, even a decisive contribution to make.

Reconciliation: Our Lord said in the Gospel, "How blest are the peacemakers; God shall call them His sons."

When I last came to this city, Europe was still at war with itself. In Western Europe, we have — please God — come to a point where war between the nations of the community is unthinkable, but there are still divisions between Eastern and Western parts of Europe which, in an era of nuclear weapons, could be not merely dangerous but fatal to us all. Part of the message of the great antinuclear demonstrations held here in Brussels and in my country a week ago was that the pursuit of peace has not been sufficiently urgent. On both sides of the divide, we seem to be drifting without the will to conclude agreements which would release immense resources and capacities, manpower and money, for creative ends.

The Christian Church is represented in both East and West, in vigorous Protestant Churches in East Germany, in Roman Catholic Poland, in Orthodox Russia. Real attempts are being made now to build on this Christian presence throughout Europe. Any Christian worthy of the name must be a peacemaker. Currently, Archbishop Sundby of Uppsala and the Patriarch of Moscow, Pimen, are working on peace initiatives, both of which I intend to support. Of course, there are political pressures and attempts to manipulate the Churches, but my hope is that one day it will be possible to organize a world religious summit for peace in some neutral place. Christians cannot strive to do less, and Europe needs their contribution to the reconciliation which may save it from destruction.

Our Lord also said, "How blest are they who hunger and thirst to see right prevail, and how blest are those who show mercy." Destruction by war is not the only way in which Europe could die. It could die of fat and hardening of the heart. A healthy and a human community shows compassion. That must mean compassion for our brothers and sisters in the great belts of hunger and poverty throughout the world, as well as those in our own countries who are handicapped and friendless.

Our Churches belong to a great worldwide family of Christians. Our Lord's insistence that we are children of the one heavenly Father and members one of another must be converted into practical terms, into active compassion and support for the brains and capacities that shrivel for lack of food. My Church has now a majority of black members, and much of the Anglican future will be in Uganda and Nigeria. You in Belgium also have historic links with Africa, particularly with Zaire. As Christians, we have the experience and the sense of belonging to one another which can equip us for encouraging and leading Europe in a more compassionate way. Do we have the will and the energy?

Lastly, Our Lord also said, "How blest are those who know their need of God; the Kingdom of Heaven is theirs." The framework of life in all the countries of Europe is changing rapidly. Technological developments make it unlikely that we shall ever return to the kind of full employment we have known in the recent past. Perhaps we must all learn to cope with much more leisure. This will be difficult for many, since a man's worth and value has commonly been measured by his work. Work has given a structure and meaning to many lives, and if the nature of work changes radically — if, for example, there is a decreasing need for manual work — then the crisis about the meaning of human life, its purpose and value, will deepen.

As Christians, we do not judge men or women by their productive capacity. We revere them as individually unique creations of God. Ultimately, we are on this earth for delight and not for any functional reason. As this service of the Holy Communion reveals, we are to take the common things of life, bread and wine, the staff of life itself. We are to offer them to God with thanskgiving. In doing so, we are to see them afresh — not as the kind of food that simply delays death, but as tokens of God's love for us. Seen in this light, the bread becomes the bread of eternal life and the wine the cup of salvation. As Browning said: "This world's no blot for us, nor blank/ It means intensely and means good/ To find its meaning is my meat and drink."

"How blest are those who know their need of God; the Kingdom of Heaven is theirs." In a Europe perplexed by the crisis of meaning, Christians have a kingdom to celebrate which is not affected by technological change or altered material conditions.

Europe was once given unity and identity by the Christian Church. I passionately believe that it can be so again, that Christians can make a decisive contribution to reconciliation between East and West, to building a more compassionate heart to our community, and to identifying an enduring meaning and purpose for human life. We are surrounded by so great a cloud of witnesses that the Christian faith and Church has had the energy to do these things in the past — do we have the will to follow the saints?

4 November 1981

 T THE PALAIS DE CONGRESSES, BRUS-SELS, ON THE ROLE OF GREAT BRITAIN IN EUROPE: If you picture the world as a great ocean liner, then most of Europe is sitting in the First Class dining rooms. Unfortunately water is pouring into the steerage where the poorer passengers are huddled. The captain and the crew must take time from devising ever more sophisticated menus for the First Class passengers in order to deal with the threat to the whole ship. My hope for the churches of Europe is that they will not be found saying grace in First Class as the ship sinks, but will be trying to raise the alarm. If we fail with the problems of the steerage, we shall not remain forever insulated from the effects of the incoming water.

4 November 1981

T THE GENERAL SYNOD'S DISCUSSION OF WOMEN AS DEACONS: The trouble about all our debates on the ordination of women is that it is necessary to convert an attitude toward the place of women in the body of Christ. Otherwise any debate — for example, on the ordination of women — is seen by the world to be prejudiced, or seen by others to be governed by emotion, rather than clear-thinking. We live with this unsatisfactory state of affairs, and we shall have to live with it a little longer if we are not to dissipate energies which are urgently needed for united Christian mission on endless ecclesiastical debate. But from time to time there are steps which can and should be taken, which are true to a proper sense of dynamic tradition, which help to shift attitudes, and which do not bring ecumenical ventures to a grinding halt. That's not to say they don't create problems. I believe that to be the case in recognizing that ordination to the Diaconate is something in which men and women can share. And it is an Order distinguished by the laying-on of Episcopal hands as a sacramental sign for the Church. Whether people should be called The Reverend, how they should dress, what should be their legal status, seem to me secondary issues. It seems also to be possible to separate this from ordination to the priesthood. Why? Because I'm persuaded that Deaconing is one sort of Holy Order, a sacramental sign in the Church, and that in dividing one sort of Holy Order we are treating Deaconesses not as ordained persons, but as female ordained persons, and that there is here a case of discrimination within an order, a case not only of diversity of function, but inferiority of function. I do not myself happen to believe that to be the case in the matter of the universal tradition of the Catholic Church about male priesthood.

Since I believe also in the recovery of the permanent Diaconate, I'm not too concerned about which comes first, but hope that postponement will not be used as a blocking device. In this whole area I have learnt that humour is very very dangerous, and although I

141

hold to the opinion that people without a sense of humour lack judgment and therefore shouldn't be trusted with anything, I'm nevertheless very cautious about advancing it. I am of course deadly serious in this speech which I am making, but I am glad that in one of those debates in 1938, someone did venture a little humour and said, "a committee." Here we might substitute the words "a Synod," for "A Synod is a body of men who individually can do nothing, but collectively can determine that nothing can be done." I believe this to be a day when something can be done, and within the constraints of five minutes I've tried to stand by the resolutions of the Lambeth Conference and to associate myself with the recommendations of the House of Bishops [that women ordained Deaconesses may be considered to be within the historic Diaconate].

12 November 1981

INTERVIEW FOR BBC-TV's "ROBERT OF CANTERBURY"

ARCHBISHOP RUNCIE ON LAMBETH PALACE: I rather enjoy some aspects of Lambeth. It's an exciting place to be. It's a pressurized place. The pressure never ceases. Of course, it's a great office-center really. . . .

AFTER TALKING WITH AN ENGLISH WOMAN ORDAINED TO THE PRIESTHOOD IN THE UNITED STATES: I found it fairly easy to meet somebody who is obviously genuine, but I'm always anxious lest they feel conned by me. You know, I'm looked upon as an oracle, a person who ought to give a lead, who is firm in faith, an example of no doubts about the ordination of women. I mean, "Where do you stand, Archbishop? Will you ordain women or won't you?" Well, I'm simply less than enthusiastic about it at the moment because I regard it as divisive and at the present time I regard the unity of the Church as more urgent than the ordination of women. Nevertheless, faced with one human being who impresses me by her sincerity and obvious commitment to the priesthood as she sees it, I cannot but give my blessing to that person. ("May God grant love from Christ to sustain you in your work for Him and courage from Christ for all that lies ahead, and the Blessing of God — Father, Son, and Holy Spirit — be with you and all you undertake in His Name now and always. Amen.") God bless you. It's very good to meet you again. I hope we shall meet when you come back to England sometime. Then you can tell me about your experiences in the States, and you'll see how far my thinking has moved.

SPEAKING INFORMALLY IN HIS STUDY: This clock, which I constantly forget to wind up, isn't a marvelous timepiece but it takes me back to the very beginning of my ministry because when I left Newcastle the parish came together and gave me the clock in 1950.

I've also got a silver pig here on the mantlepiece. I've hundreds of pigs because, although it doesn't figure greatly in my life, I have a little sideline in keeping pigs and so much has been made of it as a mark of my humanity! I enjoyed my visit to a pig farm in Iowa, accentuated by having to don a walking-on-the-moon suit — white overalls! I'm interested in the conditions in which large-scale hog-raising leaves the pigs. It is part of my concern about world hunger.

ON TRAVEL IN THE UNITED STATES: There are times when Arch-bishops have to recognize that they're a bit of a parcel. They are handled by those around them and they just submit to that — it's no use protesting. Going by helicopter from the pig farm to Ames, the second largest city in Iowa, was one of those occasions. I don't expect that the maker of my vestments thought they'd ever be used at an Iowa colosseum. When I was going into the colosseum, I couldn't help thinking of the resonance of the word across the centuries from the times that Christians were meeting the lions. The bands playing and the crowds' enthusiasm had something of the feel of the ancient colosseum. I had to be careful I didn't get too triumphal because in Iowa I had a message that might be uncomfortable — world hunger. During the Eucharist I was very much moved as we shared the bread and the cup amongst that great crowd. It was a sacred moment. But sacred moments have meaning for the whole of life, and therefore our sharing there had to suggest the sharing that is called for from being privileged in the world.

INTERVIEWED AT THE WHITE HOUSE IN WASHINGTON: You've got a lot of Episcopalians. That nice, pretty girl there, she's an Episcopalian, too, she whispered in my ear. It wasn't more than a privileged tour of the White House, but by that time I had met the Vice President and a Cabinet member, George Bush and Caspar Weinberger. They were friendly and both happened to be Episco-palians. The predominant thought in my mind was that the people

---

← *The Archbishop as he sometimes appears in television interviews from his study at Lambeth Palace. St. Thomas Hospital in background is just beyond Lambeth's garden wall, so close that Dr. Runcie jokes that if patients look closely "they can see the Archbishop having breakfast in his braces."* Press Association Ltd.

in the White House were handling fierce dimensions of power — for good or for ill.

INTERVIEWED IN LOS ANGELES: By the time we got to Los Angeles, the hunger strike in Ireland had captured the American press. Interest was at a peak because Bobby Sands had just died.

Question from a newsman: Did you ever consider or have you in the past tried to influence the Prime Minister to follow it in some way that there could be some unilateral action taken . . . ?

Archbishop: I can't speak of any private conversations, and I haven't myself engaged in that sort of debate in parliamentary forums. I wouldn't shrink from it if there seemed an opportunity. What people don't understand is that I'm not a spokesman of the British government. I'm a religious leader who has a certain place in British life and, as a religious person and as a Christian, cannot view the death of a young man, caught up in the tragedy and conflicts of Ireland, with anything but compassion for his family and with regret for the early ending of his life. I would like, as a religious leader, to appeal to all sections of the community not to allow themselves to be exploited for the purpose of retaliation and further violence.

INTERVIEWED IN A WOODED AREA NEAR CANTERBURY CATHEDRAL: It's very important, I think, for someone in my position to have secret places where he can just reflect and be himself. Sometimes I take a book and go and visit this little orchard that stands for something very precious, which is the quiet solitude that you need. It's essential to me if I'm going to fulfill my role that I have sufficient time to think of what used to be called "the great verities." Fundamentally, life is sacred, and people are sacred, and the pattern of how things should be can be seen in the life, death, and resurrection of Jesus Christ.

AT A MEETING WITH A GROUP OF PEOPLE CALLED THE CELL: It's another important part of my life. I've belonged to this group for ten or twelve years. It has a simple rule. We remember each other in prayer each day, and we meet every nine months for 36 hours, and that's an absolute priority. It's a grave sin to arrive late or leave early or say you can't attend. We tend to be people who are in positions where it isn't always easy to find free exchange in which you can be completely honest with people. I don't think I would survive without it. I believe most of the others would say the same.

If I were not doing this job, I'd still be the sort of person who got anxious about succeeding and putting his message across. My temptation would still be to depend too much on myself and not enough on God to carry me through. I would still have an over-cluttered program so that I would wake up at 4 in the morning thinking, "How am I going to survive?" I would have the same sort of spiritual problems and spiritual judgment on my life if I were the headmaster of a school or vicar of a village. You know, Bishop Pike of California used to say that he charged $500 for a speaking engagement, and if hospitality was provided he charged a thousand dollars. Much as you enjoy the hospitality, that again is somewhat wearing. And then there's also the business that if you don't have time and you don't have rest and you don't read and you don't have conversation with friends, you become bogus about your religion, which should be personal and immediate and real.

ON VISITING IRELAND: I went chiefly to learn so that in the future when I speak of Ireland I won't say stupid things. The central point of the whole visit was my meeting with the Cardinal Primate whose ancient seat is at Armagh. The picture of us praying together might seem contrived, but there was nothing contrived about it. It was a genuine moment of prayer together before we sat down to talk. . . . I was perhaps more anxious than he was, understandably, to get some real bite into our meeting, and I was perhaps a little pushy over that because he bore the responsibility of being in the hot spot if anything untoward or indiscreet or unhelpful came out of the interview.

ON HIS POSITION: . . . There will always be people who will regard you as the pantomime figure in the great national charade and be inclined to say when you talk about faith and the great Christian verities, "Oh, there's the Archbishop drippling on with platitudes." And if you try to apply the Christian faith to circumstances of the world and the need for a political will or something like that, you may get, "What does the Archbishop know about it? He's just following the latest liberal trend. . . ." So many of the things that we say about the social gospel don't carry a conviction because they seem to be too glib and insufficiently lived by the people who are saying them. That's a big problem for an Archbishop, of course, because, you know, he lives in a palace, [and] in order to operate efficiently on a wide stage he needs a car; he needs secretaries; and when he goes to places, the red carpet is put down. How can anybody believe a prophet who lives in a palace?

A Sister from Bangladesh came to see me. I hadn't seen her for 20 years. She used to be in Calcutta in the Oxford Mission, and has gradually become, you know, "the Indian Sister" who has moved to Bangladesh and realized that she can't express her faith living in great institutions built on Western wealth, however devoted they are to serving the poor. She must identify herself with the village in which she lives with a new, small community of a half-dozen young Sisters, living a life of marvelous simplicity. She came to share some of it with me, and I was terribly humbled and reduced to tears — not least when she said, "I want to have your blessing," and, in Indian fashion, prostrated herself at my feet. Now those are moments which really reduce me to pulp, because I wanted to kneel down and kiss *her* feet. She wasn't a person of built-in sentiment. She was tough as well as sensitive, so I gave her what she asked for. It was the only thing she asked. She said, "It's no use, we don't want money because that puts us apart from the people with whom we live." You have these moments, and they keep you going because you realize that if you can create conditions for those sorts of things to happen, you can carry on with all the misunderstandings about the palace and the chauffeur and the secretaries.

ON EVALUATING HIS LIFE: There are times, of course, when I wish I had never stopped being a teacher in a university where it all started, where I was married, and where I might have lived in a flat in Cambridge and written a book or two on narrow, specialist themes. Or I might have made the move from there to be the kind of parish priest of Liverpool that I first imagined I might be before I ever went to the University, where I was touched by the idea of being at the service of others for the sake of the Lord in that sort of idealistic way. You know, you look back and think nostalgically on how things were at different stages and how you might have made a simple life for yourself. But look at the compensation I have from the goodwill or the mixture of experiences that are mine. So I may often get clobbered and feel reduced and feel exhausted and grieve to be so misunderstood. But in my better moments — and I hope they're mostly when I'm at prayer or at worship — I think what good fortune God has given me.

T THE 150th ANNIVERSARY OF KING'S COLLEGE CHAPEL, LONDON: The 90th Archbishop of Canterbury, William Howley, presided over an opening ceremony of King's College Chapel in 1831. The service lasted four hours. Now, 150 years later, I believe we have at last trained Archbishops in the art of brevity!

The chapel, like the college, began its life at a time of fierce religious controversy. It was conceived as an Anglican bastion and in the beginning chapel services were compulsory. Indeed, the religious tone of the early King's was so pronounced that one noble Lord described it as "an institution for training Jesuits." He was thereupon challenged to a duel by the Duke of Wellington — the only duel the Iron Duke ever fought was for the reputation of this college.

Well, controversy does not rage so fiercely today, but there are still those who wonder whether a chapel really belongs in a place of science and learning, at the very heart of a university. I want to suggest that if we aspire at King's to educate the whole man, then we botch the job by not paying attention to the development of the human faculty for worship. That may seem a curious way of putting it. Worship is commonly understood as a somewhat peripheral activity for those who have a taste for well-choreographed togetherness. . . .

We give thanks that this chapel has been a focus for worship for 150 years, and we pray that the education offered here will always be marked by the realism that, just as man the thinker and man the athlete need education, so, if we are to avoid living at a dangerously unconscious level, man the worshipper needs education, too. The Christian worship here provides one way, which I believe to be the most profound and convincing, but which should at least be definite and vivid enough to help others in their search by allowing them to grow by defining their dissent from it.

17 November 1981

T EVENSONG AT ST. ANDREW'S CATHE-
DRAL, ABERDEEN: As Scottish Episcopalians, you
have often had a sharper sense of belonging to a worldwide Anglican family than we in the sometimes rather
provincial Church of England. I cannot forget to mention in this
place the consecration of Samuel Seabury. You led the way in ap-
preciating that the Anglican Church outside these islands had a right
to organize its own affairs and develop its own local traditions when
we were still trying to keep the reins in English hands. . . .

Our communion with the Christian centuries of our past and
with the Church in other dioceses and throughout the world is not
optional or a luxury — it is part of a fully mature Christian life. The
will to keep in step with our fellow pilgrims saves us from turning
our worship into devotion to self-indulgent fantasies, a mere endorsement of some national dream, or the desire to preserve some
particularly cherished style of life. . . .

In turbulent and fearful times, when the temptation is to retreat
into narrowly based, strident, even fanatical forms of worship, which
further divide us from one another and add fuel to the already dangerously combustible state of the world — now, more than ever before, we need to celebrate and cherish our links with the Church of
all the ages and throughout all the world. The vision of that Church
and its achievements, which we glimpse in our common worship
today, can give us hope when present realities hem us in and the
courage to act and work at a time when fear can immobilize us — or,
worse, make cynics of us.

November 1981

THE ARCHIEPISCOPAL ROUND: CANTUAR

THE CHURCH OF ENGLAND — for all the many and continuing signs of confidence and hope detected by last year's Preface writer — seems uncertain about unity and unsure of itself in mission. About the Archbishop of Canterbury, however, the Church *is* certain. The year 1981 — effectively Archbishop Runcie's second year of office — has seen fuller and more rounded manifestations of his leadership and his style. A perceptive commentator from the Free Churches has said that in Archbishop Runcie we have the most effective communicator of any Archbishop of Canterbury of this century with the possible exception of William Temple's brief reign. In his preaching and speaking, in public interviews and private conversations, there is directness, clarity, and wit. Yet communication goes beyond words: the being and doing also speak. . . . The sight and the sound of the Archbishop at Christmas 1980 not only preaching at Canterbury but also standing on the tarmac at Heathrow dispatching his envoy to visit the four captives in Iran and to intercede for their release, was a sermon in itself. Here was an Archbishop "doing something." It was a practical gesture with a practical purpose: the world was admiring and appreciative — and Mr. Terry Waite became, deservedly, a household name. But there was a symbolism in the gesture, by the accident of its timing, in the visiting at that season of prisoners and captives: "I was in prison and you visited me."

All told, it has been a busy year for the Archbishop: visits to America, Ireland, and Belgium, a meeting with the Anglican Primates, the fifth meeting of the Anglican Consultative Council, and much else. At home, there has been time for vigorous intervention in Parliament — on, for example, the Nationality Bill — and for a contribution to the work of the General Synod which comes close to mastery of it: on marriage, covenanting with other churches, homosexuality, and unemployment, the speeches from the Archbishop, delivered when the debate had got into its stride, seemed always to be determinative in the sense that they established the climate for the rest of the debate. The leadership seems effortless, though underlying it is careful staff work. His lead is always received appreciatively — or almost always. There was disappointment amongst supporters — men and women alike — of the "women's movement" at his contribution to the World Council of Churches' Sheffield Conference on the Community of Women and Men, though what he said there was consistent with his known opinions on these issues. There were anxieties, too, at the November General Synod lest the Synod's establishment should be tempted to persuade him to assert his mastery unnecessarily and too often. But these were small matters when seen against the totality of his achievement in a job which, to the outside observer, can only seem impossible. Overall, he has a sureness of touch which impresses and, at the same time, gives confidence.

NEW YEAR'S DAY STATEMENT: "You and the Church are getting too political," I was told recently. It's something I hear often and has set me thinking about the principles by which we can judge whether a Christian leader is justified in intervening in public affairs. An Archbishop is not a politician and must not become one. A large part of his work is devoted to teaching the traditional faith and to building a united community, but an Archbishop, like any Christian leader, must tease out the implications of the faith for the day-to-day life of the community. . . . He should seek to discern the moral dimension which belongs to almost every policy or problem. . . .

The Church has a special obligation to speak on behalf of the vulnerable and the inarticulate and those whose bargaining power in society is weak. . . .

We belong to a worldwide Church and follow a Lord whose commandment is "Love thy neighbor." [Hence] Christians have a special charge to discuss our problems in a global perspective. . . .

In every instance, we bear in mind that self-righteous indignation is an opium which makes people unfit for useful work.

1 January 1982

O THE BURMA COUNCIL OF CHURCHES, RANGOON: The truth about God and His Son needs to be interpreted in terms of different cultures, and that is why as Anglicans we have not translated our sense of a worldwide brotherhood into any centralized organization which will tell the Anglican Churches in various countries what to do. Local autonomy is for us a precious and fundamental principle. In England the first thing the Anglican reformers did was to compose a prayer book and a liturgy in their own language. At one time, I fear, some missionaries acted as if the only way to make good Christians was to turn people into passable Europeans. That offends against basic Anglican principles. I am convinced that God desires to be praised in Burmese and to be seen through all the richness of the cultures. . . .

1 January 1982

T ST. JOHN'S CATHEDRAL CHURCH, HONG KONG, ON THE FEAST OF THE EPIPANY: At the first Epiphany three wise men from the East traveled to Bethlehem to see and to celebrate the light of the world — the infant Jesus. Now, centuries later, three perhaps not so wise men from the islands of the furthest West journey Eastwards to Hong Kong to see the light of Jesus Christ expressed in your Church. They are not Caspar, Melchior, or Balthazar this time, but Robert, Terry, and Richard.* I am particularly glad to share such a significant moment when my good friend Peter Kwong has become the first Chinese bishop in the 140-year history of the Church here. I share your hope that a new chapter of possibilities is opening for our Church now that it is under Chinese leadership. . . .

Those who worshipped in the church on the parade grounds where now the Hong Kong Hilton stands, and those who built the Cathedral of St. John, were often men and women of energy and self-sacrifice. But that era is over. The Lord's Name is to be great among *all the nations* and here in the East, where the sun rises, the Lord should have a Chinese face. . . .

[And] if His Name is to be great among all nations, Christ's connection with the most venerable civilizations on earth must be made clearer. There should be no excuse to repeat the old slur — one Christian more, one Chinese less. . . .

When I was in Burma last week, I met the former archbishop, Francis Am Ya. I was humbled by his modest references to the occupation of Burma during World War II and by his account of his sufferings in prison. He said he was grateful for those experiences, painful as they were, because they had helped him to mature as a Christian. Indeed, the Christian gives thanks for his own suf-

---

*The Most Reverend Robert Runcie; Mr. Terry Waite, the Archbishop's Assistant for International Anglican Communion Affairs; The Reverend Richard Chartres, Chaplain to the Archbishop.

ferings and brokenness, not in a spirit of masochism, but because if we are Christian believers, suffering can spotlight and dislodge our obsession with ourselves, and make us fit for the service of others. . . .

Life taken with thanksgiving. Brokenness leading on to self-giving. Such is the faith which we must indigenize. Such was the light seen at the first Epiphany and in the life of our Lord Jesus Christ. Such is the light which we must kindle for the sake of the world today.

6 January 1982

Diocese of Hong Kong

T ST. ANDREW'S-BY-THE-WARDROBE, CITY OF LONDON, ON INVITATION OF THE HABERDASHERS COMPANY: Despite having been a Bishop now for a dozen years, I obviously am not accustomed to flattery. So when I was invited to speak here I accepted before wiser counsels could prevail. An Archbishop has limited time for the kind of reflection which leads to the organized thought appropriate for such an occasion. I have therefore taken refuge in what was, when I was a university teacher, familiar territory for me — the history and culture of Byzantium — and also in what was a responsibility before I became Archbishop for the conversations of the Anglican Communion with that legacy of Byzantium, the Orthodox Church. However, I would not want you to think this was simply old stuff taken out of a drawer. I hope to suggest how Byzantine Conversations have had some influence in my own mind of the role I have now undertaken. . . .

The Byzantine Church in the 20th century has come out of its geographical isolation. In America, by reason of the dispersion, there· are Orthodox Churches which are youthful and have much intellectual vigor. In Australia, Melbourne is now the second largest Greek city in the world. In the United Kingdom the Orthodox Community is arguably the third or fourth largest Christian group. By reason of the Eastern European interest the Orthodox are claming a larger place in the World Council of Churches. Yet it is a Church which has no experience of the Renaissance or the Reformation. It has no 19th-century middle-class religious prosperity which sent missionary movements all over the world.

Anglicanism has claimed a special relationship with Orthodoxy. It has tried to keep in touch with a Church that is Catholic but not Papal, and a Church which tries to live according to a tradition and does not elevate Biblical Fundamentalism or Pope. All these aspects had an appeal to the fathers of Anglican Reformation. So it was not surprising that the first steps in dialogue with Orthodoxy were made by Anglicans, and the first international conversations (over which I presided) between the whole Orthodox and Anglican World began in Oxford in 1973.

It would be idle to deny that those conversations have run into heavy weather, and since that time others started with the Roman Catholic and Lutheran Churches have overtaken them. The Orthodox seem to have discovered that the inroads of modern secularism have been greater in the Anglican Communion than in the more conservative and politically significant Roman Church or the more strongly theological Lutheran. The speculations of Anglican theologians and the ordination of women to the priesthood, as well as the great varieties in our liturgical life, have seemed to the Orthodox not to express spiritual vitality so much as religious St. Vitus Dance. For Anglicans there is a sense that the Orthodox Church attempts to live in a world of absolute theological clarity wholly divorced from the realities of intellectual and moral ambiguity in the 20th century. . . . and there is a question over an Orthodox Church which, however heroic some individuals may be, is thought to accept the Commissar with the same meekness with which they used to accept the minions of the Sultan. . . .

Sometime ago I visited the Patriarch of Antioch to get him to take our Byzantine Conversations more seriously. He said to me, "What we need in the Middle East is stability and charity; in my experience, theological conversations contribute to neither." Indeed, endless talk and documentation, ceaseless consultations and assemblies, may merely reveal that sharing is not enriching, because the resources are so limited. . . .

In the Roman Church the surrender of Latin and a degree of collapse in Latin culture over the last two decades, the liturgical changes, the new confidence of the non-European peoples into whose languages Christian truths need to be baptized, all these things mean that accepting diversity and plurality is a serious problem for Rome. Anglicanism, on the other hand, has to face the problem of unity within diversity. Roman and Orthodox critics are inclined to say, What kind of unity can you have with Anglicans since some seem to believe very little at all, including the theologians? Or they say the party divisions between Catholics and Protestants are so charged as to negate Anglican unity. If Rome has an authority crisis, Anglicans have an identity crisis. . . .

Byzantine Conversations always point up the question of Church/State relations, [for] numbered among their saints are diplomats as well as martyrs and mystics. I remember talking to a Roumanian Orthodox Bishop. About his desk I noticed there two pictures — one an icon of the Virgin Mary and the other a large photograph of Mr. Ceacescu, the Roumanian President. The Bishop saw me glance somewhat surprisedly at it, and shrugging his shoulders said, "Ah, Byzantium!" There was in him the idea that emperors come and emperors go, but the Queen of Heaven will remain. Undoubtedly the line is often that we were here before the Turks and Tartars, and we were here before the Communists, and we shall be here after they have gone. On the way there will be need for compromise if we are to keep alive the offering of worship, the existence of church buildings, and the training of our children through the family tradition. . . .

The Byzantine Church is called the Orthodox Church, a word that means "right belief and right worship." The two hang together. . . .

There is a sense of eternity which you get in a great act of Orthodox worship. The emphasis is that we are fellow pilgrims with all those who have worshipped God in past centuries, and who now worship him with clearer vision beyond the grave. . . .

None of what I have said means I am unenthusiastic about Christian unity, that I am not proud of Anglican diversity, that I do not applaud the courage of the Poles or admire Protestant independence. Nor that I want to discourage Christians from being change-agents in a society. But Byzantine Conversations remind me that these things are by no means the whole story of Christian witness.

28 January 1982

T THE NATIONAL FARMERS UNION: I assume that I have been invited to such an agreeable evening not so much as Primate of All England—that marvellously zoological title for this glossy purple specimen—but chiefly because I was for one brief and heady moment of glory the page three feature in *Farmer & Stockbreeder*—on the grounds that I keep pedigree Berkshire pigs!

It was very illuminating that my pig-keeping was used on my appointment to Canterbury to illustrate that I live close to reality. The *Washington Post* heralded the announcement with the words, "Easy-moving, over six-feet tall, husky, pig-keeping war veteran gets top job." I was soon deluged with books and correspondence. Choice titles like *The History of the Hog* and *A Porcine Odyssey* poured onto my desk. The Muppets sent me the *Pensees of Miss Piggy* to guide my steps through life. My children received every sort of T-shirt inscribed with "Hogs are beautiful" or "I love hogs."

The enthusiasm for the first swineherd since Thomas Becket to become Archbishop of Canterbury reached its heights on a visit to Iowa, the veritable home of the hog, last year.

The Iowans solemnly made me a member of the American Pork Chop Association, and I was presented with an American Berkshire called Martha. Getting her into Britain was a learning experience about forms and regulations, but I am told that, with the personal intervention of the head of Veterinary Services, Western Hemisphere, she is now frisking around in a beechwood near my home in Kent.

I have just returned from China where they only knew two things about me—first that I presided at royal weddings, and secondly that I kept pigs. In that country the pig is thought to bring good fortune. On reading your Annual Report, I wouldn't say that you entirely agree!

The sum of my tale is this: if you sometimes feel you are underestimated as farmers, don't believe it. My experience is that pigs are a passport — if not to wealth, at least to popularity.

Mind you, I am not to be taken seriously as a pig farmer. I am a pig *fancier*, which enables me to my first serious point.

You are engaged in the serious business of good production. You need to be hardheaded men and women engaged in the commerce and politics of agriculture, doing battle with urban-based environmental pressure groups or politically motivated low agreed prices for farm products. It is sometimes forgotten that those who farm find human fulfilment and enjoyment in it.

. . . I can't resist mentioning, as someone who often has to visit educational institutions, that the mixture of common sense, purpose, and unstuffy staff/student relations at such establishments as agricultural colleges is a model for some academic centers that I dare not mention. I was not surprised to find students from many parts of the Third World, which brings me to a second serious point. It is simply to emphasize that your argicultural expertise can make a significant contribution to closing the frightening and dangerous gap between the richer and poorer nations. I recall a professor from Iowa State University who said to me, "There is little doubt we can grow enough food to feed the hungry in the world. What is in doubt is whether we have the will."

Farmers are not characters who usually attempt to solve the world's problems by demonstrations and banner-waving, but you are in this matter one of the most powerful and influential bodies.

. . . The Church has always been particularly close to agriculture. The scriptures are full of cornfields, sheep, and, in less auspicious passages, pigs. In the Gospels, the Gadarene herd seem to have been got rid of rather rapidly. The Church of England, through its ancient buildings and country parsons, is still a significant presence in the countryside. The Church Wardens of the land may be represented by more farmers than any other single profession. We ought to be more natural allies and not let an old friendship drift apart. I was myself for nine years a country parson, and combined it with running a college for future clergy. A farming friend used to ring me up from the North and ask, "Still in your deep litter of parsons, Runcie?" But I can honestly say that in those days contact with the farming community is what kept me sane.

What I am recalling — Cuddesdon College near Oxford — is an old-fashioned place, I suppose, and I was a kind of Pooh-Bah, which may or may not have equipped me to be Archbishop. Certainly I ran the village hall, the locate fete, and the Angling Association, and was chairman of the Parish Council. At my first meeting of that group the Parish Clerk said to me, "Don't worry, Sir, until hand-to-hand fighting breaks out."

Ditching, hedging, footpaths, rights of way — anyone who, like yourselves, has handled such matters will not be terrified by the House of Lords or the General Synod of the Church of England or by Papal Visitation.

A final serious point: I believe the Church has suffered severely from having little clear strategy of the countryside and not taking seriously the need to provide appropriate training for it. There is a danger of letting the urban scene dominate the thinking and training, or of wallowing in nostalgia and dwelling in a rural dream that misses what is changing in the countryside.

. . . Having led you through pigs and prophecy, I hope that it may be said of my audience, as was said of an old Scottish preacher's congregation, that "if they did not arise instructed, at least they awoke refreshed."

9 February 1982

T HE personality of the Archbishop of Canterbury is always important to many Anglicans, and that is our excuse for including a comment which slightly overlaps with the Preface to *The Church of England Yearbook for 1982*. The choice of Robert Runcie aroused unusual interest both because it was the first time that elected representatives of the Church of England had been officially consulted by the agents of the Crown and also because it was the first appointment of a man born after the first World War. The media quickly took the new archbishop to their hearts as a wartime hero, as a part-time pig-keeper, and as a former chairman of the committee which advises the BBC and IBA about their religious programs; and additionally several television interviews have shown him to be a well-informed, thoughtful, and gently humorous man, more diffident than would generally be expected of holders of the Military Cross. There has also been a general welcome among the clergy, many of whom know of his excellent work as the chief pastor of the Diocese of St. Albans. In churchmanship he combines a firm hold of the tradition of Catholic spirituality with an open attitude to many modern realities. One of his chief interests has been in theological conversations with the Orthodox Churches, yet he has also been bold in applying pressure on the General Synod to provide a warmer pastoral care for people remarried after divorce and for homosexuals; he has surprised conservatives by publicly arguing that homosexuality is a handicap rather than a sin or a sickness (although he also annoyed "gay" propagandists by his caution). On the issue of women priests he has annoyed enthusiasts, and American women in particular have been irritated by the impression that he takes Orthodox bishops more seriously than he takes them; but he has given a few signs of being open to conversion. The only clerical element tempted to be disgruntled about the promotion of this liberal Catholic has been the conservative Evangelical movement, which perhaps had been inclined to the illusion that everything was going its way; but any such critics would have been unable to produce a plausible alternative candidate. . . .

During his enthronement in Canterbury, Dr. Runcie (as Oxford University has enabled us to call him) revealed his character. His realism is well suited to a period when the Church of England, far from triumphant in spiritual reality, is tempted to exaggerate the stories which it can tell of success, and when the Anglican Communion, unsure about its theological foundations and its future, is tempted merely to stress its present fellowship. . . .

Since his enthronement Dr. Runcie has made no dramatic calls to the nation and has seldom said anything very original in his teaching within the Church. Historians may not find much to write about as they ponder these two years. It has nevertheless been instructive to observe how decisive his interventions have become in General Synod debates (all the more genuinely influential now that the Archbishop of Canterbury is seldom in the chair) and how on a very public and very glamorous occasion such as the wedding of the Prince of Wales he struck millions as a man who could talk sense. Wisely he delegates; he has surrounded himself with an able staff at Lambeth (headed by Bishop Ross Hook, who sacrificed the status of a diocesan bishop in order to be this kind of a servant) and by an energetic team in the leadership of the Diocese of Canterbury. He has made a point of consulting his brother bishops and also has a wider circle of counsellors. It is surprising to think of such moves as innovations, but such they were to a large extent. Thus sheltered from some of the administrative pressures and spared the risks of a solo performance, he has had some time to be available as a pastor to troubled souls and to talk with people outside the English ecclesiastical machine. He has begun to gather knowledge, to win friends, and to develop a personal authority by international journeys, rightly believing that committees such as the Anglican Consultative Council can be no substitute for the person-to-person contacts made by a traveling pilgrim from Canterbury. He always strikes foreigners as being very much an English gentleman, but fortunately he is seldom called upon to move outside those circles where such an assessment is, on the whole, a compliment. The miracle wrought by his assistant and representative, Mr. Terry Waite, in rescuing missionaries from an Iranian prison after trumped-up charges of espionage is only one example of the influence which an Archbishop of Canterbury can still wield if he takes the trouble to study and prepare the ground. Another example is the respectful attention given to his addresses about world problems in the USA, where he attracted audiences wider than would normally be expected by the Episcopal Church, a comparatively small body.

This may be the beginning of a Primacy as effective as, say, Randall Davidson's (1903 – 28), although in tune with an almost totally different age. Lord Davidson was no theologian and Dr. Runcie has not been granted all the personal gifts which his five most recent predecessors exercised, but the more "ordinary" man may well turn out to be better than any of the eccentric giants at the work of the Primate of All England and the president of the Anglican Communion. Robert Runcie is splendidly gifted as a coordinating manager, and as a charming communicator. In this hope many pray for him. . . .

The comparison of personalities always tends to be odious, but when the Pope meets Dr. Runcie the Anglican leader need not feel completely dwarfed; far more than John Paul II he embodies the Catholicism of the future.

Lent 1982

ENTENARY AT WESTMINSTER ABBEY OF THE ROYAL COLLEGE OF MUSIC: Sermons divide where music unites. That was one of the messages of my predecessor, Archbishop Tait, at the meeting which founded the Royal College of Music a hundred years ago today.

It's true he undermined his authority by admitting he was tone-deaf. I cannot claim to be a musicologist, but at least I do not labor under my distinguished predecessor's difficulty, and, being married to a musician, I have a resident tutor.

Archbishop Tait was, of course, right: music in itself unites diverse forces and themes. The process of composition binds together a variety of instruments in the orchestra and brings harmony out of an interplay of musical ideas, subplots, and leitmotifs.

Music also clearly transcends cultural and linguistic divisions. You do not need to know German to appreciate Beethoven.

But I wish to spend the time allotted to me in considering another barrier which music can surmount.

The Royal College of Music was launched with words. The meeting convened by the Prince of Wales at St. James's Palace in 1882 was a veritable gabfest: nine long speeches. A century later we are celebrating the centenary with music, and the preacher has been warned to confine himself to a modest ten minutes.

I do so gladly and willingly, because we have been battered by words: newspapers, radio programs, advertisements, election addresses, sermons. We are properly suspicious of rhetoric and the obfuscating jargon of bureaucracies and official organizations. We are constantly being challenged and called in words, but very often we fail to be convinced by them as a way into truth.

Music, by contrast, does not evoke such weary cynicism. We are, in large numbers, receptive to music in a way in which we are not receptive to words. Music has become available, not just to an elite but, as the founders of the Royal College envisaged and worked for, to vast numbers of people in our country. Through a standard of performance and virtuosity which must be without equal in our history, through the concert hall, the long-playing record, and radio, music has become available to millions, and for them it constitutes a door through a world soiled, described, and imprisoned by definitions, into those uplands described by Elgar and Vaughan Williams where even somber shades are somehow more intense and more elevating.

In 1882 music occupied a lowlier place in our national life than it does now. Long past were the days of the 17th century, when music was still considered a key to understanding the universe and when there was lingering respect for music, which had been a central and integral part of medieval education. The poet Dryden, in his *St. Cecilia Day Song* for 1687, represented the end of that ancient tradition:

> From harmony, from heavenly harmony/This universal frame began/From harmony to harmony/Through all the compass of the notes it ran/The diapason ending full in man.

His rather exalted language reminds us of music's particularly close relationship as a handmaid to religious sentiment. By the 18th century, however, music had been somewhat degraded, either to a rather undistinguished role in Church or to the status of a mere amusement. By the 18th century, man might or might not have an ear for music, just as he might or might not have a leaning to piety. English music in this period became a rather dull echo of continental trends, or actually relied upon the importation of continental masters like Handel.

The pattern remained virtually unchanged until the later years of the 19th century. England did not share in the revolutionary ardours of the end of the 18th century which, on the Continent, produced a seismic shift to the grand and romantic music associated with Beethoven and his followers. We were rather a musical backwater, and, even as a handmaid to religion, music was slapdash.

When Samuel Wesley's anthem, "Blessed be the God and Father," was first sung in Hereford Cathedral on Easter Day, 1833, the only adult member of the choir present was a single bass — the Dean's butler. On another occasion, at St. Paul's, Handel's "Hallelujah Chorus" was chosen for the anthem, but during the service a message was sent to Goss in the organ loft that only one tenor and one bass were present. "Do your best," he replied, "and I will do the rest with the organ." No wonder that Prime Minister Gladstone, speaking at the meeting which inaugurated the Royal College, said, when describing the state of Church music, "I cannot use any epithet weaker than one which would perhaps shock the meeting."

One of the specific objects of the founding of the Royal College of Music was the elevation in the standards of church choirs, but I suspect that there was something much deeper involved: a profound sense that music was no longer an amusement or a divertissement; it was once again central to a culture which needed to escape from the imprisonment of rationality and definition and analysis. It is highly significant that so many of the great students of the Royal College have found it difficult to affirm any Christian conviction in creed or words but in their music have, it seems, been drawn irresistibly to religious themes — not only to the texts of the liturgy but also, like Vaughan Williams, represented in this service by his setting of Psalm 47, or, like Benjamin Britten, to an attempt to express the mystery and wonder that lies on the margins of the desert created by prose.

Music is for so many the door into the realm of the spirit, their way over the boulders, the obstacles deposited by a century of linguistic criticism. The Church has, in consequence, honoured the great musicians over the past hundred years. Archbishop Tait admitted that, although tone-deaf, he had the power to confer the degree of Doctor of Music, and no one can deny but that such privilege of the Archbishop of Canterbury has been used wisely in the ensuing years. Only yesterday I discovered that our distinguished organist, Sir George Thalben Ball, received a Lambeth Doctorate of Music on November 27, 1935. That recognition was well deserved and farsighted, just as this celebration in music and comparatively few words is exactly as it should be.

Not everyone who *sings* Lord, Lord, shall enter the Kingdom of Heaven; only those enter the Kingdom who *do the will* of the God and Father of Our Lord Jesus Christ. But for multitudes today, thanks to the Royal College, music provides a unique environment and climate in which God may be found, His healing experienced, His will known, and the power to do that will given.

28 February 1982

T CERCLE DES AMITIES INTERNATION-
ALES, GENEVA: I am grateful for the flattering introduction given me by the former Swiss Ambassador
to Britain. I am also a little shamed by his superb command of English because I remember that Napoleon used to view
Geneva with dark suspicion because "the citizens know English too
well!"

. . . An Archbishop of Canterbury is driven to ponder many
matters because, like many other religious leaders, his office and
responsibilities continually force him out of the sanctuary into the
marketplace and the debating chamber. . . .

The Church and the Archbishop become like a platitude machine
if they do not act sometimes less like cement and more like grit in
the machine when some fundamental principle is at stake. Many of
us believed that the recent bill attempting to define nationality in our
country contributed unnecessarily to the anxieties among immigrant
groups in Britain and was discriminatory in other ways. . . . Sometimes the Church should not say Amen, it should say Stop. . . .

I have not lost faith in the capacity of the communications system
and tradition of rationality represented by Geneva to make progress
in tackling the world's urgent problems. . . . Communications and
Communion obviously have a common root, and they ought not to
be isolated from one another. Communication by itself can be just
an exercise which contributes to the oppressive information overload
from which many of us are suffering. Paralysis by analysis. [But]
if communication and communion belong together, there is another
couple which ought not to be divorced — rationality and the great
religious myths. In the land of Carl Gustav Jung, I need hardly
labor the explosive and integrative power of the accounts of reality
offered by stories and symbols. . . . One of the themes of European
history has been the attempt to consign religious belief to the private
sphere of life. Delphi, the meeting place of the Greek States, was
also a sacred shrine. International conferences now are not commonly

attended by corybantic ecstasy or dependent on the pronouncements of oracles. Such is an understandable view of the divisions and violence which have flowed from religious controversies in the past. Now the times have changed, and the world needs a new partnership between religious belief and secular idealism in the common service of a creation which is in danger of being torn apart.

11 March 1982

← *The Archbishop joins in a street procession during a visit to the ancient Anglican Shrine of Our Lady of Walsingham. The vested crucifer carries the gilted plexiglass Primatial Cross made by the Canterbury College of Art after the government declared that the venerable silver gilt Primatial Cross was a national treasure that should not be taken out of Canterbury. At right is Graham Leonard, Bishop of London. At left, Eric Kemp, Bishop of Chichester.* Press Association Ltd.

O THE LIVERPOOL LUNCHEON CLUB: When you have lived the first 19 years of your life in a city, it will have marked you. And when it is a place of the character of Liverpool, it has hopelessly prejudiced you. For me, this is a day of coming home. Someone said to me recently that I talked like Malcolm Muggeridge. I am still recovering from that, but my wife assures me that you can still detect my origins. Perhaps it is because I had to go to places like Balliol Road Baths in my early days of learning to swim. Certainly it is interesting to come off the train and get into the Adelphi Hotel. In my childhood, Grand National Night at the Adelphi was our glamorous equivalent of a state banquet. Since this is such a personal occasion, I hope you will forgive me if my talk to you battered businessmen is couched in rather personal terms. I haven't come to lecture on the economy, or to pontificate about your problems in this great and lovable — notice I don't say "once great" — city and its people. . . .

In visiting and talking with you I shall try to give you an impression of how a Liverpool-bred Archbishop looks at his problems and hopes to learn something from a place in which he invests not only considerable affection but also great expectations. After my ramble 'round, you may believe the man who said that Archbishops quickly acquired the fatal facility of continuous utterance!

11 March 1982

The Liver Bird: City of Liverpool

T EASTER, 1982: Easter was, and is, an act of God that changed the world. But the sceptic will say that nothing much in fact has changed in the last 2,000 years to justify that assertion. Christians dispute it, and I should like to illustrate our faith by referring to recent signs I have seen of Resurrection power loose in the world.

Within the last week I have been privileged to visit the oldest hospice for the dying in this country, St. Joseph's in Hackney. I met there a most remarkable lady, full of the confidence and faith that there is a door through which the followers of Christ can pass to even closer relationships with God and to sharing in His divine life. She was an artist and a potter, and I was moved almost to tears when she offered to give me her last work. She has now died and her last piece of pottery has arrived, containing a final testament of her faith—a broken egg shell. It is one of the most precious gifts I have ever received, a powerful expression of the Resurrection faith that she has broken out of the shell, leaving behind her limitations and infirmities as she journeys into a fuller life in the sight of God.

The other sign is not so personal, yet we acknowledge that there is hardly a country that has suffered more than Poland. It was reduced to rubble in World War II, but its ancient Christian Church has remained firm in its Easter convictions. The Resurrection faith has rebuilt the rubble into a temple of spiritual power and energy that nothing in all creation can destroy.

11 April 1982

CREDO: BBC LONDON WEEKEND INTERVIEW:

Interviewer David Tereshuchuk: Archbishop, you've spoken of your sense that the Church has a duty to speak out for the vulnerable and the inarticulate "who are weak in bargaining power." Isn't part of the problem that here you are, a powerful and wealthy institution as you described it yourself, trying to do that but at the same time surrounded by all these trappings of secular and temporal power, that you are anxious to disassociate yourself from?

Archbishop: I'm constantly aware of that and the cry that prophets don't live in palaces. I think that for *me* it's a problem because I have to be cautious about giving the image of somebody who's lecturing from a great height to people who are struggling with intractable and terrible human problems.

Interviewer: Don't you think it's a problem for them, too, the vulnerable and the inarticulate, who seem to almost resent your intrusion?

Archbishop: I've tried to meet them on equal terms and listen to them in places like Brixton, and Liverpool, and in visiting hospices where I think that the sick are vulnerable. Also I've visited Borstal institutions and tried to contrast them with new sorts of therapeutic communities. Mind you, I don't get polite deference, and sometimes there is some hostility coming across, and I think that it's quite a tricky operation trying to listen to that, so I can articulate what they are striving for when I am in the centers of power.

← *Seated in the cloister of Canterbury Cathedral, the Archbishop talks with students who made a pilgrimage there on Easter Monday, 1982. Later that week he spoke in the House of Lords, and then left London for a three-week tour of Nigeria.* Times of London

Interviewer: Would that task be any easier if you were, for instance, less the Establishment?

Archbishop: That's a possible solution that's often suggested, that we should sell Lambeth Palace and we should distribute the assets of the Church Commissioners. I happen to think that's an oversimple way. It might win something in terms of public image in the immediate sense, but in the long-term sense I don't think it would really be so helpful. Naturally we've got to avoid waste. We've got to see what damage this kind of headquarters can create. On the other hand, let me give you an example. The assets of the Church Commissioners that are devoted to the payment of the clergy may look very considerable when toted up at the center. However, when it's distributed over the country it helps to pay modest incomes to people who can often be deployed, for community purposes, as well as representing their faith, where people couldn't pay for a man. And in Toxteth, for example, there was a certain shift in resources, in order that a priest could be put down in an area which lacked leadership. Of course, it had to be the right sort of man, a person who was experienced in working in that sort of area and did himself come from the inner city. Now to have somebody who can articulate that, and draw together a representative group from the neighborhood, by way of support, did actually depend on a proper deployment of resources. Now you need headquarters. You need places where you can have conferences and where you can have a secretariate in order that you can function efficiently. But it's a question of how the resources are gradually shifted a bit. And it's one of my hopes that we can shift our resources in a long-term way that may be more constructive in the places of need. I happen to think that the inner-city and some of the scattered rural areas of the country need much more attention and that suburbia is better able to look after itself.

Interviewer: But to, say, the youngsters of Toxteth or Brixton, you're still a member of the House of Lords, you still live in a Palace, you solemnize the marriage of Prince Charles — isn't it still a problem for you, no matter how much you do at the ground level?

Archbishop: Well, it's a problem for me, but I don't think it all depends on me. That is what I was talking about in my enthronement sermon when I spoke of authority in the world's order. You know, the idea is that the boss is at the top and the office boy down below, and the office boy exists to serve the boss. But in Christ's order it ought to be the other way around. Now I can't do it all myself, but I can create conditions for Christian people, in those areas, to feel sufficient encouragement.

Interviewer: Would you like at the very least to be Disestablished, to be disentangled from the connections you have with the State?

Archbishop: Not wholly, because I think that Establishment makes a point not of status but of a sense of responsibility for the life of the whole nation. If you're going to try to harness religious convictions with secular idealism, I think an association with the whole life of a country, through the Establishment, gives us platforms and places rather than status and control by government. I'm prepared to soldier along with Establishment. But if Establishment did seem to me really to hamper that task, and to reduce the possibility of our working for the Lord in community terms, then I would favor Disestablishment.

Interviewer: The fact remains though, doesn't it, that leading an Established Church isn't very Christlike, is it?

Archbishop: It depends on what you mean by an Established Church. If you think the Established Church is all for privilege, then that's not Christlike. But if you think of the Established Church as one that recognizes its mission and its work to be concerned with the whole of a national life, and not just with religious people, I believe that's Christlike. I don't think churchmen are to be politicians or diplomats, but on the other hand most issues in the country have a moral dimension. Take housing, for example. If I am critical, as I have been of certain housing policies — and at the same time am booming away about the importance of family life while failing to recognize that housing policies may be undermining the capacity of people to build family life — then what I say seems to be vacuous platitude. So I'm keen to point when occasion demands that here is something that is practical that at the same time may be political. But it does affect the building up of wholesome family life. People will be inclined to say, "Keep out of politics. It's nothing to do with you, Archbishop" — but I'm not in it for the sake of politics. I'm in it for something humanitarian. Again, I recognize the incredibly difficult job people have and the integrity with which they pursue getting our economic policies right. But I'm bound to think unemployment a more important issue than inflation because I'm concerned about the human dimension of economic policies.

Interviewer: You've said that you see the Pope's visit to Britain as perhaps increasing the possibility of ecumenical progress. Does that mean you expect something from the Pope himself when he comes here?

Archbishop: I hope that there will be something constructive coming out of his visit because the Pope is a great Christian figure and a great Christian evangelist. I believe we should line up behind that positive side of what he has to say. On the other hand, I recognize that if you think of the divisions we've had in the past and if you concentrate on Papal Bulls of Excommunication of the 16th century, and so on, you will have anxieties, some expressed responsibly and some irresponsibly. I understand that some people may say, Well, here's an Archbishop who's perhaps a bit high church, and here's a Pope saying he is coming to England, and here's an apostolic delegate somehow being raised in status, and here's a report that took a long time to get out and that is looking at the position of the Pope in a world Christendom: now I'm sure that those anxieties need to be tackled and need to be allayed.

Interviewer: The phrase that's being used now is an acceptance of the Pope or the Bishop of Rome, or whatever, as a universal Primate. What do you think that could mean for you and for the Angelican Church? Is it that what he says goes, or not?

Archbishop: No, not what he says goes, not at all, but something that recognizes that, in days when so many issues are global, there is an advantage in having a central focus of affection, even a central spokesman to articulate what the Churches in different parts of the world are thinking and trying to say. That seems very generalized, but I think Anglicans recognize that there is value in that sort of concept.

Interviewer: Just for yourself, how will you be greeting the Pope when he arrives? Will he have any primacy over you?

Archbishop: No, certainly not any sort of jurisdiction over me. We thought a bit about that, and one of the things we intend to do, for example, is that when he comes to Canterbury, there is the Chair of Augustine — a chair in which I often sit and in which I was enthroned — and, of course, we want to recall that it was a Pope, namely Gregory, who sent Augustine to England, so we're going to stand on either side of that chair and put the ancient Gospels in the chair, so that they will express our common loyalty to the Gospel and the recognition of the supreme authority of the scriptures. I hope that will make a point. Of course, in the whole Anglican Communion we are trying to make a distinction between essentials and nonessentials. . . . We have always suggested that you know the scriptures as the norm of our faith, that you know the Creed as the pith and epitome of our faith, that you know the sacraments as the expressions and conveyors of grace, and that you accept a particular form of ministry to unite the Church. Those are the essentials, but we allow a good measure of difference of custom and tradition.

Interviewer: Which is very different from Rome, isn't it?

Archbishop: Historically that is so, although I believe that, as proceedings of Vatican II are revealed, there was quite a revolt of Third World countries about the dominance of Latin and West European culture. If we have a problem of identity in Anglicanism — what we believe and how we make decisions as Anglicans — so the Roman Church has a problem of how to deal with diversity of custom and tradition that is bound to express itself.

Interviewer: Isn't it true that, in practice, Rome always tends towards authority and the enforcement of uniformity?

Archbishop: I'm not sure that's entirely fair to the way in which a number of Roman Catholics have argued and expressed themselves. You may have noticed that in some of the Papal visits, particularly in the United States, he didn't exactly get a free run when a Sister got up and challenged the Holy Father about the attitude towards women. I suggest we might be able to help each other in these matters. After all, I think that the Pope and the people of Poland set a fine example of being steadfast and loyal and prepared to suffer for their faith. We need that sort of example. One of our South African Bishops said to me, "I'd find it very difficult to be a Christian in England. It's one advantage of living in England because the issues are much sharper pointed. In England everybody is so nice that the gap or the line between Christian and non-Christian is blurred." I think that the present Pope may be able to speak more sharply, more decisively, but I think that we've got something to give in terms of the realities of trying to get Christianity caught, not taught, by a few people in a free society.

Interviewer: On the Pope's part, he's not very keen on diversity, is he?

Archbishop: Well, that may be so, but it may be also that he hasn't so much experience of our sort of society, and our sort of Anglican Church, just as I haven't so much experience of the kind of schooling in adversity and in hostility which somebody like himself has had.

Interviewer: There are things like whether priests can leave the priesthood and whether they may marry — surely there are going to be enormous problems?

Archbishop: Oh, there are going to be enormous problems. That means we've got to work hard at it and keep in touch. But don't forget that, within my lifetime, things have very considerably changed in atmosphere and in capacity to work together.

Interviewer: How would you propose getting over the difficulties in bringing the Established Church of England into communion with Rome, when you are entangled as you are with Crown and Parliament?

Archbishop: Yes, that will in any case be a problem so far as the Free Churches are concerned. But don't forget that our entanglements with Crown and Parliament are not very considerable now. The Queen's position in the life of our Church is very much a symbolic position. She is, as it were, a chief layperson in our Church rather than somebody who has the decisive voice in all appointments. We now have a system whereby the appointment of Bishops and other leaders is one where the Church makes recommendations. The choice is made between two names, or further names, so that in a sense on appointments we're not controlled, as we once were, by a Crown and Parliament.

Interviewer: Under a new relationship with Rome, who would choose Bishops?

Archbishop: I don't see why it wouldn't be possible for us to continue the arrangement we have here — in fact, as a result of the concordat with Napoleon, the French have rather more control in terms of certain appointments than we do. It would be a question of accepting a diversity of practice. In the Roman Church, you wait for approval — or indeed you may wait for the decisive voice. We would find that unacceptable at present.

Interviewer: How big a risk to unity is the disparity between Anglicans themselves within their own broad Church, between Anglo-Catholics on one hand and evangelicals on the other?

Archbishop: Oh, well, I wouldn't think it would negate it, but obviously it's something of a difficulty. On the other hand, some of these divisions that people talked about in the past — high church and low church — actually run through denominations and not simply within them. You could certainly claim there was a kind of high church and a low church group within the Church of Rome. You could also suggest that there was a radical, liberal, and highly conservative view of the Christian faith and its expression today — both in the Church of Rome and the Church of England and the Anglican Communion. I think that we've both got the problem of whether or not what we try to do as leaders and theologians is really in accord with what is acceptable.

Interviewer: Is it your feeling that the Anglican Church will hold together completely in the face of approaches towards Rome?

Archbishop: Yes. I don't take lightly the sort of fears and anxieties that people have about our riding roughshod over what has been said and done in the past. I'd like to give the impression that so far as I'm concerned — and I hope I speak sensitively on this point, I've already tried to do so — whereas I take seriously the need for Christian unity, I don't mean some kind of soft-boiled conformity, some kind of sellout that people are inclined to suggest when a too easy approach to the question is taken. I think there are considerable difficulties ahead and considerable conflicts of opinion, but you know that's how you grow as human beings, and it's certainly how you grow as Christians, by a certain honest exchange, and not by fudging up answers and producing some bland impression.

Interviewer: Will we see unity with Rome by the end of the century?

Archbishop: Well, I dream of unity with Rome and with the great Reformed tradition and with the Orthodox by the end of the century, but we'll have to get a move-on certainly if that's our target. I don't see why we shouldn't have that target.

18 April 1982

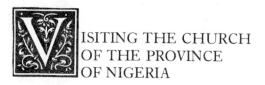

ISITING THE CHURCH
OF THE PROVINCE
OF NIGERIA

AT A STATE DINNER IN LAGOS: Apartheid is an insult to God and man whom He dignifies.

AT AN ECUMENICAL SERVICE IN LAGOS: I know of an old man who appeared in Heaven and said, "I am tired and want the fruits of the Spirit." The angel who kept the counter replied, "We don't have fruits, we only have seeds." May you plant seeds of faith in Nigeria — the fruits of the Spirit.

AT A STATE DINNER IN IBADAN: The Anglican Church was founded with certain views of authority. It recognized the traditional authority with bishops and priests. It gave to the people a Bible in the language of the people, and it gave them a Prayer Book to guide their devotions wherever they were. We have many members who are in a relationship of *critical solidarity* to the Church. We have been true to our tradition of educating our own lay critics.

AT AN ECUMENICAL SERVICE AT BENIN CITY: In God, what we all agree about is that He is resembled in Jesus Christ who came to save people wherever they are with the news that people matter because they matter to God. He took negative things in life and so dealt with them that He turned them around and increased all the goodness in the world. As the Redeemer, He gave words to the fainthearted and made realization of "the Kingdom of God" seem possible.

Aᴛ EVENSONG AT ST. MATTHEW'S CATHEDRAL, BENIN CITY: As a small boy, terrified at reading the lesson in Church, I grasped the wings of the eagle lectern and was encouraged to read its inscription, "Expect great things of God."

Aᴛ THE CATHEDRAL CHURCH OF ST. PETER, AKE, DIOCESE OF EGBA-EGBADO, "THE CRADLE OF CHRISTIANITY IN NIGERIA": I was struck by the first sentence in the Lesson which, in English, is "Walk worthy of your vocation. . . ." That is, live your lives according to what you have heard. What we have heard in this place is of how the Christian religion was more "caught than taught." If we are to be worthy, then Christian people have to show Christ in their lives. The test is whether we are signaling the Gospel fresh and new as it was with the little group in the beginning. For many it has become old and ineffectual. But remember that when Jesus spoke they said, "He doesn't sound like a religious official." The early Christians, arriving here, were prepared to suffer for their faith, and it makes me ashamed when I take exception to the heat or cockroaches in my bedroom. Most importantly, I ask if we as Christian people reflect Christ's amazing power. It is what the early Christians got across — healing, joy, faith. The first African bishop, Samuel Crowther, said he looked forward to the day when "because of the Gospel there will be rejoicing in Africa." Joy, it has been said, is the flag that is flown from the heart when the King is in residence. If we do show love, then I thank God for the birth of Christianity in this lovely land. I pray that we may walk worthily of it and show joy and express love to everyone — because it is limitless. That's our Gospel, that's our heritage in this place. Praise the Lord!

Aᴛ THE LAYING OF THE CORNERSTONE OF THE CATHEDRAL OF THE GOOD SHEPHERD, ENUGU: There are four vital characteristics of a shepherd. He will go miles over the hills to find one sheep which has gone astray. It is basic Christianity to care for the children, the homeless, the poor, the oppressed. He needs to discipline and teach his sheep. He is proud of them, for they will only prosper if they are loved. He forms the flock and

leads it. . . . I pray this Cathedral may be a symbol of a new Christianity for a great and vigorous people of Nigeria.

At an ecumenical service at jos: If our faith delivers us from worry, then worry is an insult flung into the face of God's love.

At st. stephen's cathedral church, ondo, nigeria: There is a strategy that Christianity is given through the name by which Archbishops are sometimes known: Pontifex, bridgebuilder. I remember standing on one of the largest bridges in the world, at Istanbul, a span joining Europe and Asia. There is the modern world at one end and the old world at the other end. There were armed guards who seemed symbols of the stand against peoples becoming one. It was a matter between bridge-builders and bridgebuilders. . . . The bridge between me and my God was built by Jesus Christ who gives to God a human face. The bridges in this world need to be built on earth, between Christians and others. There need to be bridges between Christians: Jesus Christ is not just Lord of Christians, He is Lord of all. We need to build bridges that will lead men and women and children to the Father. We *have* to be bridge-builders. At the Eucharist, always think of the bridge that Christ built to enable us to have Communion with God.

At the dedication of the chapter house of all saints cathedral, onitsha: In a family, when a child is surrounded by love and companionship . . . that child will grow wholesomely. So make sure you do not forget the foundation stones of the Christian faith — the Bible, the teachings of Jesus, and our prayers. Unless this building is on that foundation, it is a mockery. It is not to show that Anglicans are better than others but that we are a partnership with God built up in love and faith.

15 – 29 April 1982

← *The Archbiship in white cassock is greeted by the President of Nigeria, a Moslem, during official call at the Presidential Residence in Lagos. At left is Timothy Olufosoye, I Archbishop of Nigeria.*

MORE GRACE ABOUNDING

T HE Most Reverend Robert Runcie's Eastertide visit to Nigeria —
15 April to 29 April 1982 — was a significant milestone in the broad-
ening dimensions of an archiepiscopate then entering its third year.
He logged thousands of miles in one of Africa's largest, richest, and
most densely populated countries during a fourteen-day trip vastly
different from his coast-to-coast American journey a year earlier.

Archbishop Runcie's days in Nigeria did not constitute a "theme
tour," devoted to discussions of urban problems or world hunger,
as did the U.S. excursion. Nor was it centered on special concerns,
as have been some of the forays to East Africa, Ireland, Burma,
China, the Lowlands, or Switzerland — journeys that are making Dr.
Runcie the most traveled of the 102 occupants of his ancient office.

However, the Primate of All England did see Nigeria, as he
saw the U.S., in its cities and countryside, meeting civic and ecclesiastical leaders as well as the people in the pews and their clergy.

Archbishop Runcie left London in the midst of the Falklands
crisis (he had spoken in the House of Lords only a day earlier) and
he returned home to the shifting controversies surrounding the ap-
proaching visit of John Paul II. Through it all he continued to grow
as the most personally involved and informed prelate in the 1,385
years since St. Augustine, himself a traveler, arrived in Canterbury.

To an American observer, the most exciting aspect of the trip is
the comparison between the infant Church of Nigeria (it became an
independent Anglican province only four years ago) and the U.S.
Church's great growth of the nineteenth century. New parishes are
constantly being founded. The 19 recently established dioceses were
to grow from 19 to 23 in the year following the Archbishop's visit.

Communicants constitute record figures in a country in which Christianity was introduced little more than 125 years ago. Each bishop annually confirms an average of 1,500 persons.

It is also apparent that Britain has maintained good relationships during colonization and in the twenty-two turbulent years that Nigeria has had self-government. Its leaders repeatedly stress the contributions of the Anglican Church in education, medicine, and other areas that are now nationalized.

Although one sees much roadside poverty inherent in Nigeria's readily acknowledged role as an "emerging nation," church-goers appear well off—and somehow happier than seems to be the case in Manchester or Miami, Blackpool or Boston.

"I want to see a Nigerian face, not an English face," Dr. Runcie said at the outset. He urged indigenous expression of worship in a Church whose liturgy is largely traditional. Just under the surface, however, is Nigeria's desire to be "a singing, dancing Church"—or at least, a readiness to add its own rhythm as a postscript to liturgy. Its staid Anglicans can almost instantly become what Westerners might call "holy rollers." It is its Protestants who are on the higher side, at least in dress, as compared to Nigerian Anglicanism's preference for surplice and stole. The Nigerian Methodists, moreover, have preserved apostolic succession for their crimson-clad Bishops who preside over their own dioceses.

Beginning with a talk with Nigeria's president (a Moslem, as are 45 percent of the constituents), Dr. Runcie went on to scores of courtesy calls. The most colorful were the visits with the Obas and the Emirs, the super-chiefs who have considerable influence and the life-styles associated with the maharajahs of old India.

The tour began in the port of Lagos—a world crossroads which Dr. Runcie instantly likened to his native Liverpool. It was at a state dinner in the capital that he made the declaration that most endeared him to Nigerians: "Apartheid is an insult to God and to man whom He dignifies."

The Archbishop traveled on to Ibadan, whose two-million people make it twice the size of Lagos. Using Ibadan as a base, he ventured into tribal towns and the inner courts of the Obas. He saw the landing sites of the early missionaries. "When the heat is oppressive and there are cockroaches in my bedroom, I am reminded that it is not much when compared to all that's been endured for the faith," he said.

Accompanied throughout his visit by the Archbishop of Nigeria and several diocesans, Dr. Runcie went to such provincial towns as Ono, to a country cathedral in Asaba near the Niger River, and to Onitsha's new cathedral church that greatly resembles Coventry Cathedral. He participated in notable dedications: a bust of Samuel Crowther, the slave boy who became his country's first bishop; the laying of the cornerstone of Enugu's great new Cathedral Church of the Good Shepherd; the reredos of St. Michael's Cathedral Church at Jos; and the blessing of two new parish churches — one near Enugu and the other at Kano.

The Archbishop also gave time to women's rallies and Anglican youth groups. It was, as Baptists might say, "a total immersion" in Nigeria.

Travel, mainly by automobile, enabled the Archbishop to see the villages in their settings of sand or cleared jungle as well as the mountains of Enugu and the deserts around Kaduno. More comprehensive perspectives were offered by three helicopter lifts and two plane flights. While the majority of the trip was confined to southwest Nigeria, the last days took him into the nation's heartland (as far north as Jos) and finally to the City and Diocese of Kano. From there the Archbishop and his entourage departed at midnight for London.

The trip had its share of hilarity. At Enugu, the rooftop of the youth building was blown off by the twirling blades of the archiepiscopal helicopters. A day later the copters returned at the moment that the soup-course was being served in the diocesan parish hall. In moments great clouds of red dust turned everyone into Cardinals sipping scarlet soup.

At the grandest of all the state dinners, also in Enugu, torrents of rain drove guests to the shelter of the speakers' platform; moments later its canopy collapsed, rebaptising everyone present.

The first and last hymn heard in Nigeria was "The Church's One Foundation." It was sung more often than any others. Another favorite with the Nigerians was "Jesus Shall Reign Where 'Ere the Sun."

In summary, Dr. Runcie was present for Morning Prayer five times; Evening Prayer, eight; and was celebrant or concelebrant of the Eucharist at four altars. He preached from eleven pulpits, spoke at six luncheons, seven dinners, and three ecumenical services.

Remembering the battered, rusting wrecks of automobiles alongside the highways, the Archbishop's party looks back with thankfulness for its safety in a country that has few stoplights and no enforced speed limits. If a philosophical Nigeria can apply some degree of disciplined restraint to the costly lessons of recklessness and restlessness — as every country and individual must do — it can go forward to the leadership in Christianity and world affairs that is its true, godly destiny.

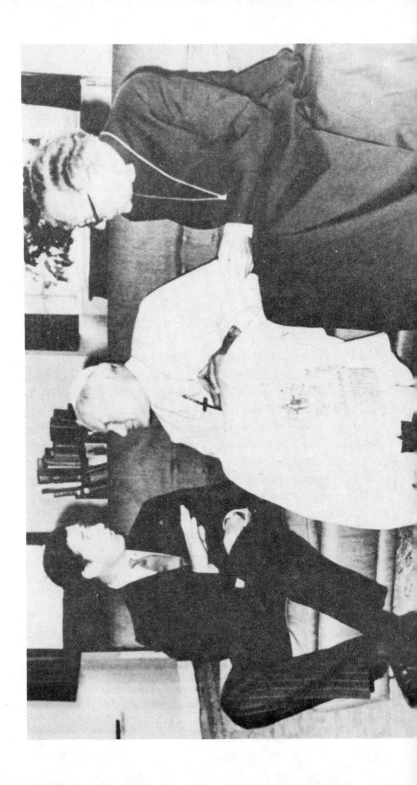

T THE VISIT OF POPE JOHN PAUL II TO CANTERBURY CATHEDRAL: Remembering our beginnings, celebrating our hope for the future, freeing ourselves from cynicism and despair in order to act in the present — this is the style of Christian living which gives shape to this service.

Every Christian service contains this element of remembering the beginnings of our community, when Our Lord walked this earth. At this season of the year, we particularly remember the gift of the Holy Spirit at the first Pentecost and the sending out of the Apostles to carry the faith of Jesus Christ to the furthest ends of the world. We recall one of the first missionary endeavours of the Roman Church, in its efforts to recapture for Christ a Europe overwhelmed by the barbarians. In the year 597, in the words of the English historian, the Venerable Bede, Your Holiness's great predecessor "Gregory, prompted by divine inspiration, sent a servant of God named Augustine and several more God-fearing monks with him to preach the word of God to the English race." Augustine became the first Archbishop of Canterbury, and I rejoice that the successors of Gregory and Augustine stand here today in the church which is built on their partnership in the Gospel.

We shall trace and celebrate our beginnings in this service by reaffirming our baptismal vows made at the font at the beginning of Christian life and by saying together the creed, an expression of the heart of our common Christian faith, composed in the era before our unhappy division.

The emphasis, then, will be on the riches of what we share and upon the existing unity of the Christian Church, which transcends all the political divisions and frontiers imposed upon the human family. One of the gifts Christians have to make to the peace of the

---

←*The Archbishop listens as Prince Charles talks with Pope John Paul II during the papal visit to Canterbury, May 29, 1982.*

world is to live out the unity that has already been given to them in their common love of Christ.

But our unity is not in the past only, but also in the future. We have a common vision, which also breaks up the lazy prejudices and easy assumptions of the present. The Chapel of the Martyrs of the 20th century is the focus for our celebration of a common vision. We believe even in a world like ours, which exalts and applauds self-interest and derides self-sacrifice, that "the blood of the martyrs shall create the holy places" of the earth. Our own century has seen the creation of ruthless tyrannies by the use of violence and of cynical disregard of truth. We believe that such empires, founded on force and lies, destroy themselves. The kingdom spoken of by Our Lord Jesus Christ is built by self-sacrificing love which can even turn places of horror and suffering into signs of hope. We think of Your Holiness's own fellow countryman, the priest Maximillian Kolbe, who died in place of another in the hell of Auschwitz. We remember with gratitude our own brother Archbishop Janani Luwum in Uganda, who worked in the worst conditions for Christ's kingdom of love and justice and whose death inspires us still and will mark the future more deeply than the lives of his oppressors.

We remember all the martyrs of our century of martyrs, who have confirmed Christ's Church in the conviction that even in the places of horror, the concentration camps and prisons and slums of our world — nothing in all creation can separate us from the active and creative love of God in Jesus Christ our Lord.

If we remember that beginning in Jesus Christ our Lord, if we can face the suffering involved in travelling His way, if we can lift our eyes beyond the historic quarrels which have tragically disfigured Christ's Church and wasted so much Christian energy, then we shall indeed enter a faith worthy of celebration, because it is able to remake our world.

29 May 1982

T THE ANNUAL GENERAL MEETING OF THE COMMUNITY RELATIONS COUNCIL OF BIRMINGHAM, ENGLAND: Many hopeful initiatives in community relations have been launched in Birmingham, which has continued to be an energetic pioneer when so many others have become weary and dispirited. While commending Birmingham it is, at the same time, not hard to understand civic depression about current attitudes and the future pattern of relations between communities in the new multiracial Britain. There is still a frightening lack of awareness about the nature and seriousness of the problem. There is still a tendency to place all the blame for the disturbances on "criminal elements." It would be foolish to deny that there is some truth in that analysis, but in Martin Luther King's words, riot is also "the voice of the unheard."

As I visit different areas of the country I still frequently meet housing authorities and councils who claim that there is no racial problem in their leafy avenues. Their lack of urgency and conviction to redress racial disadvantages is itself a major contribution to the problem.

Lack of urgency and inactivity, however, are sometimes less frightening than simplistic prescriptions, whether hostile or well meaning. It is the daily experience of many that when you examine the community patterns of a particular locality the "racial problem" dissolves into a bewildering welter of crosscurrents and subplots. Asian and West Indian populations are as different from one another as they are from the indigenous Anglo-Saxons. Not only are there tensions between minority groups, but also within families there are often acute differences of attitude and conflicts between the generations. In particular, there is a subculture of disadvantaged young West Indians who do not participate at all in society as we understand it. Moreover, it would be naive to refuse to accept the evidence that the brew is being stirred by extremist groups at both ends of the political spectrum. I am glad to be able to say that in Birmingham where your Chief Constable led the way for many other parts of the country in successfully applying to the government to ban marches by extremist groups bent on winding up racial tension.

The complexity and difficulty of the problems has immobilized some, while others have been wearied by the impotence of so much talk about racial attitudes and problems, and bored to the point of exhaustion by the virtuous and detached. An Archbishop is particularly exposed to such danger since he can rapidly develop what one critic described as "the fatal facility of continuous utterance."

There is abundant pessimism about the possibility of society remaining coherent and united in the future, much of which is justified, but it is also true that defeatism insures defeat. Complacency is inexcusable, but we can be encouraged by what has already been achieved and the way in which attitudes have been changed, particularly in the aftermath of last year's year's riots.

. . . It is easy to be critical of the police, but when on the streets they are faced directly with threats, abuse, and violence, it is not so easy to preserve a philosophic attitude. Young blacks and young police officers have much in common. Both are minority groups under pressure, wary of any threat from the other. It is understandable that both groups in times of stress should retreat behind tribal stockades of prejudice and bigotry.

The question of relations between the police and the ethnic communities is obviously of crucial importance if Britain is to be a coherent and peaceful entity with all the racial elements contributing and going forward together.

It is to the credit of many leading policemen that they have not retreated into defensive positions. In particular, I have been heartened by a recent lecture by Sir Kenneth Newman as he prepared to head up the Metropolitan Police Commission in London. After emphasizing that there are "thousands of young black people living in sensitive areas in London who are basically law-abiding and who are by no means alienated from white society," he went on to sketch a new police strategy. He contrasts proactive with reactive policing and favors the former policy in which the police take the initiative in acting rather than merely responding to it. In other words, he believes that the police should try to do more in preventing crime by having greater contact and cooperation with the public and social agencies. He also states that, in our society, visible accountability is one of the conditions for effective policing. At the same time he endorses the view that new forms of consultation should be worked out to insure that the police and their policies and operations are in touch with and responsive to the communities they police. As many officers recognize, a policing style has to be negotiated with the local community to provide the basis for the greatest possible cooperation in the vitally important matter of maintaining social order and respect for the law. Violence ought not to be condoned. The police have the responsibility for combatting crime and protecting society from those who commit crimes, but it cannot be done effectively without the cooperation of the community in general. Part of Sir Kenneth's prescription for achieving cooperation is that the police should, especially in multiracial inner city areas, reduce abrasive street encounters to a minimum while focussing their efforts on the selective targetting of the people actually committing the street robberies.

In the words of Sir David McNee, the present Metropolitan Police Commissioner, "the best defense against a repeat of last year's public disorder is not riot squads and water cannons, but public opinion and officers who get alongside the communities."

Relations between the police and the ethnic communities is only a small, albeit important, part of the picture of race relations in this country, but it is an area where I believe there has been movement and modest progress that should nerve us with the conviction that there is a way forward. Britain is inescapably a multiracial country. Any talk of repatriating people who have sometimes lived here for more than two generations or who are no longer welcome in their countries of origin is a dangerous fantasy. We are in fact a multiracial society, and the choice we have is between working to make that fact a matter of pride and celebration, or drifting into a situation where the fact is a matter of lament and despair.

John Brown, the social analyst, who has been working on police and community relations, described a scene in Handsworth in which "people of all races moved freely at ease, stopping to watch the entertainments or just to sprawl on the grass to take the sun, while the kids rushed off for lollypops and the ice cream van. Girls in ethnic dresses brushed past Sikh elders with long white beards. And there in the midst of it all an old English couple selecting their spot to sit, spreading a cloth on the grass, laying out their picnic with care, eating in peace: key symbols of personal security: the acid test of it all."

Such happy coexistence can be achieved if we take immediate action, employ symbolic gestures, plan long-term strategic approaches, and always retain the visionary element.

. . . As for the churches, it is futile to point a finger at others when one's own house needs to be put in order. I believe that the churches currently do make a contribution to improving attitudes and building bridges between different sections of the community, but their untapped potential is even greater.

The churches begin with considerable advantages. They have substantial buildings in the inner cities — sometimes the only local buildings that can be used for community purposes. Most of the clergy, unlike many other professional workers, live in the areas they seek to serve and thus have special opportunities to discover the problems and the anxieties of their neighbors. I know from personal experience that we have some very able and dedicated men and women working in the inner city who can and do play a crucial part as intermediaries between different parts of the community, while providing neutral ground where mutually hostile groups can meet.

There are, of course, temptations to withdraw from the inner cities. The work is costly and difficult. There is often little response. In some areas we have had to close churches and to reassign workers, but as far as I have any influence, I am determined that we should maintain our presence in the most sensitive areas and allocate our resources accordingly.

. . . As for being visionaries, every society needs a story that vividly explains where its members have come from and for what they stand. Sharing a common story gives a community both direction and purpose. It is precisely what happened to the wanderers who formed the nation of Israel under the impact of the story of the exodus from Egypt and the exile in Babylon.

During its history, Britain has been influenced by a number of stories. Some have purchased national cohesion at the cost of asserting Anglo-Saxon superiority. As Milton said, "God speaks first to His Englishmen." Or in the words of the 19th-century hymn, "Can we whose souls are lighted with wisdom from on high, can we to souls benighted the lamp of life deny?" The arrogance of these stories has been found out by history. The sun has set on the British Empire and the imperial story has been overtaken by the march of events. But those old stories also had a nobility about them. We were the island of the free, where tyranny was restrained by equality under the common law and a great range of opinion was tolerated, and eccentrics cherished, not persecuted. The story was taught in music, words, and pictures. It was part of the reason that many of our black and brown citizens wanted to make their future in Britain. It is no part of equipping ourselves for multiracial harmony to respect every tradition except our own. The period when our institutions and traditions were scoured and scrubbed by satire was doubtless valuable, but the time has come for "affirmative action" as well. Our national story was not all romantic cover for exploitation and oppression. There are precious elements in it that could help us to realize that racial prejudice involves letting ourselves down.

However, that is not enough. Tolerance is first cousin to indifference, and the way forward must be through building up one another and championing one another's strengths and talents. The religious view of life provides a basis for treating men and women from different cultures as brothers and sisters. It makes talk of fraternity a reality and not just a pious or sentimental aspiration. Indeed, our human brotherhood flows from our dependence on God as His children. I believe these concepts have been enlarged by the arrival of Asian, African and Caribbean groups in our cities. . . .

I have hope that the presence and the fresh insights of the most recent members of our national family will recall us to the best in the English story and help us to see that it has a future with the help of our new members in building a vision of world brotherhood. They bring rich gifts. They include refinement and spiritual wisdom, hard work and acumen of the Indian subcontinent. We see also the religious enthusiasm and exuberance and the sporting achievements of the West Indies and Africa. To give only a short list runs the risk of caricature, but new citizens can save us from ourselves and can have much to offer in building up a nation for the next century. We can persist in attitudes that will almost certainly insure that immigrants do their worst, or we can seize the opportunity and the choice of helping to create conditions in which they can give of their best.

2 July 1982

COMMEMORATION DAY SERMON FOR
THE COMMUNITY OF THE RESURREC-
TION, MIRFIELD, YORKSHIRE: Commemo-
ration is about remembering. So let's start there.

The last two months have added to my stock of dramatic
memories.

First, a visit to Nigeria, where I received from our growing and
lively Church a wonderful welcome. . . . Then there was that great
service in Canterbury where we welcomed the Pope, and if you had
any sense of history you had to pinch yourself to believe that it was
all happening. For it was one of those religious events that can
outflank so many theological debates so that things can never be quite
the same again.

So this day will be for me a vivid memory of Mirfield. It has
already called out of the past the reminder that the first priest who
taught me the Christian faith, prepared me for my first confession
(we were systematic in those days), and gave me a task to do, was
a Mirfield man. I am reminded too of my only other visit here
when, as a student, I alighted from a Leeds bus with the words "Off
'ere for t' Resurrection" ringing in my ears.

Memories make us the sort of people we are. The musician
remembers tunes; the good cook, recipes; the financier, figures; and
the good family person remembers birthdays, anniversaries and to
send a get-well card to Aunty Kate when she is in hospital. If you
don't remember, it shows that you don't really care. So if you tell
me what you remember, I will tell you what sort of person you are.

Now the first disciples were called Christians because they remembered Jesus Christ. They remembered him easily, deeply, tenaciously. It was the most fundamental thing about them. And we
are so called because *we* remember Jesus Christ. But there is this
fundamental difference from our other memories. We don't gather
round a plaque to recall someone from the past who is absent, but
rather through the sharing of bread and cup, we commune with

someone who is present. That is why in the New Testament they needed a different word for this remembrance, so powerful an experience was it.

So we give thanks for our Mirfield memories, and we remember Jesus Christ is risen from the dead. It means that His caring, His redeeming, and His bringing hope to the world, can live and reign in us. That's why at Mirfield, Incarnation and Resurrection — theological terms as they are — form the great witness of this Community of monks since its foundation.

We are here to commemorate, but we are also here to link this Community with all the communities in so many places in this country and beyond, to which each and every one of us belongs. How can we bring the incarnation of Our Lord and His living presence into them?

I believe there are four ingredients which are needed to achieve true community, and they are reflected in the history of Mirfield, but, more, they are found deep in the Gospels and the New Testament.

First, any community worthy of the name needs to cultivate the family virtues of acceptance, tolerance, forgiveness, welcome, companionship. These give people anchorage and security. Without them no child will ever thrive. Care for the sick, the misfit, the poor, the damaged, the dying. This is basic Christianity. Our Lord accepted people before he made demands on them, made them feel that they mattered.

So this Community, which stretches out its arms to welcome us today, has from Sunderland to the shanty towns of South Africa been found in the dismal places, as well as in the ordinary parishes we know, and has inspired us to care, to rejoice, to mourn with those who mourn. Wherever your priests and friends have gone, this Community has respected and not straight-jacketed the human gifts of the Spirit. Unity in diversity, said Keble Talbot.

But the family virtues on their own can be too soft and flabby. They can keep people in dependence and immaturity. Father Talbot reminded us that the secret of your liberty is a steely discipline, though there was nothing grim or strained in his authority. All of us need standards and discipline, a readiness to undertake tiresome duties and stick at them, as well as the proper development of talents and gifts.

So from the beginning this has been a teaching Community, and your founding fathers, Gore and Frere, explored an honest catholic faith, which avoided neither the hard sayings of Jesus nor the wrestling that goes with faith in God-given reason, as well as the documents of our tradition. If the Church today is to preserve us from the short cuts and easy slogans which are pressed upon us, and to preserve us from the tide of rhetoric and abuse which threatens to engulf the affairs of men, we must ensure that the renewal of the Church for which we pray, is not mindless renewal but something rooted in doctrine and discipline.

The third ingredient for true community is loyalty. Communities, like individuals, only thrive if they are loved. That's true of a parish church, a school, or a country. When Jesus the Jew wept over Jerusalem he accepted and blessed our local loyalties.

It seems unnecessary to labour this point on a day which is the ecclesiastical equivalent of the Miners' Gala in Durham. But perhaps I can recount a visit I paid to a dreary housing estate on the outskirts of London some years ago. I went on a grey, drizzly day, and my heart sank when I saw the dreadful, dull building which was the modern church; but once inside, the loyalty of the people to that place and that estate lifted my heart, as their singing lifted the roof. There was an adult baptism, and the candidate was so excited that after her baptism she threw her arms around me and knocked off my mitre! The barriers were down, we were members one of another. It was not surprising to find that after the Mass it was their custom to invite anyone who on that estate would otherwise have spent Sunday alone, to their parish dinner. Here, again, was incarnation and resurrection in a very ordinary local community.

But loyalty on its own can be narrow, exclusive, complacent. If so, it should be mocked. And this Community has never lacked a sense of humor. People who lack humor have no judgment, and therefore should not be trusted with anything. So be prepared to laugh at your loyalties, and remember that the fourth ingredient is *vision*. Christians can never be obedient to their Lord if they rest content with things as they are. Without vision a people perishes, and Our Lord was always leading people to look beyond Himself into looking for and working for the Kingdom of God. It is characteristic of so many institutions today, whether secular or religious, that they are defensive, anxious to protect their rights, or obsessed with the necessary management of limited resources. It can mean that narrow planning blocks generous vision.

One of the reasons why unemployment is the greatest scourge of our day is that it has a deadening, depressing effect on people, and they become locked into a kind of fatalism. Great government is greatly human, said Keble Talbot. He loved human society and each individual of it.

It is possible, said Anson in his book on Religious Orders, that the Community of the Resurrection would not have come into being without the influence of Christian Socialism — to claim for the Christian Law the ultimate authority to rule social practice and to present Christ in practical life as the enemy of wrong and selfishness — the power of righteousness and love.

We all have our visions, and many have been disappointed this week that our Church was not prepared to take a new step forward in the Covenant for Christian Unity. We must not lose that vision. But also remember that even Christian Unity is not the ultimate vision of those who seek to follow an incarnate and risen Lord. A united Christian Church, out of touch with the world, would be worse than a number of separate Christian Churches in touch with God's world. So those visions of peace for the world, or of a multi-racial society in this country, or Southern Africa are signs of hope that are never to be lost.

So let me draw together my thoughts on this Community and your communities.

Here is a welcoming place where people feel at home and wanted. May it be so among you. But that on its own could be too soft.

Here is a place of high standards where teaching and discipline are cherished. May it be so among you. But that could be too stiff and impersonal.

Here is a place that nourishes loyalty and affection. May that be true of your local church. But that on its own might be complacent.

Here is a place where they have dreamed dreams and seen visions, whether in work for a new kind of church or a new sort of ministry. But that on its own could be mere talk and hot air.

The world cries out for more kindliness or more discipline — for more loyalty or for more vision — and falls apart. But the faith which we hold is one that brings all these qualities together because they are found in Jesus Christ himself. We see it in His life and we can now see it in our lives, for Jesus Christ, the incarnate Word, is risen from the dead. So shall we in our thanksgivings and in our prayers be renewed this day.

And I pray that our memories of this time together will make us once again and more deeply into Resurrection people.

10 July 1982

"RESURREXIT ALLELUIA"

Community of the Resurrection

T ST. PAUL'S CATHEDRAL FOR A SERVICE OF THANKSGIVING ON THE 60th ANNIVERSARY OF THE BRITISH BROADCASTING COMPANY: Our perceptions have been so transformed under the influence of public broadcasting that it is difficult to imagine the world before its advent. Yet it was only a comparatively short time ago that the transformation occurred with the birth of the BBC in 1922. What is commonplace now was astonishing then. Indeed, when my predecessor Archbishop Randall Davidson, then in the nineteenth of his twenty-five-year Primacy, was invited to listen to the wireless for the first time in the home of the BBC's pioneering founder, Lord Reith, he was "amazed and thunderstruck." Mrs. Davidson asked whether when listening to the radio it was necessary to have the windows open.

Broadcasting was also as controversial at the beginning of its history as it has been ever since. In April, 1923, the Chapter of Westminster Abbey objected to the broadcasting of a royal wedding on the grounds that "the service might even be received by persons in public houses with their hats on."

During the last 60 years, however, by maintaining itself as a free institution, the BBC has come to be one of the most powerful instruments for extending freedom in the world. It has succeeded in remaining independent from excessive commercial pressure on the one hand and the government of the day on the other. It has been necessary to fight for such independence on many occasions. In 1926, for example, the objectivity of the BBC's reporting of the General Strike gave the radio news greater credibility in the eyes of the public at the cost of considerable hostility in some sections of government. The independence of the BBC has become an important constitutional safeguard, and the Corporation deserves our support in its struggle to maintain that independence.

By remaining free the BBC has become more effective in spreading freedom. Its reputation for objectivity has underwritten freedom in Britain, but its significance is perhaps even greater abroad where the External Services, now noting a 50th anniversary, broadcast in 37 languages and are heard by over 150-million listeners in the course of a week. Millions have come to trust the news on the World Service and know that it will be free from distortion and lies that are the instruments of tyranny and totalitarian regimes. Perhaps the greatest tribute ever paid to the BBC External Services, who celebrate their half-century this year, came from Hitler's Germany, where listening to the BBC was made a capital offense.

Broadcasting has also brought us out of our isolation. In our own nation it has been a force for increasing the sense of sharing and belonging to the national family. The presence of Her Majesty the Queen reminds us of the royal broadcasts that passed into folklore and that helped to knit us together as a people in times of the greatest danger. As a participant in international broadcasting, it can bring new people and attitudes into our homes, thus helping us to break out of insularity and offering us material to nourish our sympathies and understanding. We can now rapidly share the sufferings and disasters, as well as the achievements, of peoples in the remotest parts of the earth. Broadcasting continues to have great potential for being a world community builder and for helping us to become world citizens.

Broadcasting, however, not only brings us out of our geographical isolation, but can give new cultural freedom by making accessible to large audiences work of the highest quality that expands the sensibilities. The BBC's role in creating one of the most knowledgeable and discriminating audiences for music in the history of the world has been crucial. The potential of its educational role also can hardly be exaggerated. New horizons have been given to us, and like much of my generation I owe a large part of my own further education to broadcasting. . . . At the same time, for a nation that cherishes its reputation for having a sense of humor and in the main rightly believes that people without such ought not be trusted, the BBC has made a massive contribution to our culture.

It is at this pivot of my address that I wish to put before you a sentence from St. Paul, "You my friends were called to be free, only do not turn your freedom into self-indulgence, but serve one another in love." The BBC for 60 years has demonstrated great power for good. It has remained free and it has brought freedom to others. Like all other institutions with great power, it only thrives if it continues to respect those it serves. . . . The individual, who expresses his freedom in contempt for his fellows and in rejection of the values of his community, is a monster. Institutions can become similarly deformed if freedom and technical brilliance are used in the service of arrogance and cynicism. Freedom is to be used in the affectionate, but not uncritical service of the community and its inherited values. It should not be used to cultivate a detachment about loyalties and values that is the mark of those who are clever, but shallow. In the welter of distractions that abound in the life of any institution, it would be a disaster for us all if the BBC lost its vision of building up in our society "whatsoever things are true, whatsoever things are just, whatsoever things are lovely and whatsoever things are of good report."

Broadcasting has a vocation that is capable of uniting both people of religious convictions and all men and women of good will. I believe that the BBC has been conspicuously loyal to that ideal over the last 60 years, and I pray that in the decades to come it will not allow it to be dimmed by the enemies to freedom both external and internal.

Again, in the words of St. Paul, "You my friends were called to be free, only do not turn your freedom into self-indulgence, but serve one another in love."

12 July 1982

T THE FALKLAND ISLANDS SERVICE OF THANKSGIVING AT ST. PAUL'S: The first theme of this service is thanksgiving. We began with particular thanksgiving for the courage and endurance of those who fought in the South Atlantic, and that is where my sermon starts.

What I have heard about the conduct of the British forces in and around the Falkland Islands has moved and heartened me. I have experienced battle myself and know that it is no mean achievement to preserve the restraint and display the courage shown by so many involved in this conflict. I was particularly impressed by the report of one journalist just returned from the Falklands. He admitted that he had started the campaign with a fairly standard stereotyped view of the forces — effete officers leading unreflective men. He was converted by the Falklands experience and returned with a deep respect for those who had fought bravely, without turning into "automata." He was moved by the mature way in which grief was openly expressed over the loss of comrades, and he admired the lack of rancour shown in attitudes towards the enemy. Another eyewitness described to me the determination shown at every level to achieve objectives with minimum force at the hard-fought battle of Goose Green. The reaction was not the conquerors' triumph, but "thank God it's stopped." It is right to be proud of such men.

There is much to give thanks for in all this now that the attempt to settle the future of the Falkland Islanders by armed invasion has been thwarted. Those who served in the campaign would be the first to say that while we are paying tribute to the armed forces we should not forget the perseverance and courage of those who have been defending the lives and laws of the citizens of this country, in Northern Ireland, over a number of years.

While giving thanks, however, we also mourn for grievous losses. Thank God so many returned, but there are many in this cathedral who mourn the loss of someone they love, and our thoughts go out to them. We will not forget that our prayers and remembrance must not end today.

They remind us that we possess the terrifying power for destruction. War has always been detestable, but since 1945 we have been living with the capacity to destroy the whole of humankind. It is impossible to be a Christian and not to long for peace. "Blessed are the peacemakers, for they shall be called the Sons of God."

Yet war, demonstrably irrational and intolerable, has left a terrible mark on this century; it has claimed tens of millions of victims and even now occupies some of the best talents and resources of the nations. The great nations continue to channel their energies into perfecting weapons of destruction, and very little is done to halt the international trade in arms, which contributes so much to the insecurity of the world.

Our hope as Christians is not fundamentally in humankind's naked goodwill and rationality. We believe that we can overcome the deadly selfishness of class or sect or race by discovering ourselves as children of the universal God of love. When we realize that we are beloved children of the creator of all, then we are ready to see our neighbors in the world as brothers and sisters. That is one reason why those who dare to interpret God's will must never claim God as an asset for one nation or group rather than another. War springs from the love and loyalty that should be offered to God but instead is applied to some God-substitute, one of the most dangerous being nationalism.

Ours is a dangerous world where evil is at work nourishing the mindless brutality that killed and maimed so many in London only last week (near Buckingham Palace and in Regents Park). Sometimes, with the greatest reluctance, force is necessary to hold back the chaos that injustice and the irrational element in man threaten to make of the world. But having said that, all is not lost, and there is hope.

Even in the failure of war there are springs of hope. In Shakespeare's great war play, Henry V says "there is some soul of goodness in things evil, would men observingly distill it out." People are mourning on both sides of the Falklands conflict. In our prayers we shall quite rightly remember those who are bereaved in our own country and the relations of the young Argentinian soldiers who were killed. Common sorrow could do something to reunite those who were engaged in that struggle. A shared anguish can be a bridge of reconciliation. Our neighbors are indeed like us.

I have had an avalanche of letters and advice about this service. Some correspondents have asked "why drag in God" as if the intention was to wheel up God to endorse some particular policy or attitude rather than another. The purpose of prayer and of services like this is very different, and there is hope for the world in the difference. In our prayers we come into the presence of the living God. We come with our very human emotions, pride in achievement and courage, grief at loss and waste. We come as we are, not just mouthing opinions and thanksgiving which the fashion of the moment judges acceptable. As we pour into our prayers, our mourning, our pride, our shame, and our convictions, which will inevitably differ from person to person, if we are really present and really reaching out to God and not just demanding His endorsement, then God is able to work upon us. He is able to deepen and enlarge our compassion and to purify our thanksgiving. The parent who comes mourning the loss of a son may find here consolation, but also a spirit that enlarges our compassion to include all those Argentinian parents who have lost sons.

People without God find it difficult to achieve revolutions inside themselves. But talk of peace and reconciliation is just fanciful and theoretical unless we are prepared to undergo such a revolution. Many of the reports I have heard about the troops engaged in the war refer to moments when soldiers have been brought face to face with what is fundamental in life and have found new sources of strength and compassion even in the midst of conflict. Ironically, it has sometimes been those spectators who remained at home, whether supporters or opponents of the conflict, who continue to be most belligerent in their attitudes and untouched in their deepest selves.

Humankind without God is less than its potential. In meeting God, people are shown their failures and their lack of integrity, but they are also given strength to turn more and more of their lives and actions into love and compassion for other men like himself. It is necessary to the continuance of life on this planet that more and more people make this discovery. We have been given the choice. We possess the power to obliterate ourselves, sacrificing the whole race on the altar of some God-substitute. Or we can choose life in partnership with God the Father of all. I believe that there is evidence that more and more people are waking up to the realization that this crucial decision peers us in the face here and now.

Cathedrals and churches are always places into which we bring human experiences—birth, marriage, death, our flickering communion with God, our fragile relationships with each other, so that they may be deepened and directed by the spirit of Christ.

So today we bring our mixture of thanksgiving, sorrows, and aspirations for a better ordering of this world.

Pray God that He may purify, enlarge, and redirect these in the ways of His kingdom of love and peace. Amen.

26 July 1982

HAT THE THRONE OF JESUS IS; SERMON FOR ENTHRONEMENT OF THE RIGHT REVEREND MOSES TAY LANG KONG IN ST. ANDREW'S CATHEDRAL, SINGAPORE: The prophet Isaiah sees a vision of glory in the Temple — "The Lord sitting upon a throne high and lifted up," surrounded by the Seraphim. Stately services like this one at St. Andrew's Cathedral can help us to catch a glimpse of the breath-taking and humbling majesty of God, but the throne which Isaiah sees is God's alone. We must beware of putting ourselves or the leaders of the Church, especially bishops, on the throne which belongs only to God.

Bishops have their deepest authority from walking in the way of Jesus Christ who, seeing the crowds, "went up on the mountain and when He sat down His disciples came to Him and He opened His mouth and talked." This is a homely throne on a hillside and no guards surround Him as He talks to His friends and followers.

I know from experience that when you are a focus of loyalty and affection for Christ's Church, as a bishop is, you can easily come to accept the attention and respect of believers as your right and due. A bishop must always remember that to become more and more like Christ he must sit on a throne as simple as His and speak as He did. Jesus Christ would not recognize the imperial style of some of those who presume to speak in His name. He warns us that "they which are accounted to rule over the gentiles, exercise Lordship over them. . . . But so shall it not be among you, but whosoever will be great among you shall be your minister and whosoever of you will be the chiefest shall be the servant of all."

I am happy to be here as a fellow worker with a small share in the Christian life of this great city. I saw something of your new Bishop when he was in England. I formed a deep affection and respect for him then, and now, after these days in Singapore, I am delighted to know him as a fellow Bishop and as a friend. . . .

I am convinced from what I have seen that you have indeed

heard Christ speaking in Singapore. There is a vitality and a boldness about those who have felt the breath of the Spirit on their faces which is refreshing and for which I give thanks. One of the signs of this is that the Church has been nerved for more energetic work in the community which it seeks to serve. To be turned inwards and to be full of feelings of spiritual achievement and possession, to say with the Pharisee, "I thank God that I am not as other men are" is to reveal an un-Christlike exclusivity. All the beatitudes that Christ commends in the gospel are dispositions which make us vulnerable to the world around us and put us in touch with God and with our fellows. Christians must embrace God's world, not exclude it. . . .

This is a service that revolves around a personal dedication, the dedication of your new Bishop, Moses Tay. We are here to surround him with our prayers and affection and to support him in the best way possible, to commit ourselves as he is doing to the way of Jesus Christ.

31 October 1982

UST AND UNJUST WARS; AN ADDRESS AT CHATHAM HOUSE, THE ROYAL INSTI-TUTE OF INTERNATIONAL AFFAIRS: When I was invited to give this talk well over a year ago, I warned Chatham House that they could not expect an Archbishop to show the wily sophistication of a Foreign Office official or the technical expertise of a defense strategist. My business is trying to relate the moral teaching of the Church to present circumstances in a creative way. In my own defense, however, I ought to say that I come to this subject of just and unjust wars having experienced war at first hand and then more happily in 1945 having learned something about a successful East/West negotiation when I was part of the team that settled the question of the Italo/Yugoslav border.

"War as a method of settling international disputes is incompatible with the teaching and example of our Lord," says a resolution passed in 1930 when Anglican bishops from all over the world gathered in London for the Lambeth Conference. In subsequent decades, the Lambeth bishops have reiterated that judgment and that is where I wish to begin. War is always a failure. It would be a mistake to understand my title in a complacent sense. The just war tradition does not legitimize war as such. It rather seeks to prevent wars and has a built-in reluctance to resort to the use of force.

It is an essential precondition to thought about war in a Christian context to appreciate the biblical insistence that we live in a world in rebellion against its own best interests — a world which has rejected the order given to it by its creator. War is a vivid sign of this rebellion. Our world is marked by a yearning for unity and harmony but it is also disfigured by endemic conflict in which one man or group seeks to dominate others.

Christian thought has not lacked realism about the intransigence of conflict. Christians have usually argued that in what they regard as an interim world, force may be necessary to restrain the violent and protect the weak from injustice. There is in our faith a hope for the future but no naivety about the present. Men of principle, men who have known what is best for their neighbors have wrought havoc in our world. But the alternative of mere pragmatism is not enough. The ethics of the Kingdom are a judgment on the inescapable limitations both of ideology and pragmatism. The Pope said, "War should belong to the tragic past, to history," but we have to deal with the fact that it is manifestly a part of the tragic present as well. In that present of ours two symbols of hope and fear have been burned into the consciousness of our contemporaries — the planet and the cloud.

By "the planet" I mean the earth, sapphire blue and beautiful, photographed and seen whole for the first time from the moon. By "the cloud" I mean, of course, the mushroom cloud over Hiroshima.

The vision of the earth as a whole is a symbol of the essential unity of our planet. It has already helped to heighten our perception of a world made one by the interdependence of its economy, the new possibilities of global communication and the problems of pollution and energy which cannot be solved by individual states and which demand a common response. At no time in history has it seemed more realistic — and necessary — to regard the world as a unity.

The cloud, however, is a reminder not only of the intransigence of conflict but also of the volcanic forces which threaten to tear the world apart. We now have the power to destroy civilizations which have been painfully constructed over thousands of years. This terrible power has to be managed. It cannot be disinvented.

The biblical tradition puts a heavy emphasis on the management of power. God is seen at work, bringing order to the elements of creation: "He gave to the sea his decree that the waters should not pass his commandment: . . . he appointed the foundations of the earth" (Proverbs 8:29). Some Christian treatments of conflict neglect this inheritance and see power as primarily something to be renounced. This is a dangerous oversimplification, which often arises from a refusal to distinguish between the ethics appropriate to a private individual within society and those applying to competent authorities — in our case mainly sovereign states.

The Old Testament is insistent that we have a responsibility for seeking justice and the well-being of creatures in the world as it exists. There is no doubt that force may be used to ensure the preservation of these ends. While the New Testament is not primarily concerned about the right use of power, even in the Sermon on the Mount, Matthew takes care to set the whole discourse in the context of the Old Testament Law. He does this in words he attributes directly to Jesus: "Think not that I am come to destroy the Law. . . . whosoever therefore shall break one of these least commandments and shall teach men so, he shall be called the least in the Kingdom of Heaven" (Matthew 5:17 – 19). Even though he was speaking to Jewish people before the inauguration of the Church, it is clear that Jesus accepted the Law as God-given. What Our Lord goes on to say cannot be taken in any way to undermine the Law's concern for the responsible use of power to preserve justice and freedom.

I underline this point because some Christians would deny that there was any possibility of "just" war and would claim that Christianity was not compatible with any support for the use of force and was essentially pacifist. Bonhoeffer, the German martyr to Hitler's tyranny who wrote a book, *The Cost of Discipleship*, advocating total renunciation of personal rights because of the Sermon on the Mount, had to struggle with this problem. Finally he came to accept that evil must be combated. One may renounce one's own rights. One cannot renounce one's responsibility for preserving the rights of others.

The Christian must respect the world of law and limit. In our contemporary world, he must be concerned with sovereign states and how they use their power, but in certain respects, as we shall see later, a Christian can never rest content with the provisional kind of peace which can be guaranteed by states. The way indicated by Our Lord transcends the world of law and limit, but recognizes it as a condition of the discovery of a richer kind of God-given peace. . . .

Christian thinkers, notably St. Augustine and St. Thomas Aquinas, borrowed, largely from Stoic sources, a language with which to analyze the question of justice and war, and over the past 1,000 years a so-called "just war" theory has been elaborated. . . . The theory falls into two parts, the *Jus Ad Bellum* and the *Jus In Bello*. It has to be established that there is justice in the resort to force, sufficient to override a brutally realistic view of the moral ugliness of war. Those who go to war must also not only have a reasonable hope of success, but they should also believe that the damage to be inflicted and the cost in lives lost and wasted resources will be proportionate to the good to be gained by taking up arms. When the war actually begins, this principle of proportionality should continually be applied along with the principle of discrimination, which prohibits all actions directly aimed at killing noncombatants.

By these criteria, very few wars are 95 percent just on one side and in the same degree unjust on the other. In my judgment, the Second World War approximates, as near as may be, to a just war. The Germans claimed that theirs was a just cause, basing their case on the injustices of the Versailles settlement. This was a pretense, however, and not supported by another principle in *Jus Ad Bellum* — right intention. In Hitler's mouth, these claims were a cloak for war aims totally unjust and inhuman. Even so, the justice of the Allied Cause contained some ambiguous elements. If the war was so right in 1939, why was it not undertaken sooner, in 1936 for example, when more resolute action might even have stopped Hitler in his tracks and avoided the pain of Czechoslovakia being sacrificed? More awkward by far, there is a question which presses upon all of us who were taught during the war and in the years after to regard Hitler's tyranny as by any standards worse than Stalin's. How has it been "better for humanity" that Hitler's demonic regime was eliminated at the cost of reinforcing and extending Stalin's?

Nevertheless, I am convinced that World War II comes as close as anything to a just cause, although there were some events within it which are difficult to justify on *Jus In Bello* criteria. It is always important to recognize that war is inevitably a mixture of accident, personalities, moral coarseness, and pure tragedy and that just war contains these elements as well. Despite these ambiguities, the categories and principles of the just war tradition do help us in the necessary business of educating the Christian conscience in making moral judgments about the right use of force.

It is too soon to extract all the lessons from the Falklands conflict, but in the light of the just war tradition I still think that it was right to send a task force after the Argentinian invasion because it was necessary that aggression should not be permitted to short-circuit the processes of negotiation. I also believe that there was justice in the conduct of the war and general respect for the principles of discrimination and minimum force. But, as I said at the time, it was — and is — important to count the cost at every stage. The principle of proportionality demands that we measure the immediate damage inflicted and the cost incurred against the good intended by taking up arms, but today we must also, in an interdependent world, reflect on the wider consequences for the international community.

Although this way of thinking may be a useful tool for helping us to form moral judgments about the so-called "conventional" wars which continue to distract the world — wars like that between Iran and Iraq and the Soviet operations in Afghanistan as well as the revolutionary struggles in Southern Africa and Central America — I am convinced that full-scale nuclear war cannot possibly qualify as a just war. Here we come to a real difficulty of maintaining the distinction in my title in a nuclear age. There could not be any *Jus In Bello* in either full-scale nuclear or biological war, because it would be impossible to discriminate between combatants and noncombatants. I have children and the elderly particularly in mind. Also the scale of the destruction inflicted on both sides would inevitably nullify any good intended by entering the war. There is no such thing as just mutual obliteration.

Human history has been full of just and unjust wars, but since 1945 we have been confronted with the possibility of a kind of warfare which is, soberly speaking, madness. What are we to do? We are faced at present with the problem of how to get from where we all know we are, in a world capable of destroying itself, to where we all want to be, in a world where conflict is channelled into creative directions and where potentially lethal power is used to improve the life of mankind. . . .

We ought not to be complacent about such a situation. If retention of nuclear weapons can be justified at all, then more urgency has to be shown in stabilizing the situation. We are faced with the twin dangers of vertical proliferation as the overkill capacity of the existing nuclear arsenals are developed and the horizontal proliferation represented by the increase in the number of states capable of initiating nuclear war.

One of the most horrifying aspects of the present situation is the apparent placid acceptance of the dangerous status quo. When disarmament initiatives are produced by whatever government, it is frightening to hear the immediate dismissive responses. It is becoming incredible to write off every Soviet suggestion as a propaganda ploy. To do so underestimates the extent to which everyone has an interest in seeing the present tensions relaxed.

As Pope John Paul II has said in his message to the United Nations' Special Session on Disarmament, there must be "an immediate and urgent struggle by governments to reduce progressively and equally their armaments." The Pope properly includes so-called conventional armaments as well. I am particularly concerned about the effects of the international arms trade, but a first priority must be the reduction of the dependence on nuclear weapons to a minimum level compatible with national security. There must be progress to a mutual, verifiable nuclear disarmament between world powers.

I do not despair of negotiations in the present climate. Responsible public pressure is denting unpardonable complacency about this issue in the countries where public opinion is free to express itself. This is not, alas, happening to the same extent in the Soviet Union. But, even there, a perception of the danger from the cloud which faces us all is reinforced by the economic difficulties and the competition for limited resources.

A measure of disarmament is, however, only one side of the picture. The cloud represents the outcome of man's attempt over hundreds of years to manage and dominate his environment and to impose himself upon nature and his fellows. Ironically, the effort to achieve mastery has brought us to a point where we have unbounded unmanageable forces. We do not know for certain (with only the experience of Hiroshima and Nagasaki to go by) how far-reaching the effect of a nuclear war would be on the genetic future of mankind, or how irreversible the damage to our planet. The cloud is a judgment on centuries of aggressive intention. But perhaps, if the significance of the cloud is properly understood and accepted, there is hope here as well as fear. Curiously, in the Bible, the cloud is a sign of God's presence. Psalm 99: "He spake unto them out of the cloudy pillar."

This is a moment to seek not only to stabilize as far as possible the balance of terror, but to gain fresh determination to build more effective international institutions to reflect our perception of one world as seen in the photograph of the sapphire planet. World government may not be as utopian for those born after 1945 as it seems to be for those of us who were born before, but for the moment I am not thinking so much of world government as of a new world order. I believe we should be paying more attention to the plea contained in the first report, issued last September, of the new Secretary-General of the United Nations, Senor Perez de Cuellar. He described what he called "the new international anarchy" and listed some steps which governments ought urgently to consider: greater use of the United Nations mediation facilities, more immediate resort to the Security Council, and the building up of the United Nations' policing capability. . . .

A new world order is not, of course, only a matter of a more efficient police force. We should not forget the contention of the Brandt Commission that the denial of justice to the hungry and poor in the world will have more and more explosive consequences from which none of us will be entirely insulated. This is another way in which we should seek to develop the capacity to feel and act as world citizens. It is not that we have to abandon a patriotic love for our own homeland, but we should try to transcend national self-interest as the determinant of policy.

There are, however, so many barriers to our sympathy and compassion; so many stereotypes of one another that make talk of brotherhood merely theoretical. . . . I have had some experience of theological conversations with Russian churchmen and as a consequence I have come to glimpse the differences between our mental furniture and basic categories of thought. It seems worse than ironic that we are running down Russian studies in our schools and universities just at a time when we are increasing our defense spending.

But peace is not just something for high-powered dialogue or international commissions. We have to acknowledge that the springs of violence and war are in everybody. This is implied in the UNESCO constitution which states that "since wars begin in the minds of men, it is in the minds of men that the defenses of peace must be constructed." . . .

To do anything about the violence in each one of us is to go beyond the world of law and limits represented in the time of Christ by the government of the Roman Empire. Wars and conflicts arise in a world which yearns in its smallest particles for union and relationship, because that principle is confronted by another in which the individual parts of the world strive for mastery over one another when they should be looking for marriage. The way of renouncing power and the lust for mastery is one that is being followed even now by many people in the Christian world. But this way demands a profound and costly personal repentance and sometimes even peace groups can manifest the kind of unrepentant and unreflective aggression they so readily ascribe to others. Few have the wisdom of Gandhi, who, when he was discussing with the British Government in India the use of violence by the Government against the Indians, stressed that the violence in the heart of the Indian people, and of himself, contributed to the overall violence of the conflict. But the way of renouncing power and subjecting self interest to the interest of others must be pursued if the peace intended by God is to be established. This path, however, can only be trodden in the context of and perhaps partly in reaction to a world which has first been restrained and ordered by law and limits.

I believe myself to be a preacher of the Kingdom of God to which Our Lord pointed supremely when he said "My Kingdom is not of this world," and also I pray those mysterious words "Thy Kingdom come on Earth as it is in Heaven." The road to the realization of this Kingdom is heavily mined, and we have to tread carefully, defusing the mines one by one.

10 February 1983

AT OXFORD UNIVERSITY MISSION 1983:

I

CARDINAL Hume and I have been invited to lead a Mission and I am here to ring up the curtain. We were both educated here but we have agreed not to spend our time wallowing in anecdotes. I was, however, myself, deeply influenced by the postwar Oxford Mission conducted by a Bishop who still lives in this city, and it is rather awe inspiring to find myself now in this place.

While I was reading the autobiography of an Anglican monk, Fr. Harry Williams, I came across another reference to the effect these Missions have had throughout the years. He recalls a sermon preached during the course of the Mission one Sunday evening by William Temple, then Archbishop of York. "I couldn't understand a word," Williams said, "but the sight of an Archbishop in Convocation robes, uttering a ceaseless stream of words in a rotund style and fruity voice, absolutely mesmerised me. From that moment I knew I wanted to be a clergyman." I would not say that that was the kind of conversion experience that either Cardinal Hume or myself are aiming to induce!

These addresses here in the Sheldonian will not be lectures nor will they be sermons. We seek, together with the team who follow, to provide a presentation of the Christian faith from several angles in the hope that this may be a week in which many of you may seriously consider its claims. . . .

I am not so confident or perhaps conceited as to suppose that my contribution will produce instant conversions all over the Sheldonian but, like Cardinal Hume, we are concerned that this might be a week where those questions about fundamental attitudes to life and, above all, to truth may be reflected upon, discussed, and some decisions made. This central place will, I hope, fertilize that sort of reflection and discussion.

One of the reasons why I could not turn down the invitation to come is that I myself owe something to this sort of experience. I promised no anecdotage, but perhaps I can call it a brief biography. I did not have the advantage or disadvantage of being brought up in any sort of churchy atmosphere, but I did in my teens acquire a rather fragile Christian faith and a modest loyalty which sprang from my confirmation. . . . As for the excitements of Oxford, when I gave my time to work, most of my ideas were exposed to the ruthless questioning of logical positivism which was in high fashion in immediately postwar Oxford. I would certainly testify to its lasting impression on me. You will at least know of some of its texts and perhaps that of Wittgenstein above all. "Of that about which you cannot be certain, it is better to keep silent."

I owe much to the teachers of those days for such disciplines as I have acquired in mental agility. I remember Isaiah Berlin exhorting us that we should not spend our lives lying on a bed of unexamined assumptions. I recall how we were taught the principles of empirical verification: In those days a language which professed to treat of truths or realities which are not susceptible of such verification was deeply suspect. It was a reaction to a period when the fluent Idealists, or many of them, managed to dovetail their philosophical way of looking at things into their Christian assertions. The new school of philosophy challenged that sort of dovetailing. Thus they would say that Christian assertions are not so much untrue as meaningless. "OK," said one of my tutors, "you can be interested in religion and I can be interested in billiards but, as a matter of fact, I am not interested in either." It tended to make religion a matter of taste rather than truth.

Unfortunately, English churches have sometimes, by their blandness, connived at this notion that religion is an interest or a hobby for those whose tastes lead them in that direction. Graham Greene in *A Burnt Out Case* gives us a picture of those whose faith has been honed to a terrible smoothness: "Those who marry God, he thought, can become domesticated, too — it's just as humdrum a marriage as all the others. This marriage, like the world's marriages, was held together by habits and tastes shared in common between

God and themselves — it was God's taste to be worshipped and their taste to worship, but only at stated hours like a suburban embrace on a Saturday night."

In this, of course, the Church mirrors the spiritual stagnation of large parts of our society. As I go about my work, even when I am straying up and down the corridors of power, I very rarely meet any wicked people. You may think that such would encourage me, but it doesn't. Goodness is closely related to the capacity to perceive the opposite and both are dependent upon considerable spiritual vitality. Both sanctity and wickedness seem in short supply in high places, but everywhere a great deal of the blurred, ill-defined, and invertebrate, a longing for rest and tranquility on easy terms.

In some ways, this is less promising soil than the ground prepared by the audible clash of principles or the oppressions of tyranny. Bishop Tutu once said to me, "I would find it very hard to be a Christian in England. In South Africa, everything is so clear cut." From tedium and boredom it is very hard to emerge. From the horror of the camps and the gulag, sometimes the most extraordinary spiritual beauty can arise.

This is the irony, that what is equated with billiards in Oxford is worth dying for in the gulag. I remember when I was at Cuddesdon a Rumanian priest saying to me, "You treat one another very nicely, but I wonder if anyone would be pepared to die for the sake of the Holy Trinity."

But all is not lost. Although there is a very great deal to fill our lives — distractions and entertainment and amusement and, until recently, a career structure to be a substitute for any other kind of structure — I still meet people who are dissatisfied, particularly in universities. Thank God for that, because, as I have said, the living quickness of dissatisfaction should be experienced here above all other places. I meet many people who are conscious that, although there is much to live with, there seems often little to live for.

I believe that you are being offered an opportunity in this week of making a more conscious decision about something which is of fundamental significance in every life. It is my conviction that everybody necessarily lives by faith, only some have articulated and explored their decision more thoroughly than others.

By saying that everybody necessarily lives by faith, I do not mean anything as trite as to suggest that even hardened atheists will say a prayer when facing death or great danger. I have too much respect for atheists and do not believe this proposition to be true. Faith can be of a negative or of a positive kind but it is the only form of response appropriate to a certain range of questions about life which, although they have often been declared to be meaningless, continue to be obstinately asked.

When you asked questions like: "Why life?" "Is life intelligible?" you are asking about something which is innaccessible to the usual range of empirical tests and the process of reasoning which we habitually use to answer other kinds of questions. If you ask: "How did our present form of life develop?," then you would want to talk to a biologist, a historian, and many others. When, however, you ask about the intelligibility of life, why this whole process in which we are involved, then, because of the impossibility of observing the whole process of which we are a part or conducting experiments on something which comprehends both experiment and experimental, then a decision of faith is the only possible response. Faith is not some irrational reaction which is displayed by the immature when confronted with difficult or complex circumstances, it is the only kind of answer we have to some fundamental questions about ultimate meaning.

Some people implicitly or explicitly answer by saying there is no purpose, that the world is not intelligible and possesses no order, no direction and no meaning. A random collision of molecules in the cosmic soup stands at the head of a process of life in which we are alone and have to make the best of it. When the word "no" is the answer to the question "Is there intelligibility, order and purpose in the universe?" then, quite often, the result in human terms is heroic. It takes a very great deal of faith to be an atheist and some of the atheists I have known who have taken their decision seriously and have pursued its implications to their logical end have been among some of the most admirable human beings I have ever met.

If the answer is "yes," however, then again all kinds of consequences flow. One of our contemporary social and spiritual problems is that the response of most people to the question I have posed is still "yes" but only a muted and frivolous "yes." It is a "yes" which has not been fully articulated and which does not exercise a vital influence on life. It does not bring to life the sap and the vigor and the dynamism which are seen in the lives of the greatest saints who have followed their "yes" through to the end.

So in this week I hope you will be given the material from which to review the decision you have already made, the decision of faith to say "yes" or "no" to the question of the intelligibility of the universe which is so intimately bound up with the question of whether the universe has an author and creator and order and purpose. Religious people would say that you were saying "yes" or "no" to God. I hope also that you will be given the encouragement to follow your answer through to the end, whatever it is, because rejecting a position held by people you respect can also often be a way of growth. But, naturally, I hope that you will be able to say "yes" and to see more clearly the consequences of this decision for your own way of living. . . .

I am an Archbishop. It is no secret that I have given the answer "yes" and I believe that this answer is not only true but has positive gains for the life of individuals and societies. One of the greatest gifts, I believe, is that of coherence. For me, Christianity makes sense of more things about my own personality and about the world in which I live and about my society than any other faith or ideology which I have had the chance of studying. But I think also that one of the greatest strengths of the Christian faith is that it does not attempt to explain everything. Christianity has as its core a heart of mystery. That heart of mystery is not over there on the horizon where the big brains will sooner or later see through it but there is a heart of mystery in the most elementary and the most common experiences which we all go through.

I believe that this is most commonly perceived in our relationships with one another. Is it not true that however well you know another person, however intimately, and however long, there are always depths of the personality undisclosed? So, in the happiest of marriages, life always has marvellous surprises. No one knows the heart of anyone except that person himself or herself. And if we talk at all of knowing another person, it is only because that person gives himself away. There has to be revelation.

That brings us right to the point of believing and Christian believing. Enter my second text of the week: "Things beyond our seeing, things beyond our hearing, things beyond our imagining, all prepared by God for those who love Him." That is St. Paul again and it brings us right to the subject of tonight.

God is a God of ultimate mystery but Christians believe He is also the God who gives Himself away and who enters into personal relations with men and women so that, without ever exhausting the mystery of His being, nevertheless they can have the conviction that in this or that experience of life, they have met the God who has given Himself to the world. It is because I come to faith in this way that I emphasize it as a gift which is received rather than something which is confected or established by logical deduction.

You will recognize that I am only here to raise the curtain tonight and to make a beginning. I hope that you may consider that the gifts of Christian believing may offer more coherence for human experience. I hope that you may believe it to be reasonable and that you may be prepared to consider some of the next stages in the argument. For all those experiences of a God who gives Himself away and is prepared to enter into relationships with men and women have their center for a Christian in the person of Jesus Christ.

The Gospels tell us of one who made such a profound impression on his contemporaries that, when they were in his presence, they felt themselves to be in the presence of God. So out of this story we come to a conviction that all our aspirations towards the infinite and the transcendent and the eternal are justified and grounded in the point where God comes to meet us in the person of Jesus Christ. That is a trailer for my next talk tomorrow night. . . .

May I remind you of my two modest biblical texts for tonight. "You my friends were called to freedom. Only use not your freedom to indulge yourselves, but through love be servants one of another." And the second, "Things beyond our seeing, things beyond our hearing, things beyond our imagining, all prepared by God for those who love him." And, finally, a third one which will prepare us for tomorrow, this time from St. Peter: "Sanctify the Lord God in your hearts and be ready always to give an answer to every man that asks of you a reason of the hope that is in you with meekness and fear."

OXFORD MISSION
II

I am here this week to join with others and speak about a faith I think is true, a faith to guide you through the real world. I was claiming last night that it is ultimately no bad thing that you and I if we are to believe in God deeply, have to face difficulties.

Those who have wrestled with these mysteries in the Christian tradition have often found in the end a faith deeper than would have been possible had they remained superficial and conventional. This was so even in the so-called "ages of faith" when it was conventional to say that you were a Christian and believed in Jesus Christ. Some of the medieval people who were most truly Christian have left records of great agonies of heart and mind as their thinking about God was purified in prayer and tested in suffering. St. John of the Cross claimed that everyone who really thirsts for the living God must experience a "dark night of the soul" when images of God seem utterly unsatisfactory. There is a strong streak of that kind of agnosticism in the mystical traditions of the ancient Eastern churches. So I beg you to remember that if you find the going hard as you seek God genuinely in Oxford towards the end of the twentieth century, you are surrounded by many, many believers who also found faith hard — not dull or joyless, or something only for intellectuals, but somehow sharing in the pain which seems to go along with all creativity. It is creativity and human enterprise with which I want to start tonight.

I have spent time in the last twenty years in countries which have attempted to banish God and live by Swinburne's line "this thing is God, to be man with all thy might." I also know from many of my contemporaries that the modern sense of technical mastery and economic progress can result in a new pride in being human. We can do so many more things than our fathers could. We have so many more opportunities opening out before us. There is a thrill of being alive. "Glory to man in the highest and on the earth prosperity." Well perhaps that has been rather dented recently, but it is certainly the faith that was flourishing when I was an undergraduate. It seemed that religion was the enemy. Enter progress, exit God. So since those days, it has been possible to look around the world and find substitutes for old religious traditions. I see communism, which is a kind of religion with Marx or Lenin or Stalin or Mao or the Party in place of a God, with the dream of a perfect society in place of heaven. I see nationalism which has often called for a religious self-sacrifice, human sacrifice to the god of patriotism. I see a generation growing up which is putting religious energy into protest against the wars and injustice and material and spiritual poverty in our world. I go in and out of universities and find most students would run a mile from the thought of the organized church or the official looking parson but I observe that many of them are rejecting the materialism which religious believers also reject.

Is not there something valid in this contempt among intelligent young people for the exploitation of sex in commercial advertising or for the rat race of commercial life? Isn't sex or money often worshipped in adult society as a substitute for God? Would you say that in this country that we have largely escaped from the illusions of communism or nationalism or student protest or obsessive sex or money making? Perhaps so; but would you go on to say that we have no need to be worried about the condition of our society? Aren't there many signs both of a basic cynicism and of a search for something which we could feel deeply in our emotions and serve in our lives? Historians among you will know that religion has been at the heart of the story of mankind, until the end of the seventeenth century at least. Men and women have united their societies around a religious vision of life and as individuals they have been most creative and most noble when they have thought that they were being obedient to the religous vision. It just is not fair to emphasize only the cruelty which has gone on in the name of religion or only the superstition, without admitting the massive fact of religion's enrichment of human life. The question is whether religion is redundant. Has human nature become utterly different since the modern scientific and industrial movement began about 200 years ago? I don't think so and let one example stand for many in my experience.

Recently, I was sharing a discussion with doctors and lawyers and philosophers on the subject of transplant surgery. One of their number was a surgeon who had just joined us from his hospital in Hammersmith. That morning a kidney had been taken from a child after a road accident in Vienna, frozen, put on a plane and brought to London, where this surgeon had put it into a young Englishman. It all seemed technically superb, but as he described it he said, "I couldn't do this work if I thought I was simply dealing with a bundle of parts. I am not very 'religious' " — people often say that in my presence — "nor do I know how to define life, but what I have of faith teaches me that I must respect, know, reverence every person with whom I have to do." One is reminded of how John Stuart Mill in his early days said "I would like to write a book which will make the human person as clear as the road from Charing Cross to St. Paul's." (In those days it was very clear!) Later in life he had to confess — his enterprise unachieved — "it is better to be Socrates dissatisfied than a pig satisfied." He had come to understand that in the curious questing, mysterious human person there lay more than a mechanism or a mixture of chemicals.

The history of our own time is stuffed full of the disasters which follow from eliminating the religious dimension from faith in man. Those modern substitutes for religion, which I have mentioned, have this in common, that they all dehumanise man. Communism crushes the freedom of man for the sake of a political slogan. Nationalism cuts man down into being a mere citizen or a mere soldier. Youthful idealism, shouting for a revolution, forgets that no revolution in history fails to persecute because no revolution is patient with the awkward individual. The worship of sex turns every woman into just a body as the worship of money turns every home into just a collection of furniture.

Many scientists are, I find, extremely worried about what may happen unless the advance of our knowledge and technical skills is stripped of any careless arrogance. For they know that it will take more than their ability to stop the destruction of the city by selfishness in transport and housing and living, to stop the division of the world into affluent and hungry, to stop the exhaustion of the earth's natural resources, and to stop the use of nuclear, biological and chemical weapons. Will the solution of these problems, so sickeningly familiar to us, be found in the development of a truly significant understanding of man and society? Many in the days since I was a student here are turning from natural science to social science in the hope that these problems, which concern them deeply, can be answered by a growth of knowledge; and of course, I too agree that psychologists and sociologists and other experts can help very greatly to cure us of our follies. But I note that little of the wisdom which we need has yet been produced by these experts; and I note also that usually in history when they hesitated to think of other human beings as mere producers or consumers or as mere members of a class or a nation or as mere bodies or brains, it has been because of a belief in man with a religious dimension. It is possible that science may save us; but if the sense of religious mystery no longer surrounds humanism, if the sense of religious obligation no longer disciplines our selfishness, I for one believe that the suicide of civilization is probable. And now as a Christian I believe that man has been regarded as sacred when he has been regarded as a Son of God. Karl Barth the Swiss theologian used a very daring phrase, "the humanity of God." By that he meant that there is a real kinship between God and man and that this family likeness was revealed to us when God used the human nature of Jesus Christ as he did.

That is why we must look seriously tonight at the marriage between the religious spirit and the highest humanism. We must look at the person of Jesus Christ. I am sure that Christianity — the whole colossal organization, all the art, architecture, music, and literature, the whole emotional fact that covers the prayers and lives of thousands of millions of human beings, including many of the best who have ever prayed and lived — all this Christianity depends on the figure of one who lived as a Jew for just over 30 years, just over 1900 years ago; who died and is said to be alive in some sense now. Christianity is about Him and were He to be pushed out of His dominant position, we would need a new religion. . . .

We each of us make Christ in our own image. Can we get at a

controlling truth? I believe that we can and it is crucial. But we must not dodge the problem or deny that we can no longer accept some kind of vacuum-packed miracle from Palestine with words of Jesus literally dictated to Gospel writers. Paradoxically, I believe that it is at once both simpler and more sophisticated.

The Gospel writers were composing their Gospels thirty or forty years after the crucifixion and were presenting a picture of Jesus which would be appropriate for the particular people for whom they were writing. Each was selecting and interpreting and using material which they had to hand — sayings, stories which had been used at their gatherings — which material may well have been substantially altered in the process of transmission. However, what they were doing was (a) to point their readers back to one who undoubtedly lived and acted and spoke in the past, who, when He was alive in the flesh, sought to evoke a response from those who encountered Him; (b) to mediate the demand and promise and appeal of Jesus to the people for whom they were writing; and (c) to elicit from them the same response to the living Lord as He had sought to elicit when He was alive in the flesh. . . .

We can move from ancient accounts of a first-century man in an alien culture with remote economic and social conditions to finding the key to humanity in Him now. First, human motives and emotions and the nature of personal relations is broadly constant, and what Jesus showed and practised of relations between man and God and man and man, still applies to us. Whatever the differences, the character of personal relations remains virtually unchanged. Secondly, in any case *this* man is not merely a figure of remote antiquity: because of the resurrection, Christians have known him as their contemporary, continuously, since the beginning. It is not that successive generations have preserved His memory, or perhaps created each its own Christ in his subjective imagination. Jesus transcends time in such a way actually to go along with time. It *is* the same yesterday, today and always — and to be shown the man of Nazareth in His ancient environment is to begin to find the very same person who is with us paradoxically as we read about it. As a famous theologian has said, "Jesus is in a sense His own tradition." It is not memories about Him or fantasies about Him, it is Himself: "Lo I am with you even to the end of time" or "where two or three are gathered in my name, there am I in the midst of you."

Certainly there is mystery here, and I said last night that we cannot expect to eliminate that; but there is also something which intelligent and sensitive people should be ready to explore seriously and to test in their own lives if they are to discover the possibilities for a human being and the objects of the human enterprise.

But what of Jesus Christ the disclosure of God? All I can do in this final half of my address this evening is to share with you the ways in which I have come to terms with what has been and still is hotly debated from all sides, enshrined in the formulas of many different philosophies, and made the subject of every sort of emotional appeal, i.e., the divinity of Christ.

First, this Jesus in whose life the Christian finds such significance, did live and did die and this is one thing which I cannot deny. If I start from there, I find that however radically critical my approach to the Gospel tradition may be, one of the things which we cannot eliminate is that Jesus believed in another whom He called father. He saw Himself as the expression of the Father. Thus one comes to a belief in this invisible other who is shown to us as far as He can be shown to us in the life and death and resurrection in the person of Jesus of Nazareth. I would still not want to eliminate altogether the effect of that argument which says either He was God or He was a deluded madman. The evidence of the New Testament is varied in character. It includes the attribution to Jesus of divine functions and attributes, the use of titles with divine implications, the use of Old Testament texts about God as if they applied to Jesus, the coupling of Jesus and the Father in a way which apparently makes their names interchangeable, prayer to Jesus, and ultimately formal worship. These and other traits occur in the New Testament in an untidy profusion which makes systematic presentation difficult and gives the New Testament theologians their living. Seriously, they testify, not to a carefully formulated doctrine, logically applied to life and worship, but to the gradual consciousness of the more than human significance of Jesus; a consciousness born more of spiritual experience than of logical deduction, but one which from the time when Jesus was visibly present among His disciples would never be denied and grew inexorably until John could proclaim clearly "the Word was God."

Second, in addition to this sort of evidence from the Bible, I find that the real Jesus, while making great claims for Himself, always leads people beyond Himself into the mystery of God. There are qualities of wonder, mystery, and humility which are occasionally lacking in some expressions of Christianity which treat Him either as a moral example or as an emotional experience. This means that in the great art and music and sacramental worship that goes on in His name — perhaps rather formally in a Cathedral — there is a sense in which the figure of Jesus both fits and has to keep all such elaborations true to the Gospel if it is to have its validity. I often recall my rather pious Scottish grandfather, who when he saw Christian activities which he felt were questionable — I regret to say that often meant Bishops capering around in copes with incense and candles — would say, "What has this to do with Jesus of Nazareth?" It was a simple expression of someone who recognized that any worship of God had to fit the picture which we are given through our impression of Jesus Christ as Lord.

Third, my way to the disclosure of God has come through my greater awareness of other religions. I cannot understand those who think that you need first to dismiss all other religions as totally false, create a vacuum and then in your preaching insert Jesus Christ. I do not believe with the old-fashioned preacher that there is only darkness in other faiths. I have found that there is much light, and the light that comes to me through my experience of that finds its fulfilment in Jesus Christ. . . .

I find very interesting the division which is made by the theologian Ninian Smart between those religions which are ethical and prophetic and those religions which are contemplative and numinous. He believes that the fullest truth of these religions centered upon God may be found in one which is able to weld together the insights both of the ethical prophet and of the contemplative person at prayer. Of course it is not a knock-you-down argument. But it is one of the ways in which I believe that, in Jesus Christ, vague and various intimations of God have been given a human face in Jesus Christ, the image of God. Images in India are places for gods to live in. So Christ is the place where God is to be seen. I find that the study of other religions gives me a nonexclusive confidence in Jesus Christ. Of course there are other ways into the divine, but this is for me the way, the truth, and the life which discloses God.

I always remember being told long ago — in fact in this University — that the divinity of Jesus cannot be stated in the third person singular as the conclusion of a theoretical argument "He is divine — QED!" It is a conclusion which can only be expressed in the second person, as Peter expressed it when he said, "Thou art the Christ, the Son of the living God." And so, in the end, all that can be done is to try and show you Jesus Himself in action. The procedure is standard in all preaching of the Gospel. It consists in seeing Jesus at work and implying that this is how He still works today. It consists in inviting you to identify yourself with the people who met Him and to hear Him not addressing them only then, but you, too, now. And the experience of Christians is that if you now make a positive response you will find that He is a present person and a living power who demands that you too should recognize Him as your Lord and God. You can only recognize Him as perfection when you take your standard of perfection from Him. And you can only find that God becomes real through the experience of obeying Jesus which leads into a sense of obeying God. That is preaching, but at least you have been warned. To understand the divinity of Christ there must be not only reflection but an act of will. Perhaps we can acknowledge the moral authority of Christ when we cannot yet see His divinity, or perhaps we can pray, as we thought yesterday, as the seeker. In the last resort, in one way or another we have to face the question of Jesus saying "Will you trust me?"

The life of faith begins with an act of trust. As it goes on, the evidence accumulates; we find we are living in God's world, that there are signs all around of His working, which we recognize because we have the clue in the word of the cross and the resurrection. We often have to renew the act of trust. The things which happen to us, and the things which are demanded of us, never compel us to acknowledge that they are from God. But gradually our world is reorganized round Christ at its center, and we have, not the proof we asked for at the beginning, but an assurance which is held by faith and the hope which is stronger than men's proofs. . . .

How do we know there is a God? First, we know because we are told — that is through religious traditions. Second, we know because God finds us in the experience of inspiration. Third, we know because we find God in the adventure of faith.

1) I find myself saying that I know because I have been told, because there is a certain givenness in the tradition of Christian truth, which has been built up through long and varied experience of living and suffering and praying and thinking — a way of talking about God which is to be found in the Bible and crystalized into creeds and doctrines and prayers of the Christian Church. This tradition speaks to us about the ways and purposes of God. It may be expressed in all sorts of ways. We need for example to tell the Bible stories, to recite the round of psalms in order that convictions there expressed may be established in us. During the last war there was an attempt in Germany to produce a national Church in which they held that Jesus Christ was a pure arian, but all over Germany there were confessing pastors who were reading the Bible to their flock and in the Bible it is clear that Jesus was a Jew. There are those today who would insist that Jesus was a black man and so would drift from the tradition and use the faith to make a racial or political point. But we need to stand under the truths that we have received if we are to conserve that sense of God which has brought us to where we are.

2) But we also know there is a God because he finds us. We experience a presence, a power, a personality who is with us and for us. The experience of prayer and worship seem to me of value like political freedom or aesthetic appreciation which, if denied or smothered, impoverishes the human spirit. I have lived in a communist country where an attempt has been made to eliminate this dimension from life. It is significant that, in these countries, faith is kept alive not so much by words or policies or ecclesiastics as by groups meeting together for prayer and worship. To move into the Orthodox liturgy in the Soviet Union and hear a congregation lift the roof with their singing of the Creed is to have your heart lifted by an experience of a people whose soul is still being nourished by the experience of God amongst them. Here is a place for Pentecostal groups and other revivalist groups as they are a protest against a traditional religion or of formal intellectual belief or one that is simply concerned with social action. If we have ever prayed we know that God has found us and even if we are a bit flat at the moment, He may find us again

and therefore we know that the traditional Gospel is about a living Lord.

3) But the tradition handed down to us and the experience of God finding us are held together by the fact that we also find God. "He who does the truth will understand the doctrines" says St. John. There are times when there is simply the Christian thing to do — feeding the hungry, protesting against nuclear weapons, starting a movement like Amnesty International or Oxfam, taking an unpopular line, giving up comfort to help in a crusade for others. We may not always understand the tradition or feel much presence, but as we seek to make the Christian stand, there, in company with others, we find that life is sharpened, experience is deepened and the tradition at last begins to make sense. So I believe that the tradition, the experience and the Christian action assure us that the Gospel is true and that there is God.

Christian tradition on its own can be blinkered, narrow, and fussy; the agents of no change for those who are locked in old categories. If the Church is deaf to God's voice speaking through the events and discoveries of the contemporary world, it will find itself in the end speaking only to itself.

Religious experience on its own can be soft and sentimental; it can nourish piety and be blind to poverty on the doorstep. Above all, this sort of religion can fail to see that a total faith applies to the mind and imagination, when God is active in the world and not just in religious people.

Then Christian action and policies — Oxfam and Amnesty International and the peace movement — can be as arrogant as all ideologies are. All men are brothers except those who in the name of brotherhood need to be eliminated.

So the reason why I am a believer in God and find it through the Christian way is that I hold to this blend, a threefold strand which cannot be broken of tradition, inspiration, and action, correcting and assisting each other. We must be careful that this is not just an abstraction — nor should it be a coalition government. Christianity must be personal and interpersonal and a whole way of life. It demands a response to the question, "What think you of Christ?"

OXFORD MISSION
III

SOMEONE described this operation to me as a *cool* Mission. They contrasted it with the sort of campaign evangelism that we associate with someone like Billy Graham — that they might think of as a *passionate* Mission.

I want to make it clear that I am rather a fan, as well as a personal friend, of Billy Graham. We need to bear in mind his great statement, "If we were being persecuted because of our Christianity, would the police have enough evidence on which to convict you?"

However, I defend this Mission as reflective. I think that we need *both* passion and reflective coolness. In my last address I tried to explain how I personally came to look on Jesus Christ as the key to man and the disclosure of God. . . . In talking about the life of Jesus, I said that you could not eliminate that part of the story in which He mysteriously related Himself to the Father. All those prayers in which He uses the intimate word "abba." If you eliminate that, the whole event seems a fraud.

Now tonight I want to say that there is another part of the story which you cannot eliminate. There is the relationship of Jesus to the disciples — the welding together into a group, a fellowship, of an astonishing assortment of characters — impetuous Peter, dreamy artistic John, doubting, dare I say, donnish, Thomas, Matthew the city slicker, Nathaniel the countryman, Andrew the fisherman and Philip who seems to have had a muddled mind and usually got things wrong. Well, that's a bit of poetic license but, when John Wesley said that the New Testament knows nothing of the solitary Christian, he was thinking of them. He was thinking, too, of the first Pentecost when the puzzled disciples, not forgetting Mary and the women, were given an assurance, strong like the wind, warming like fire, that they were to be Christ's body in the world. That event is a mixture again of what I referred to on Monday. People living in the past with a tradition of Jesus — people with a sense of His presence within them — and people with a mission of action for the Kingdom.

Now this company did not spend their time saying how righteous they were, nor were they thought by others to be specially righteous. They were not self-centered. They said, "We preach not ourselves but Christ crucified, the power and wisdom of God." No, they were a company who believed themselves to be forgiven. The group of disciples that arose from them in Ephesus, Corinth, or Antioch were concerned that God through Christ had forgiven them and so brought them into a new relationship with Him and with one another — the forgiven community, the forgiven fact; nothing mass-produced or machine-tooled about these varied characters. Listen to St. Paul: "Be kind to one another, tender hearted, forgiving one another even as God for Christ's sake has forgiven you." The forgiven community working for and with the Lord to bring in his Kingdom.

Well, what happened? They were looking for a Kingdom and they got the Church — groan! At this point in composing my address, I put down my pen. I scratch my head. How can I relate these communities to all your varied experience of the Church? How can I deal with that cynicism which associates the early Church with attractive, charismatic groups of undogmatic leftist saints, with what goes on in your local parish Church, or with your sense that Christians had control of Western civilization for over a thousand years and they did not stop wars. They could not cure sickness of body or mind and they seemed to have as many breakdowns as anyone else.

I decided to concentrate on one other undeniable fact about the early followers — an unbroken link with today. They were given a special action for their special day — the new Resurrection Day which they called Sunday. It was a service of the bread and wine which has developed into what we call the Mass, the Eucharist, the Lord's Supper, or the Liturgy of Holy Communion. Now, one of the unusual experiences of an Archbishop is that he still, on the Lord's day and many other days, shares in that service but very seldom in the same place or in exactly the same way, twice running.

Take the last year. I have taken part in the Eucharist informally in China, in a hotel bedroom where the Church after the cultural revolution is like a patient recovering from a near fatal illness. So, as we met together, it seemed ridiculous that I should say to any of those around the table or altar, "By the way, are you a Methodist?" or, "Incidentally, are you a Roman Catholic?" or, "You look like an Anglican." Then I have shared the Eucharist with thousands in a stadium in Nigeria where the amazing growth of Christians gives an exuberance and liveliness that overwhelms the visitor. They flew balloons around the stadium to welcome me, balloons stamped with my image and sold with the ambiguous caption, "Help the Anglican Communion blow up the Archbishop of Canterbury." I have shared the Eucharist in Bulgaria where, as in the Soviet Union, there was something timeless about the numinous music and the flickering candles — and, of course, I have shared it with stately English restraint in Canterbury Cathedral and with a small congregation in a parish church in Margate.

I want to argue that, in all of these, as in the early Church, the Eucharist has three ingredients. They are all necessary. They give a picture of what the Church is all about and remind us of its purpose in the world.

1) The presence of the Lord — not a gathering for some social or political purpose but one distinguished by that promise that, "when you break the bread and share the cup and repeat my words, there am I in the midst." It is the Lord living and forgiving.

2) The presence of the local community — not just those who think and act the same way. St. Paul was always warning people that there are varieties of gifts of the spirit. The Church in Jerusalem or Corinth or Rome was very different. The thing that marked off Christian groups from others was that, however much disciples might differ on worldly issues, they remain a fellowship.

3) You needed the presence of the Bishop (or give him a less debatable name, the Minister) who is a link with the wider communities so that the local regards itself as part of the universal.

So the Lord, the locals, and the link make up the Church, and I believe that things have gone wrong and distortions have arisen in Christian history when these three strands of the Eucharist have not been held together.

So there have been Christians with a deep sense of the living, forgiving Lord; that is necessary, but we are not meant, if I may put it so, simply to hug Him to ourselves, and sometimes there have been those who combine that sense of unity with a feeling of superiority. Now Jesus reserved some of His strongest condemnations for religious know-alls; the exclusive, the self-righteous carry within themselves the seeds of Christian corruption.

Then, second, there have been Christians with a strong sense of local loyalty. In our own country, we can see how Christians have engaged in social service, pioneered as Samaritans, or cared for the aged. All this is defensible but they have sometimes forgotten the hard sayings of Jesus, the revolutionary character of His Kingdom, and so they have become "yes" men and women. Establishment Church folk carry within them the seeds of Christian corruption.

Third, there have been Christians with the sense that the Church must be influential in the affairs of the world. That's right for politics of importance since politics affect people. Yet there have been times when archbishops, popes, patriarchs, and perhaps world councils of churches have become distanced from the ordinary Christian and have attempted to manipulate them to achieve worldly power. Such international Churches can carry within themselves the seeds of Christian corruption.

All of us can think of disgraceful episodes in history. All of us can think of Christian scandals today. I believe that they all spring from the failure to hold together the Lord, the locals, and the link.

This picture also gives us the threefold thrust for faith in community.

1) We need to strengthen our grasp on the faith and deepen our relationship with the living and forgiving Lord in teaching and in worship. For this is a community based upon revealed truth, not just a collection of anyone's ideas. When the vocabulary of Christianity is gradually eroded, adulterated, and made to mean what it never meant before, watered down, brought to the level of our understanding or our taste, our faith becomes so anemic that there is really no reason, no impetus, to believe in something that has practically no content. The Gospel is proclaiming something that is beyond us and is there to stretch our mind, to widen our heart beyond the bearable

at times, to recondition all our life and give us a world revolving not around ourselves but around God in Jesus Christ.

2) We need to contextualize our message in the life and culture of our particular community. Let me illustrate this by confessing the failures of my own Anglican Communion. We are a Christian tradition that spread around the world largely during the days of the British Empire. Too often, we exported with our faith the context of Englishness. I remember seeing church wardens in Sierra Leone in English morning coats. What we should have done is to export the principle which was held dear by my first predecessor, St. Augustine, that our grasp on the essentials of faith should be expressed in service to the society in which we are placed and with a proper respect about its customs. That's why I have to say now to Anglicans stumbling around in Burmese Churches trying to sing hymns ancient and modern with surpliced choirs, let your Church have a Burmese face, or in other circumstances an Asian face, or an African face.

The same, of course, is true in a local community. I believe Christians will often need to find strange allies in building up healthy community life. William Temple said that the Church is the only society which exists for its nonmembers. When Jesus the Jew weeps over Jerusalem, he accepts and blesses our local loyalties. Communities only thrive if they are loved. That's true of a college or a parish or a country.

So there is a duty for those who try to build the Kingdom to do so within the circumstances in which they find themselves. Your generation cast the net of sympathy much wider than mine for people in distant parts who get a raw deal in life. It is important, however, that we don't combine this theoretical sense of justice for people in distant parts with an inability to get on with our family, the neighbor next door, or the stranger in our midst.

3) Christians must not be absorbed into their local loyalties and fail to challenge all insularity. I can tell you that is not popular. Alas, it is not vote-catching. There are no votes in aid to the Third World. I found this myself in attempting to oppose the Immigration Act because of its effect on family life among immigrants with relations in other countries. I have found it in attempting to build up our commitment to international institutions like the United Nations. I

have found it in urging Christians to work for a new world order or in concern about human rights. . . .

So, a personal faith, local loyalty and witness, and wide horizons. That's why the Lord, the locals, and the link are significant.

Always my prayers try to include the three dimensions. Sometimes, of course, in history one needs special emphasis but never in the Church to the exclusion of others.

I recognize that I have spoken of the Church without saying much about Christian disunity. This has been on purpose. Of course I give much of my time to bringing Christians together. Disunity is a scandal. In places like Northern Ireland it costs lives. But I also recognize there is a certain apathy. Talk of institutions is so boring. I believe the key to Christian unity lies in spiritual renewal. We must never forget about each other, never lose contact, but the deepest ecumenical question is not "how are we going to unite with that lot?" but "how can our Church become more Christ-like in its fellowship, its mission to the world, its care for suffering, its proclamation of the Gospel?"

I would like to round out my thoughts on faith in community — which might be a definition of the Church — with a testimony of faith: that, with all its faults and with all its failures, I love you still. Sometimes I go into Canterbury Cathedral to the Chapel of the Twentieth-Century Martyrs. The list is as honorable as any I know of worthwhile lives — but I also have my own private picture gallery of people in whom I have seen something of Christ, the living and forgiving Christ. There are a great variety — English, Indian, African, old and young, some very simple, some learned professors. Some show it in their active service of others, some in their patience under suffering, some have shown it in the way they die. All are extremely different, all very much themselves. There is no one Christian type of saintliness but all reflect unmistakably the one Christ.

I am sure that the weakness of the Christian Church can be exaggerated — by critics who do not know enough about its life today, or by Christians who are too romantic about the past in comparison with the present. The true history of the Church has been the story of a minority in every age, for only the minority has ever taken an active part in the deeper spiritual life of the Church. Today, the world over, I believe the Christian minority is still as courageous as it has ever been. Even here in our rather blurred society, in villages, suburbs, housing estates, and inner city, small congregations are being renewed as they come together week by week in a deeper fellowship and, above all, as they go out together in service to the neighborhood and in concern for the world — and millions of individual Christians are going to work in the modern world. Many nurses, many teachers, many of the people who staff the social services, many of the people who are doing something about peace or about world poverty — many of these people are Christians, a higher proportion than you would expect in these days of small congregations.

So let me ask you to consider not so much the scars and scandals of the Christian community (we have always a need to remember those) but whether a combination of personal faith, local commitment to your neighbor, and a wide vision of God's purposes in the world are not the ingredients for Faith in Community.

Now for a final five minutes. I want to put it in three parts.

1) Jesus Christ — The Light of the World. We haven't had many words about it. But we did have that service on Wednesday when each one of us in the darkened Church had a candle — symbolizing that each one of us who is a baptized Christian can expose the darkness, illuminate the truth, and get some sense of direction. It is not achieved through words. It can't even be packed into the capsules of ideas. It's communicated through a kind of life.

2) You may remember that I said we needed passion and coolness. How is it possible to be a Christian without passion? How is it possible to love God and see His works and see His finest creation, men and women, so starved that their brains shrivel without passion — to see its best talents and a large proportion of its resources wasted on the mass production of weapons without passion. Who could witness men and women belittled by reason of their sex or skin colour without passion?

3) But passion is not enough. Some inside and outside the Church are shouting so loud they have made themselves deaf. Inside and outside the Church we suffer from the cults of unreason. We need renewal but not mindless renewal, for Our Lord appealed to the whole man: "What think ye? Have ye never read?"

So, a cool-headed Mission may not pack the Sheldonian or prove very exciting, but it has its place. It should reflect a readiness to be still, to receive, to be silent, and so to free ourselves from the strident slogans of half-truths, to recover a fuller vision of the truth, and put energy into well-considered and purposeful action.

Of course, we need both, for the Christian hope lies in a passionate coolness; and the questions which come at the end of both sorts of Mission are the same: 1) Are you going to say yes to God and follow that through in all the pressure points of life? 2) What think you of Christ? 3) Are you prepared to express your faith in community?

We don't have public prayers at the end of each of these evenings, but there is only one prayer to say in the moment of silence which we can now keep. O Lord, change the world; begin, I pray, with me.

Lent, 1983

T THE 150th ANNIVERSARY OF THE OX-
FORD MOVEMENT, OXFORD: "Whoever eats
this bread shall live forever."

That great disciple of the Oxford Movement, Wil-
liam Gladstone, recalls traveling as a young man in a coach where
he overheard a snatch of conversation between two of his fellow
travelers. "Well," said one, "what *is* the Church of England?" "The
Church of England" said the other, "is a damn big building with an
organ inside."

After John Keble and his friends had done their work, such a
utilitarian definition was not possible. The Church is a divine society
in which heaven and earth and all the centuries meet. She is nourished
and sustained by the Eucharistic food we receive today and is given
her character by feeding on the body and blood of our Lord Jesus
Christ. Today, we celebrate our communion with those fathers of the
Oxford Movement, particularly John Keble, who opened the eyes
of so many to the mystery of the Church and who protested at her
degradation.

Keble himself lived with a profound awareness of God's presence
in the Church and by his preaching, poetry, and person reminded
some of the best of his contemporaries that it was not sufficient to
think of the Church as a merely useful institution, a department of
state, an educational or welfare agency, or a society for the improve-
ment of morals.

Appealing beyond his own time and place to the evidence of the
springtime periods of Christianity, in particular to the scriptures,
seen through the eyes of the fathers of the primitive Church and the
Anglican divines of the seventeenth century, Keble — probably un-
wittingly — stimulated a movement back to the Christian roots which
released great energies in the Church of England. Men and women
were given strength and grace to spend their lives in gruelling missionary work in the great new cities of industrial Britain. Great

numbers of churches, schools, convents, and almshouses remain as a testament to the vigour which flowed from the Oxford Movement. Christian poetry and art as well as beauty in stone and glass brought into the world of getting-and-spending a sense of the delight that there is in the presence of God.

Keble, his friends and followers, kept open the channels of communication and inspiration which flow from God and from the Church of all the centuries at a vital moment. He preached his sermon in 1833, at a time when a new, post-Christian view of the truth and meaning of things which had no place for the presence and activity of God was growing in potency and confidence. His view derived its authority from the scientific world picture of the Enlightenment, and it was pitted against the traditional, Christian understanding of the meaning of the world and the place of human beings within it in a stark and vivid way. In the Assize sermon, Keble imagines the spokesman for this alternative view as saying of Christian doctrine, "Once and for all we will get rid of these disagreeable, unfashionable scruples which throw us behind other people in the race for worldly honour and profit."

Over the last 150 years, the clash has perhaps become moderated and less explicit. Religion has been pushed even further out of the center of the picture into a sphere of private life where it affords psychological satisfaction for some who are built that way. For much of the time, the Church has consented to this exile to the comfortable periphery. But that is where we in fact find ourselves now. One of the most common defensive comments you ever hear as a clergyman is "I think religion is very much a personal matter." This is no doubt true on one level, but often what is being stated is a denial that God has any claim on us or any right to be taken seriously as an element in our understanding of history or social affairs.

The Church has lived so long and so comfortably in its privileged privacy that sometimes it comes as a shock to realize that we do not live in a country most of whose citizens subscribe to another religion. It is often not perceived to be such and, like many powerful systems of thought before it, the truths of this modern religion are commonly believed to be self-evident. One of the central beliefs of this West European creed which is given almost unquestioning assent is the notion that "the individual has a right to happiness." Our contemporary secular religion also nourishes the hope and expectation that such happiness can be a possibility for the whole world.

I do not wish to sneer at this modern religion. In many ways, the modern creed is humane and admirable with a vast amount of achievement to its credit. Nobody wants to return to a world in which the conditions of life for the mass of the population were nasty, brutish, and short. Anyone who presumes, however, to speak from a Christian pulpit must say that biblical Christianity starts from a radically different point of view and has different emphases. I passionately believe that Christianity is a better description of reality than its secular alternatives and does in fact nourish human beings in all their God-given dignity. I also believe that this contrast is becoming more and more evident.

Very briefly, I wish to place side by side some of the central ideas of the modern creed and biblical and apostolic Christianity.

The modern creed starts with an "individual" who possesses all that is needed for making moral choices and for personal development.

Biblical Christianity, on the other hand, begins with man's dependence on God. Men and women do not grow to their full stature until they surrender their own "rights" in the service of the love of God and the neighbor. The service of God, as the Prayer Book reminds us in one of its noblest prayers, is perfect freedom.

In the modern creed, happiness can be achieved by consuming and possessing, although there is now increasing cynicism about the claim that man can live by bread and circuses alone.

In the Bible, however, joy and fullness of life is the gift of God which comes to some of those, like the poor in spirit mentioned in St. Matthew's gospel, whom modern man would count most miserable.

One of the ways in which the modern creed is being revealed as increasingly threadbare and exhausted is the ebbing of the element of hope in it. The modern creed used to be full of hope that it was possible to attain on earth by rational organization and the advance of technology a utopia of independent individuals in a worldwide society of plenty. This hope in gradual progress and the beneficence of technology has evaporated, leaving large numbers of people immobilized by fear and anxiety.

The biblical vision of deepening conflict, leading to darkness, in which God will inaugurate a new era — the pattern seen in the life, death, and resurrection of Jesus Christ — appears once more to be in tune with the times. As Keble said in his great sermon 150 years ago, "The churchman is a man possessed of an unfailing, certain hope; he is calmly. . .sure that the victory will be complete, universal, eternal."

There is a missionary challenge in this contrast between the modern creed and biblical and apostolic Christianity which could be indefinitely extended. This challenge is addressed, not merely to members of the Church of England but to the catholic and universal Church as a whole. Our membership of the Church gives us access to a divine reality through the bread of eternal life, which is not made stale by any passing fashion or contemporary orthodoxy. In the Church of England, at a time when we were in danger of being assimilated to passing fashion and conditions, Keble and his friends recalled us to the inheritance of all the ages which we share and taste in common with others who are members of the one, holy, catholic Church.

Keble was the most reserved of men. He would not have wished the 150th anniversary of his sermon and his serious appeal to an apostate nation to have been marked by an after-dinner style of reminiscence or something merely historical. Keble bent all his powers to reflecting the divine life which he received as a member of the Church and through the bread and wine. He protested against the subordination of the Church to a system of belief reared on different foundations from those we find in the Bible and the Apostles. He rejected the idea that the Church should merely be a useful agency in the service of the state.

We are not faced with precisely the same problems. There is very little danger now that the State would even wish to see the Church as a yoke-fellow in its activities. We are, however, faced with the danger of the Church becoming just a Friendly Society in a culture whose public structure of truth and meaning excludes God and centers on the autonomous individual. There is for us a danger that Christian doctrine could become so attenuated that the divine reality will be diluted into a dull echo of the liberal consensus.

In its own day, the Oxford Movement stimulated a great missionary effort to our own country and culture. We need to do this now — it is the best way of celebrating 150 years of Tractarian influence. This is by far the most important field of missionary endeavor in our own day, because, being missionaries at home, we are engaging with that West European secular dream which has penetrated to every part of the globe and overturned almost every other culture in the world.

This missionary effort is not something for the intellectually gifted alone. Keble perhaps taught more effectively in the sweetness and gentleness of his life than in his preaching. We are in Oxford. We need thinkers in every department of life, ready to challenge our present decaying assumptions. But we follow Keble most surely by being missionaries of love, showing in our lives what it means to put the center of self outside self, and what spiritual beauty follows. The world is once again waking up and needs to hear this truth.

So be of good courage. We are meant to praise a movement that goes on, not to bury it. Be hopeful. Be loyal to your Church. Be thankful to those who have gone before you in the faith, but above all be thankful to God who gives us the body and blood of His own Son to nourish us in the way and give us a foretaste of heaven.

16 July 1983

RCHIEPISCOPAL HUMOR: People don't believe you if you say to a stranger on the telephone, "This is the Archbishop of Canterbury." There is a silence and then something like, "Is that a public house?"

The story is told of one of my predecessors that he entered a railway carriage and took the last seat. In a few moments he realized that the other passengers in the carriage were from the local mental hospital. He buried himself in his papers, but suddenly the carriage door was thrust open and an official began counting, "One, two, three, four. . . . *Who* are you?" "I am the Archbishop of Canterbury." "Five, six, seven, eight. . . ."

When I was on a visit to Scotland a man held up a placard proclaiming that Runcie was a Romanizer. I was a little upset about it until one of my companions remarked that it could have been worse and it might have been the far more damaging if the placard declared Runcie is a womanizer.

Reading in advance of my stop in Chicago I learned that I was an "unstuffy Englishman" subject to "lacrhymal spill" in moments of emotion. I enjoyed that phrase, although I hope it will not reach home. It rivals my favorite piece of misinformation gathered from a San Francisco newspaper that revealed that the Church of England was founded not by St. Augustine but by St. Benedictine — doubtless in one of his moments of leisure from the liquor business!

Things are not so simple now or leisurely as they were when Voltaire, one of the most distinguished refugees ever to have been offered

The Archbishop pours tea for his predecessor, Lord Ramsey of Canterbury, during a visit to Lambeth Palace. The clock on the mantlepiece was a farewell gift from parishioners of All Saints, Gosforth, Diocese of Newcastle, where the Archbishop served as a curate in 1950-52.

shelter in Geneva, wrote his contemptuous but highly amusing essay on the Church of England. He is good enough to admit that the morals of the English clergy were more regular than those of France, but he adds, "Most of the clergy are married. The pedantic airs contracted in Oxford and Cambridge and the little commerce men of this profession have with women commonly oblige a Bishop to confine himself to one wife only and that usually his own." Yes, gone are the days when one of my predecessors and one of Voltaire's contemporaries was so consistently drunk in the House of Lords that his bench alone was fitted with an arm to prevent him falling off the end on to the floor. Even today the Archbishop's bench in the Lords is still the only one with an arm, but the Archbishop has no leisure for generous imbibing!

Sometimes I fear our pulpits should be hung with a notice of a pharmacist's shop. It read, "We dispense with accuracy."

Instead of a nice litter of books on the parish shelves — William Barclay's *Plain Man's Guide to the Apocalyptic* and the like — we behold a line of paperbacks in ice-blue covers in a similar format on everything from Euthanasia to the Virgin Birth.

Once I visited a certain rather dilapidated church and spoke to one of the wardens. Gazing lugubriously around him at the evidence of neglect and decay, he said, "You know, Sir, I think that it is inertia that keeps us going."

It is important to express simple truths, I believe, always remembering the man who once told me he had suffered all his life for never having been treated as ignorant!

One of my heroes among parish clergy was a priest who refused to have an electoral roll which distinguished between the so-called "committed" and the uncommitted. He did not neglect to teach the catholic faith, but baptised all the children presented to him. He loved the resonances of the *Book of Common Prayer* and observed stillness and stateliness in the celebration of the sacraments. He had a mortal horror of the exclusiveness of the phrase "the people of God" and tried to so conduct himself that he was at the very least a friend to all the inhabitants of his parish. He also made a lethal homemade wine out of the rose petals of withered wreaths from the crematorium, and called it "In Memoriam." Just before retirement, he sighed for the day when parish priests would give up their modish obsession with synods and turn to their true business — bee-keeping, cricket, and siring future Lord Nelsons!

In recent months I have cherished the story of a 19th-century Archbishop of York. Emerging from Evensong in a country church, he found his coachman drunk and incapable. There was nothing to do but to put dignity aside, and so, in top hat and gaiters, he took the driver's seat to get them both back to Bishopthorpe. In the dark, they went past the Gatekeeper at a furious pace. But the gatekeeper was heard to shout, "Whoa, Bob, wearing the old boy's hat is making your driving even worse!"

A Somerset farmer touring the Vatican was shown some hens and told that they were direct descendants of the cock which crowed at Peter's betrayal. The sturdy farmer was unimpressed. When the claim was repeated, he replied, "Ah, but be they good layers?" He was more interested in apostolic success than in apostolic succession!

There is a danger in refusing to apply our minds to the scriptures. When I was Bishop of St. Albans, I encountered a lady who had taken Christ's words, "Drink ye all of this" to mean that when she came to the altar rail she should drink *all* the wine in the chalice!

After World War II, when I came to study theology at Cambridge, we all read C. H. Dodd for the New Testament and Reinhold Niebuhr for our social gospel. Those were the days when we irreverently stated the Commandments as "Thou shalt love the Lord thy Dodd and thy Niebuhr as thyself."

Constant cope-and-mitering in England has, alas, all but eclipsed the academic hood, so much that when a bishop of conservative habits went for a school's Confirmation, one of the boys wrote him, in words suggesting the excessive influence of Hollywood, "Now I know what a real hood looks like!"

The organizing committee of the World Affairs Council in Los Angeles is obviously very well briefed, even down to the fine gradations of the English social hierarchy. It is quite remarkable that you should have been charged $20 each to hear Prince Charles and only $16 to hear me!

In remembrance of the American visit of Archbishop Davidson, I am wearing purple frock coat and gaiters—what my Chaplain calls my "bird of paradise" attire. I've been frightened, even in England when I've braved myself for some great banquet, that if the car broke down I might be arrested as a transvestite!

I have been visiting the cathedrals in Washington and San Francisco and have discovered that the fellowship of Head Vergers is something that undergirds the Anglican Church worldwide. Both the top men at the National Cathedral and at Grace Church Cathedral were personal friends of the Head Verger at Canterbury Cathedral. I find it just a little sinister, and I hope there will not be any kind of coup or Day of the Verger!

The Archbishop waves from an automobile as he sets out on the 35-mile drive from the Old Palace, Canterbury, to his week-day residence, Lambeth Palace, in London. Seated behind him is his chaplain, The Reverend Richard Chartres. Press Association Ltd.

INDEX